Writing for Interactive Media

This thoroughly revised fourth edition teaches students and professionals how to create interactive content for all types of new media and become successful writers or designers in a variety of fields.

This comprehensive guide is grounded in the core principles and skills of interactive media writing, in which writers create text and structure content to guide users through interactive products such as websites or software. The book examines case studies on interactive formats including complex informational websites, computer games, e-learning courses, training programs, and immersive exhibits. These case studies assess real-world products and documentation used by professional writers such as scripts, outlines, screenshots, and flowcharts. The book also provides practical advice on how to use interactive media writing skills to advance careers in the social media, technical, instructional communication, and creative media fields. This edition includes new chapters on UX Writing and Content Design, Social Media Writing, and Writing for Mobile.

Writing for Interactive Media prepares students for the writing challenges of today's technology and media. It can be used as a core textbook for courses in UX Writing, Writing for Digital Media, and Technical and Professional Communication and is a valuable resource for writing professionals at all levels.

Supplemental resources include a sample syllabus, class assignments, student exercises, scripts, outlines, flowcharts, and other interactive writing samples. They are available online at www.routledge.com/9781032554242

Timothy Garrand is a Lead UX Product Designer who has led numerous projects for major corporations including JPMorgan Chase & Co., Merrill Lynch, Bloomberg, Proctor & Gamble, and Iron Mountain.

Writing for Interactive Media

Social Media, Websites, Applications,
E-Learning, Games

Fourth Edition

Timothy Garrand

Routledge
Taylor & Francis Group

NEW YORK AND LONDON

Designed cover image: bestdesigns / © Getty Images

Fourth edition published 2024
by Routledge
605 Third Avenue, New York, NY 10158

and by Routledge
4 Park Square, Milton Park, Abingdon, Oxon, OX14 4RN

Routledge is an imprint of the Taylor & Francis Group, an informa business

First edition published by Focal Press 1997
Third edition published by Focal Press 2009

Library of Congress Cataloging-in-Publication Data
Names: Garrand, Timothy Paul. author.
Title: Writing for interactive media : social media, websites, applications, e-learning,
    games / Timothy Garrand.
Description: Fourth edition. | New York, NY : Routledge, 2024. | Includes
    bibliographical references and index.
Identifiers: LCCN 2023019022 (print) | LCCN 2023019023 (ebook) |
    ISBN 9781032554259 (hbk) | ISBN 9781032554242 (pbk) |
    ISBN 9781003430612 (ebk)
Subjects: LCSH: Interactive multimedia. | Writing.
Classification: LCC QA76.76.I59 G37 2024 (print) | LCC QA76.76.I59 (ebook) |
    DDC 006.7—dc23/eng/20230502
LC record available at https://lccn.loc.gov/2023019022
LC ebook record available at https://lccn.loc.gov/2023019023

ISBN: 978-1-032-55425-9 (hbk)
ISBN: 978-1-032-55424-2 (pbk)
ISBN: 978-1-003-43061-2 (ebk)

DOI: 10.4324/9781003430612

Typeset in Sabon
by Apex CoVantage, LLC

Access the Support Material: www.routledge.com/9781032554242

To my wife, Elizabeth, for the patience, support, and understanding while I took time away from fun and family life to write this book.

To my daughter, Danielle, who is a successful writer for social media and, who along with her writer/producer friends, contributed numerous insights to the social media chapter.

Contents

To Instructors

In addition to being popular with professional writers, earlier editions of this book have also been successful in the classroom.

Teaching Resources

Writing for Interactive Media includes separate content for instructors with sample syllabi, assignments, exercises, script samples, and other material to enhance the use of this book in the classroom.

Online resources for instructors are hosted on the Routledge Instructor's Hub as downloadable files. A link to the hub will be accessible from the book's product page on Routledge.com. From there, instructors can apply for login credentials to access the files.

Courses Using This Book

This book has been used for several types of courses including:

- Writing for the web and multimedia
- Writing for interactive media
- Interactive design
- Interactive media production, as the content component paired with a more technical text
- Interactive Media Studies, providing a solid overview of many types of interactive media

Acknowledgments

When I first got into the field of interactive media, my daughter, Danielle Garrand, was in middle school. Now she is a successful writer/producer for social media working for companies like CBS, NBC, and *theSkimm*. She contributed interviews and advice for the social media content, as well as introducing me to her fellow social media writers Sophie Lewis and Stephanie Orozco, who contributed interviews and insights as well.

I also had considerable help with the UX Writing/Content Design section from colleagues past and present who gave helpful interviews and suggestions. They include Justine Hyland, Rachael Hyland, Susan Passmore, Laura Wixted, and Carole Balawender.

This book also could not have been written without the generous donation of script samples and images by various companies. Many thanks to The Federal Reserve Bank of Boston, Her Interactive, Jeff Kennedy Associates, CyberFlix Inc., Indie Built, Trilobyte Inc., Chedd-Angier Production Company, T. Rowe Price Associates, Access Software Inc., National Scouting Museum of the Boy Scouts of America, Ziff-Davis, Houghton Mifflin Company, Encyclopaedia Britannica, Philips Media, and Prudential Verani Realty.

Equally crucial was the time generously donated by the many writers and designers interviewed for earlier editions of my writing books, these include: Shawn Hackshaw, Andrew Nelson, Maria O'Meara, Steve Barney, Anne Collins-Ludwick, Matt Costello, Dave Riordan, Aaron Conners, and Andrew Nelson.

Last, of course, I want to thank the editors at Routledge, Alexandra de Brauw and Sean Daly, for publishing this book and their help and support through the long writing process.

Introduction

You read interactive media writing every day when you use websites, social media, software, e-learning courses, mobile apps, and even interactive museum exhibits. Writing for interactive media is a booming field with many unique challenges. The linear writing skills (essays, reports, articles etc.) you learned in school provide a good foundation, but to be a successful writer for interactive media, there are a whole range of additional skills and insights that need to be mastered.

This book will first take you through the key challenges facing all interactive media writers and then discuss the unique aspects of the various type of interactive media writing, including:

- Part I: Challenges Writing for Interactive Media
- Part II: Conversational Writing—UX Writing [Applications], Social Media, Mobile
- Part III: Writing and Structuring Long Form Interactive Information—Websites, E-Learning, Simulations
- Part IV: Writing and Designing Interactive Narrative—Games, Immersive Experiences
- Part V: Interactive Writing Careers

The insights in this book are gathered from the author's more than 20-years' experience working in interactive media for a wide variety of major corporations. These insights are enhanced with dozens of interviews with other interactive media writers and extensive examples of interactive media scripts, outlines, and other important interactive media writing artifacts.

The last section of the book offers career tips on how to break into this field or build your career if you are already an interactive writer.

DOI: 10.4324/9781003430612-1

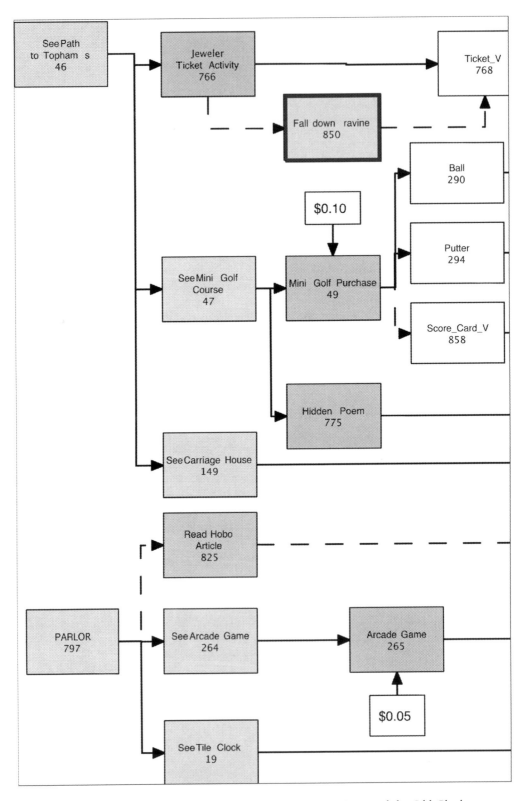

Figure I.1 A portion of the writer's flowchart for *Nancy Drew: Secret of the Old Clock* computer game

Part I

Challenges Writing for Interactive Media

Part I Overview

Part I explains key interactive writing challenges. They include:

- Interactivity
- Writing for the small screen
- Writing for many types of media (text, pictures, video, audio)
- Interactive writing tools
- Interactive writing script formats
- Collaborating with a team

DOI: 10.4324/9781003430612-2

1 The Challenge of Interactivity

Chapter Overview

This chapter explains how interactivity and the limits of the small screen are challenges for the writer. Topics explained include:

- Linear media
- Interactive media
- Writing for interactive vs. linear media
- Interactivity vs. control
- Types of interactivity
- Understanding the user

Linear vs. Interactive Media

Linear Media

Linear media dominated a generation ago. Movies, television, books, newspapers, magazines are all meant to be primarily consumed linearly in the way the author created them—read a book from first chapter to last, follow a movie from opening scene to final climax. The consumer has little input into how and what order the content is presented. Linear media is also either presented as a complete physical artifact, such as a book or a newspaper, or if screen based, the screens are usually large, such as a movie screen or big screen TV.

Interactive Media

Interactive media has existed for a while, but really took off in the late 1990s when the Internet became commercially viable. Interactive media is any form of media that responds to a user's input in a way that substantially alters the experience. Interactive media is also usually presented on smaller screens that allows only a portion of the content to be shown on one screen. You use interactive media every day. It is probably the primary type of media you engage with. Common examples include: software, mobile apps, websites, social media, video games, and immersive museum experiences.

In all these examples, a computer is used to make possible the interaction between the users and the material being manipulated. Computer is used here in the broadest sense, including computers in cell phones, game consoles, and other devices, as well as traditional PCs. Limited, manual interactivity experiences, such as paint by number paintings or

DOI: 10.4324/9781003430612-3

choose your own adventure books fall outside our definition of interactive media and the scope of this book.

Writing for Interactive vs. Linear Media

For most of your education and career you have practiced skills for writing linear media. All your school papers, emails, work reports and presentations are all linear media. You learned to organize and clearly present your points sequentially and to control the presentation from start to finish. Good writing skills to have, but not enough to succeed in interactive media, which has unique challenges that don't exist in linear media. In this chapter we will examine two of those challenges: interactivity and writing for the small screen.

Working with Interactivity

Interactivity vs. Control

Perhaps the biggest obstacle and opportunity for the new writer of interactive media is understanding interactivity. In a product like a website, the problem is that unlike linear media you have no guarantee that the users of your content will see your material in the order you designed it or even see all of your content at all. The key challenge is to allow the user to find the content they need when they want it. This means that each of your pieces of content have to both stand alone and also work with other pieces of content if accessed by the user. You also have to have intuitive information organization and navigation, including descriptive navigation labels.

The UX designer or game designer will generally be the one to create the overall structure and set the level of interactivity, but the writer needs to understand the interactivity and structure to prepare effective content. Having a deeper understanding of the overall structure is also a good way for a writer to move up into a writer-designer role.

Even writing for a simple website is challenging, but writing for a complex informational piece or a video game, requires additional skills "the hardest challenge for the writer is the interactivity—having a feel for all the options in a scene or story," said Jane Jensen, game writer-designer, in an interview with the author. Unlike a linear piece in which it is crucial to pare away nonessentials, in complex interactive media, the writer must think of all the possibilities.

But unlimited interactivity may also not be the best way to achieve your goals depending on the type of product you are working on. For example, if you are trying to tell a story in a narrative adventure game, the degree of interactivity you can allow and still create believable characters, intriguing plot, and suspense will be far less than if you are simply creating a world for viewers to inhabit, such as *SimCity*. Similarly, a website with the focused goal of getting you to buy a car will have far less interactive options than an online encyclopedia that wants you to explore its information. In an interview with the author, game designer David Riordan echoes the feeling of many designers when he says, "Infinite choice equals a database. Just because you can make a choice doesn't mean it's an interesting one." He says that the creators of interactive media must maintain control of the overall structure and communication goal for the experience to be effective.

Degree and Types of Interactivity

Interactivity can vary by degree and by types. Some projects, such as a mobile app can be highly interactive with many options for users to affect the flow of content and function. Other projects, such as a blog or online news story may have limited interactivity with mostly a linear presentation with a few links to additional resources. The degree of interactivity will affect the difficulty of the challenge for the writer.

In addition to the degree of interactivity, there are also different types of interactivity that add to the complexity of interactive media. The most common are direct action, indirect action, or reaction

Direct Action

In a Direct Action, the viewer makes a choice, and that choice produces a direct and immediate response that the viewer expects. For example, on the Amazon mobile app or website, when the user clicks on the image and text about a razor, the user expects to and will get a page of information about razors and the opportunity to buy them.

Reaction

Indirect Reactions also called "if-then" links, are more complex. Users do not directly choose an item, as in the example above. Instead, they take a certain action that elicits a re-action they did not specifically select. The following example is taken from the walkthrough for the computer game *The Pandora Directive*. The walkthrough describes the program's story and the main interactive options for the user. At this point in the story, you, the user, are trying to escape with the woman Regan, but you have been cornered by the villains Fitzpatrick and Cross.

Excerpt from the Pandora Directive walkthrough

```
You get the choice of shooting Fitzpatrick, shooting
Cross, or dropping the gun. If you try to shoot
Fitzpatrick, you get trapped alongside Regan and Cross;
then everybody dies, safely away from Earth. If you try
to shoot Cross, he kills you before you ever get into
the ship. If you drop the gun, you get to the
spaceship.
```
© Access Software, Inc.

An example of an indirect reaction in an informational piece is a student who fails a test in a certain subject area and is automatically routed to easier review material, instead of being advanced to the next level. The student did not make this direct choice. It is a consequence of his or her actions. Figure 1–1 shows how a student who could not answer an arithmetic question in a math tutorial is sent back to an arithmetic review module as opposed to being advanced to the more difficult material. This review material is something the writer would need to create and it would have to address the needs of the student who did not succeed with the original math content.

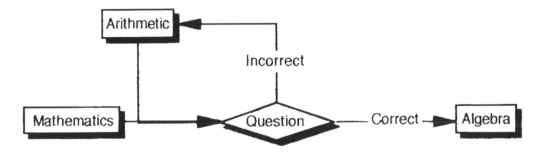

Figure 1–1 A reaction to user input

Indirect interactions can also cause multiple things to happen when the user clicks or taps a single choice. For example, on the T. Rowe Price website, users can fill out a form and establish the list of mutual funds and stocks that they are most interested in. After they have done this once, when they log on to the site in the future, they are activating a program that searches out the most current data on their topics in the database, organizes this data, and presents it to them. Depending on the type of data, the writer may have to create some of this content and make sure the information and writing tone align with the user's needs.

Delayed Reaction

Delayed reactions remember what choices the user made earlier or on previous plays/visits to the program/site and alters future responses accordingly. These links can be considered delayed "if-then" links. In a story, intelligent links create a realistic response to the character's action; in a training piece, they provide the most effective presentation of the material based on a student's earlier performance.

In *The Pandora Directive*, for example, you as the player are a detective who is trying to get in touch with Emily, a nightclub singer. You meet Emily's boss, Leach, well before you meet her. If you are rude to him, he mistrusts you. Later in the script when you try to rescue Emily, he will block your entrance to her room, and she will be strangled. If, however, you are nice when you first meet him, he lets you in, and you save her.

As a writer, you have to understand the web of connected content, such as that described above, and create appropriate content for each linked screen, bit of information, or narrative plot point.

Understanding the User

Viewer Input

It is difficult to predict how the viewer will interact with all the interactive possibilities in a piece. This is true in both narrative and informational interactive media. In an interview with the author, game writer-designer Jane Jensen warned that this can sometimes make certain type of interactive media, such as video games "a frustrating and difficult medium . . . You have this great scene, but you have to write five times that much around it . . . to provide options. When your focus is on telling the story, that can feel like busy work and a waste of time."

For example, you have a telephone in one scene that your player must dial to call his or her uncle and find out who the murderer is. This is near the end of the game and getting the telephone number itself has been one of the game's goals. The writer needs to anticipate all the things players might try to do with that telephone. What if players get the telephone number from having played the game earlier, and they then jump ahead to the telephone scene? What should happen when they dial? Should they get a busy signal? What if they dial the number after they have gotten it legally in the game, but they don't have all the information they need, such as knowing that the one who answers is their uncle? Should the writer give them different information in the message? What if they dial the operator? What if they try dialing random numbers?

This can be equally complex in an informational piece where you must anticipate the related information that the viewers will want to access and all the different ways they may want to relate to the key information. Compton's Interactive Encyclopedia, for example, allows users to explore a particular piece of information through text, pictures, audio, videos, maps, definitions, a time line, and a topic tree. The design of the program allows all of these different approaches to be linked together if the viewer desires. This means that students studying Richard Nixon can click their way from an article about Nixon, to his picture, to an audio of his "I am not a crook" speech, to a video about Watergate and Nixon's resignation, and finally to a time line showing other events happening during his presidency. This type of broad interactivity works fine for a general exploration such as this, but if the writer is creating a goal-oriented program, such as a training or education piece, the interactive options have to be more controlled.

Knowing the User

To present the right content presentation and type of interaction, a writer needs to anticipate user behavior and content needs. To do this, the writer needs to know as much about the user as possible. This is also important in linear media, but it is even more crucial in interactive media because the interactive relationship is more intimate than the more passive linear one. Knowing the audience is absolutely essential. Knowing what the user considers appealing and/or what information they need will affect every element of a production, interaction design to the writing.

On most interactive projects considerable effort is put into researching the user. Some sources for user information include: interviews, surveys, support logs, user groups, etc. This information is usually put together into documents, such as personas and use cases that describe a typical user, their needs, and common interactions. A journey map is another useful synthesis of user data that tracks a user's experiences with a product from beginning to end. Documents like these helps writers understand how they need to present the content to meet the user's needs. Before a project is released to users, it is also usually tested with a limited set of users using various techniques. The feedback from these studies allows the designers to refine the design and for writers to revise the content.

Conclusion

Working with interactivity is one of the key challenges facing interactive writers. Although deciding the approach to these challenges are not always under the full control of writers, they must understand these concepts to write effectively for interactive media. The next chapter will address the challenge of writing for many types of media.

References

Jensen, Jane. Game Writer-Designer. Interview with the author
Riordan, Dave. Game Writer-Designer. Interview with the author

2 Writing for Many Media

Chapter Overview

The interactive writer must be able to write effectively for a variety of media. Because interactive media programs often include some combination of text, graphics, audio, and video/animation. This chapter outlines some of the basic principles for writing:

- Text
- Graphics
- Audio
- Video

The Skills of the Interactive Writer

Although writing for some software or basic websites may only require the writer to write text, often the necessity to write for many media in the same production is as demanding on the writer as is dealing with interactivity. Unlike a print writer who can focus on honing communication skills with the written word, or the screenwriter who can specialize in communicating with images, to be truly successful, the writer of interactive media must be expert in a variety of techniques: writing to be read (journalism, poetry, copywriting); writing to be heard (radio, narration); writing to be seen (presentations, film, video); plus writing for the special demands of the computer screen. This is because interactive media may incorporate many types of media in a single production or even a single screen.

Depending on the project, the interactive writer may write link and button labels, on-screen text, audio narration, video action and dialogue, and even the conversation for a chatbot. Often writers also write ancillary material, such as hints files and help screens. There are basic style differences in each of these types of writing. Following are useful guidelines.

Text

Websites, social media, blogs, email, and chat have brought about a major resurgence in the writing and reading of text. Even with the increased use of web video, audio, and animation, on-screen text still plays a major role in most interactive media where the primary activity of most users is interacting with the text.

DOI: 10.4324/9781003430612-4

In an email to the author, Andrew Nelson, the writer of *The Harlem Renaissance* site, profiled in Part III Writing and Structuring Long Form Interactive Information, suggests that when writing for online you should remember that most people view interactive media as one person sitting in front of a computer or phone. To connect to your users, Nelson said, it is important to "write as if you are talking to an individual, not a collective group of anonymous Web surfers."

Clear, Concise, and Personal

An author writing blocks of text in interactive media can take a few tips from print journalists:

- Be accurate, check your facts, and be sure you understand what you are writing.
- Keep sentences short and use simple sentence construction.
- Use the lead or first sentences to tell simply and clearly what the following text is about.
- Use the active voice (for example, "The dog bit the man," not, "The man was bitten by the dog").
- Use descriptive nouns and verbs; avoid adjectives and adverbs.
- Choose each word carefully, and avoid jargon or technical terms unless you are writing for a specialized audience.

You can use the search function on your word processor to avoid many of the errors described above. For example,

- search for "is" or "are" to find passive voice. "He is listening." becomes "He listens."
- Search "ly" to find adverbs modifying weak verbs. "He walks slowly." becomes "He saunters."
- Search weak adverbs and adjectives, e.g. "very," "really," "just." "I'm just starving." becomes "I'm starving." "She is very pretty." becomes "She is gorgeous."

Use any tool you can to trim your word count and make your text an engaging read for the online reader.

Web Writing Tips from Usability Experts

There are a number of text-writing techniques that are unique to writing for the computer screen. The main reason for using many of these techniques is that most people cannot read as quickly and as comfortably on a computer screen or phone, as they can from the printed page. Adding to the problem of writing for computer screens is that many readers are looking for quick information. They do not want to sit down and read a six-page essay in a wall of text. They want to get the information they want quickly and then go about their business. The term "usability" describes how easy it is for users to perform tasks or get information on your website or multimedia program. A number of usability experts have conducted tests with users and come up with conclusions about the most usable way to write and organize text for the Web.

Write to Be Scanned

Several classic usability studies by Dr. Jakob Nielsen, usability engineer and information architect, discovered that many users don't read websites, rather they scan them for the information they need. To write effectively for these scanners, Nielsen suggests in *How Users Read on the Web*:

- highlighted keywords (links serve as one form of highlighting; typeface variations and color are others)
- meaningful subheadings (not "clever" ones)
- bulleted lists
- one idea per paragraph (users will skip over any additional ideas if they are not caught by the first few words in the paragraph)
- the inverted pyramid style, starting with the conclusion and most important information
- half the word count (or less) than in conventional writing

These concepts are particularly true on the first couple of levels of a site or mobile app where users are trying to find the information they want. Once they have located their information deeper in the site, users may be content to read longer text material.

F-Shaped and Other Reading Patterns

Nielsen Norman Group, the same research group that identified that Web users scan, also identified common web and mobile reading patterns based on eye tracking studies. These studies refer to how users view a content page on both web and mobile.

A frequent pattern is the F-Shaped Reading Pattern. This pattern visualizes how users move through the page, starting with a long horizontal scanning across the top content, followed by a shorter horizontal scan below, then finally a longer vertical view down the left side looking for any information triggers, such as headers.

According to the Nielsen Norman Researchers:

"The implications of this pattern are:

- **First lines** of text on a page receive more gazes than subsequent lines of text on the same page.
- **First few words** on the left of each line of text receive more fixations than subsequent words on the same line."

Knowing the "F" and other reading patterns can help inform the content design as to where to place the most important content. But as always these are some basic concepts that are worth validating on your site or app with your own users.

Usability Studies Related to Text and Online Writing

A more recent and more comprehensive study of online writing was organized by the U.S. Department of Health and Human Services and involved a large team of academics and practicing professionals, who analyzed all the usability research currently available and came up with a number of conclusions that are useful to the interactive writer. The study confirmed Nielsen's earlier work, but added a number of additional suggestions that are listed below.

Know and Respond to All Your Users

- Writers must understand user's expectations of their program. These user expectations can be formed by prior knowledge and past experiences. This requires user research by the writer or other members of the production team.

- Present help for all users. Be sure to define any unusual terms within the text.
- Have text or other alternates for information that is communicated by color. About 8% of males and a smaller number of females have trouble distinguishing color.
- Format information for multiple audiences. For example, if you have a medical website, it might make sense to have differently written sections for doctors and patients.

Home Page, Navigation Pages, and Links

- Describe your site or other program's purpose clearly and simply on the first page. This can be done with a tag line or a brief piece of highlighted text high on the page. Don't make users dig through the site to determine that your site has research information on televisions and is not a place to buy televisions.
- Don't have a lot of prose text on a home page or a navigation page. When most users come to a home page, they scan quickly looking for links to the information they want. A lot of text will either slow down their information search, or they may skip it altogether.
- For long pages that extend way below the fold, it helps users to have a clickable list of page topics or jump links at the top of the page. This allows them to quickly jump to the information on the page that they want.
- Write tool tips on links. Tool tips are bits of explanatory text that appear when a user mouses the cursor over a link. This helps the user understand where the link is going. Tool tips are not, however, an excuse for poorly labeled links and tabs.
- Use a consistent clickable style. If your links are underlined and blue in one section, keep them the same throughout. Avoid using underlining for general, non-link text because that suggests a link to most users. Text at top of page or in left and right column are common locations for link lists.
- Make links in the body of the text descriptive. If you need to make the links a few words long that is better than having an unclear link. Users tend to ignore the text around an embedded link so don't rely on that context to help. Avoid "Click Here". Instead use descriptive text that describes where the link will take the user, such as "Reptile Food" on a pet products site.

Information Display

- Display quantitative information in a standard and easily understood format for your users.
  - For example, presenting time in a 24-hour clock (e.g. 16:25) for an American audience is not appropriate because Americans use 12-hour clocks and will have to translate the information to the time format they are used to (e.g. 4:25).
  - Information, such as statistics, with multiple information entries is often better presented as a table, chart, or other visualization.
- Keep information needed for comparison on the same page or available in a popup link. Users can only remember three or four items for a few seconds. If you ask them to read product information on one page and then make decisions about products on the next page, they will have difficulty. Tables are useful for comparing lots of information.
- Set appropriate page lengths: shorter pages for home pages and navigation pages; longer pages that require uninterrupted reading of content.

- Place important information higher on the page so users can locate it quickly. Top center is the most prominent part of a page.
- Group information consistently. For example, if supplemental information is in a column on the right with a yellow background on one page, place it in the same location throughout the site to speed users' information search.
- Align items on a page. Bullets and menu items should be lined up along the left, such as the bullets in this list. This makes it much easier to scan information than if bullets are arranged in a diagonal or other artsy formation.
- Use appropriate line lengths. Users tend to prefer short line lengths, but they can actually read faster with longer line lengths. One study shows that line lengths as short as 20 characters consistently slowed reading speed. So, home pages and navigation pages may want to use shorter line lengths to engage users, but pages with more text may want to use longer lines to speed up reading, but obviously extremely long lines will have their own challenges.
- Limit page information only to what information is needed on that screen. Do not add extraneous information unrelated to the screen's purpose.
- Group related information and groups of links and give them meaningful headings.

Label

Label, Label, Label. A repeated result from a number of usability studies is the need to clearly and consistently label chunks of information or portions of a task. This includes:

- Frame labels (frames divide a page into sections).
- Input boxes on a form. Put the labels for input boxes close to the entry box that they define, on top of form is most common.
- Navigation tabs and menu links. They should be descriptive of the content they are leading to and use language all your users can understand.
- Category labels for groups of links and other information. If you have more than a few links on a page, group them and give each group a clear, descriptive heading.
- Unique and descriptive headings of blocks of content. Don't use the same or similar labels for different content. Clear unique headings facilitate scanning.
- Rows and column heading on tables. Don't use abbreviations unfamiliar to your user.
- Pushbuttons and other widgets. Try to use standard meaningful labels, such as "Enter", "Cancel", etc.
- Clickable images. Labels on clickable images makes it clear what information the image leads to and emphasizes that it is clickable.

Write for All Members of Your Audience

When you are writing, keep in mind that some members of your audience may be from another culture, speak another language, or have a disability, or have a different sexual orientation that the binary male-female. Fortunately, there are well established principles to help you write for all these audiences. This is called writing for:

- Localization: considering different cultures and languages
- Accessibility: including differently abled individuals
- Inclusion: using language that includes users of all types of sexual and gender orientation

These topics will be covered in more detail in Chapter 6: UX Writing/Content Design, but they are important considerations for all interactive writing.

Mobile Text

As discussed in Chapter 1, when writing for the small mobile screen all the guidelines above are even more important because of the extreme space limitations and that mobile users are often distracted. They generally do not give the phone the same focused attention as when viewing content on a PC.

Because of this, it is even more important when writing for mobile to:

- make it clear on the start page what you can do on this app, either through text of clearly laid out menus or feature links
- write succinctly with as few words as possible
- use descriptive text, no room for fluff or marketese
- strictly prioritize information with the most important on the first screen
- use simple conversational language
- in a content rich app, use outline or menu on the first page to allow users to get to desired content easily.

Who Edits Interactive Media Text?

If you are a writer who is coming to interactive media from the print world of books, newspapers or magazines, you probably expect an editor to be as important a position in interactive media as it is in print media. Apart from a few exceptions, this will not be the case.

Most interactive media projects will not have anyone on the team with the title of "editor." This does not mean you will not get feedback on your writing. A variety of other individuals take on this role including:

- The Clients or Project Manager. They often know the product and message better than you do. The client will usually review your writing and offer detailed comments primarily on the accuracy of the content and the way certain products and business practices are described. But keep in mind that the client will probably not be a trained writer, as a book editor might be. The client will give feedback, but it is up to you to revise the writing so it accomplishes the client's goals.
- UX/Product Designer, Instructional Designer, Information Architect, or Content Strategist. If your project has one of these content experts on board, it is likely that they might review your text to make sure it accomplishes their vision for the information presentation. People in this position are likely to have good writing skills and may be able to give some of the detailed comments you might expect from a print editor.
- The Game Designer or Exhibit Designer. If you are building a computer game or a museum exhibit, the high-level designer will often look at your text and give comments.
- Development Editor/Subject Matter Expert. The place you are likely to see a traditional editor role is in e-learning and training. In this case, it is not uncommon to have a subject matter expert editor, such as a Math editor. This person will review your text and suggest detailed text and content changes, as would a book editor.

- Copyeditor. Although some projects have some sort of copyeditor who will read through your text for typos and obvious grammatical errors, typically copyeditors do not offer substantial suggestions about your writing.

So, a good first step when you take on an interactive writing assignment is to determine who will give you feedback and get some sense of their expectations. But as noted above, you are likely not to get the kind of detailed editing you would get on a print project. Instead, many interactive writers need to learn to be their own editor as well as the writer.

Style Guide

Although there may not be a human editor, most projects give editorial guidance through a writing style guide. This guide defines specific text usage for writers. Usually, a project will have a custom style guide, but will also rely on a standard print style guide, such as *The Chicago Manual of Style*, for basic writing issues. Be sure to get a copy of the project style guide when you start a project. If there is no style guide, offer to write one. Without a project style guide, it is impossible to have writing consistency across the production.

How Editing Comments are Presented

If you do get editing comments, they will be delivered in one or more of the following ways.

- Track Changes. A common feature in most professional software, track changes allow an editor to enter and highlight changes. It then allows the writer to accept or reject changes and to compare multiple drafts of documents.
- Hand Written Notes. Sometimes clients like to print out a screen of text and edit the old-fashioned way with hand written notes. If this is the case, make sure you know the standard editing symbols, such as delete, replace, insert, and transpose. These are available in any manual of style and on the web
- Comments in a Second Document. Clients also often simply write or list their comments in a separate document. The writer then has to integrate them into the final document. If you get these types of comments, it is helpful to create a table with the client's comments in one column and your solution in the next column. The solution describes how you addressed the comments or reason you did not address the comments if you felt the suggestion was incorrect. See the sample below. It is good to capture the reviewer's initials in case you need further clarifications. It is also a good idea for each comment to have a unique number so you can easily refer to it in discussions with the client or development team.

Number	Reviewers Initials	Location	Reviewer's Comment	Writer's Resolution
1.	D.G	Home Page	Line 2 of body text, should be "multiply" not "divide"	Fixed
2.	D.G	Addition Problem #1	Problem explanation is unclear. Clarify amounts of different types of fruit.	Broke into bulleted list

Web Text Writing Example

The following excerpt from the T. Rowe Price website illustrates many of the elements of good text writing for the computer screen described above, including the inverted pyramid, concrete statements, simple sentence construction, reduced amount of text, highlighted text, different fonts, bulleted lists, one idea per paragraph, and conversational style. The underlined text in the sample below are blue hyperlinks on the actual site. Note these techniques also apply for writing for the even smaller mobile screen, which will be addressed later in a separate chapter.

ONLINE COLLEGE PLANNER

    This on-line College Planner can help you learn about meeting the costs of college. Our five-step <u>College Planning Calculator</u> calculates how much money you'll need to save, and suggests ways to invest your savings. Meanwhile, our <u>College Planning Library</u> gives you more information on other helpful resources, including:

- Tax Issues
- Education IRAs
- State Tuition Assistance Programs
- Sources of Financial Aid
- Ways that Grandparents Can Help

    A wealth of additional college planning information is available on-line. See our <u>Additional Sources of Information</u>.

© T. Rowe Price Associates.

Blog Writing Example and Writing Tips

The following fragment of a blog is from the Google Official Blog. This blog is limited to Google employees and includes new product information, public relations information, and just plain goofy things that Google employees do. The goal is to connect with Google customers on a more personal basis than traditional corporate communication.

    The blog below demonstrates most of the good online writing style techniques discussed earlier in this chapter.

- Descriptive heading.
- Clear direct, short sentences.
- Gets right to the point.
- The tone is very personal and keeps its audience in mind. A good blog is usually written in a conversational not formal style.
- Links to other sites. This establishes a blogger as an expert because it shows you are knowledgeable about information resources about your subject. Linking also helps you get return links.
- Uses keywords pertinent to the subject. This will help the search engine rating.
- Not in the example below, but another common technique is to try to end with a question or something controversial to encourage reader response.

Searching for music

Posted by David Alpert, Search Quality Product Manager

```
It may come as no surprise, but I like to search for things on Google.
Yep, when I'm looking for something, I always try it on Google first.
And sometimes, that thing I'm looking for is music. Many of our users
feel the same way, and we get a lot of search traffic on music terms like
popular artists and albums.
    A few of us decided to try to make the information you get for these
searches even better, so we created a music search feature. Now you can
search for a popular artist name, like the Beatles or the Pixies, and
often Google will show some information about that artist, like cover
art, reviews, and links to stores where you can download the track or
buy a CD via a link at the top of your web search results page.
```

Audio

Writing in which the audio carries the bulk of the meaning, as it does in radio, occurs fairly often in interactive media for two practical reasons:

- Audio is much cheaper to produce than video.
- Audio files are much smaller in size than video files. Because of this, these files load more quickly than similar video files.
- The popularity of podcasts. A podcast is a feed of audio files that a user can download and play on their computer or their mobile device. Podcasts are now used for a wide variety of content, including radio programs, education, politics, religion, and much more. Note that podcasts usually have limited interactivity, but they are mentioned here as a popular form of audio only programming present on computer or phone.

Writing where audio carries the primary meaning, demands the skills of the radio writer, or the ability to write to be heard as opposed to being read. In addition to the print writer's skills of being accurate, simple, and clear, the radio writer must:

- Write conversationally, the way people talk. Radio is the most intimate medium. When most radio announcers talk through the mic to thousands of people, they imagine they are talking to just one person, because that is how most people experience radio: one person and a radio. This is similar to the way most users experience interactive media programs on their phone.
- Write material to be understood on first listening. Audio is more difficult to replay than text is to reread.
- Keep it simple. Be aware that the writing will be heard and not read. Avoid abbreviations, lots of numbers, unfamiliar names, parenthetical expressions, and anything else that cannot be easily understood just by hearing it.
- Read all your work out loud when you are rewriting, or better yet, have someone read it out loud to you. You'll be amazed at how much of your perfectly acceptable written prose is unspeakable as dialogue or incomprehensible as narration.
- Write visually. A well-written audio-only piece can stimulate vivid images in the audience's minds. A famous radio ad once convincingly portrayed a ten-story-high hot fudge sundae being created in the middle of Lake Michigan. Create such pictures in the audience's mind by using:
  - Concrete visual words

- Metaphors and other comparisons to images the viewer already knows
- Sound effects
- Different qualities of voices (sexy, accents, etc.)
- Music
- Words and phrases that appeal to other senses, such as touch, smell, and taste.

Examples of audio-only or audio-dominant interactive media include audio interviews and seminars; audio and image scenes in which narration carries the bulk of the meaning; and even streaming video, which can easily degenerate to a series of still pictures with audio voice-over if the user has a slow connection or if the network is congested.

E-Learning Narration Example

The following example of narration is from Houghton Mifflin's Interactive Math and Statistics Lessons profiled in Chapter 14. This narration accompanies on screen text and graphics. So, it does not really have to stand alone. Notice the short uncomplicated sentences and clear straightforward language. The target audience is college statistics students.

```
     Bar graphs and pie charts are two common methods of representing
data graphically.

A bar graph is used to display quantitative or qualitative data.

Bar graphs have the following features in common.

   • The bars may be placed horizontally or vertically.

   • The bars are all the same width and are evenly spaced.
```

© Houghton Mifflin Company

Narrative Audio Only Example

Narrative scenes sometimes emphasize audio to save space or for dramatic effect, such as the following example from the interactive narrative *Voyeur*. In this scene the player is looking at closed window blinds and listening in. Notice the use of visual writing, sound effects, and different voices to create images in the audience's mind. (These items are in boldface type.)

```
All SEE ARE THE CLOSED WINDOW BLINDS OF CHLOE'S ROOM

LARA AND CHLOE.

SLIGHT KNOCK ON DOOR.

                          LARA
                    (knock on door)

     Chloe?
```

                              CHLOE
                Yeah. Come on in Lara . . .

                              LARA
                          (embarrassed)
        Oh, I'm sorry I didn't know you weren't **dressed**
        . . .

                              CHLOE
        No, no, no don't worry about it, man, don't worry
        about it.

                              LARA
                      (nervous **laughter**)
        Maybe if I had a **tattoo** there, Zack would take a
        closer look . . .

                              CHLOE
        Yeah? You like that? I'm not sure what hurt more,
        the tattoo or the hangover . . .

                              LARA
        What am I doing wrong with him?

                         CHLOE
        Oh, Lara would you stop it right now! Don't buy into
        Zack's bullshit. You're a babe. You're gorgeous.
        You've got a **terrific body.** You just don't know how
        to package it. . . . I have got the most terrific
        outfit for you. It's going to look killer on you.
        I swear to God.

RIIING! She's interrupted by phone call.

                              CHLOE
        Look, . . . Hold on a minute.

                         (**into phone**)
        Yeah? . . . Oh, hi. . . . Well, not exactly . . .
        Hey man
        I'm working on it. . . . will you give me a fucking
        break . . . Hold a sec.

                         (**to Lara**)
        Lara, could you . . . come back here tonight . . .

                              LARA
        I don't want to be a pest . . .

                              CHLOE
        Oh, come on, come on, it'll be fun . . . please,
        come on, come by around eight.

```
                    LARA
      OK. . . . see you then . . . (door closes)


                    CHLOE
      (back to phone)
      Like I told you, give me a couple a more days . . .
      I'll get you the damn money. Fine.
```

© Philips Media

Video

Writing for video or scriptwriting is an important skill for the interactive writer because of the popularity of live action and animated video on both desktop and mobile devices. Of course, many amateur videos are not written at all, but longer professional pieces certainly are, making scriptwriting a crucial tool for the interactive writer.

In a video, the viewer is seeing the results of the writing, not just reading or hearing them as in print and radio. Writing for video is a complex subject, about which many books have been written. Further complicating this topic are the very different demands on the scriptwriter of writing documentaries and narratives. It is difficult to reduce the specifics of scriptwriting to a few rules, but some of the scriptwriter's concerns include:

- Show, don't tell. Discover action to present the information. Don't have long-winded interviews about poverty in the ghetto; show scenes of poverty in the ghetto. Don't have your character tell us about how sad they are; have them do something that shows their sorrow.
- Structure. Have a clear grasp of how to structure a video. Several screenwriters have noted that scriptwriting has more in common with architecture than with writing. Screenplays are built, not written. Shots build scenes, scenes develop sequences, and sequences create plots and subplots. Much of film and TV follows established structures that writers should be familiar with. (These structures are discussed in Part IV Writing and Designing Interactive Narrative.)
- Interactivity and chunking. Keep in mind that your video is often part of a larger interactive program. In most cases, you will have to chunk it or break it down into smaller units so that the users can access just the piece of video they need.
- Setup. Exposition is one of the hardest elements to portray in video, and without proper exposition, characters are shallow, themes are undefined, and the setting is unclear. Exposition includes background information on the characters, setting, and the back story (events in the story that happened before the beginning of the current narrative). An example of important back story occurs in the classic film *Casablanca*. This film begins in Casablanca, a port city in Morocco, but essential back story includes the lead characters' romance that occurred in Paris a year earlier.

Setup is equally important in an informational video, where we need to understand the context of the material that is being presented. In the New England Economic Adventure profiled in Part IV Writing and Designing Interactive Narrative, the program designers had to introduce users to economic history of New England before they could play the game.

Unlike print, where it is fairly easy to "tell" the reader about background information, in video this material needs to be shown. In interactive media, novice scriptwriters often have the characters talking incessantly about things that happened years ago instead of finding a way to visualize this information.

- Characterization. There are a limited number of original stories but an unlimited number of unique characters. Finding and developing unique characters is essential in narrative films and most informational documentaries. It is also important that you pick the right characters for your audience. An informational program aimed for high-school students, such as the *New England Economic Adventure* has young, energetic characters. The training program, *Vital Signs*, is aimed for medical professionals, thus has more mature characters who can relate to that audience.
- Conflict. Conflicts must be clearly defined. Many videos focus on conflict, whether it is a fictional battle between humans and aliens or a *60 Minutes* documentary on the concerned citizens of India versus their nuclear power industry. Conflict arose from obstacles and opposing forces. Even short how-to videos have the conflict of a person trying to overcome the obstacles to accomplishing a task, such as changing the headlight on your car.
- Cost. Unlike radio and print writing, professional video production can be costly, and scriptwriters must be aware of this. Even though cheaper video cameras and software plus high-end video-enabled phones have brought costs down, a writer with a limited budget probably will have to forget about complex lighting, action, or special effects.

Informational Program Video Example

In the New England Economic Adventure, video, interactive games, and live hosts present information to high-school students in an immersive theater program. The excerpt below follows a short section that introduces the history of the times. Notice how they set up the background in this piece by making the main characters time travelers who can talk to us (the audience) directly.

HOST	VOTE; PDA	VIDEO & LIGHTING	AUDIO, NARRATION & SFX	EFX
HOST Now let's begin the Decision Round In this round, you'll have a chance to go back in time . . . to the year 1813, . . . where you'll decide how to invest your money. . . and you'll see if you make a profit. Ready to make some more money? Let's begin our trip.		LOGO Decision Round	SFX Decision Round SFX	1813 gobo effect timed to movie Lights fade out.

Continued

(Continued)

HOST	VOTE; PDA	VIDEO & LIGHTING	AUDIO, NARRATION & SFX	EFX
		CHRIS and SARA on screen in modern-dress against plain background. They matrix out of the scene.	CHRIS Ready? SARA Ready.	
		TRANSITION TO PAST Lights dim as sound effects fill room. We enter a door, and then a dark, private office.	EFFECTS *:5–:10 seconds* Lighting and sound effects in room take visitors back to 1813 Boston.	
		MAIN SCREEN VIDEO ADVISORS matrix into an area outside of LOWELL'S office. CHRIS and SARA materialize in costumes of the day that would make them fit in with Lowell and his friends. The sounds of "aheming" and murmuring from inside the office. They open the door and enter the office.	CHRIS (looking at his outfit, brushing himself off, maybe little flecks of electronic time transport material fly off) (to audience) Well, it looks like we all got here in one piece! SARA (brushing herself off) Let's fill you in quickly. We are all prosperous associates of a man named Francis Cabot Lowell. CHRIS We've made our money in trading, but Lowell has called us together to hear a startling new proposal. SARA C'mon. Let's go in.	
		LOWELL is presiding over a meeting. He sits at a functional office, or desk	LOWELL (to the advisors/audience) Welcome, welcome. Come in. Sit down. Meet my	

HOST	VOTE; PDA	VIDEO & LIGHTING	AUDIO, NARRATION & SFX	EFX
		with ledgers, papers. There are two or three other men in the room. CHRIS and SARA enter the room, the camera following as if they are leading us to our seats. They slip into a couple of seats.	associates. This is Patrick Jackson and Nathan Appleton. Sit down.	
		Props may hint at China trade, a porcelain tea service, a silk pillow or wall hanging of a Chinese scroll.	LOWELL I've called you here with a business proposition . . . After long hours of planning, I have devised a way by which we may avoid the catastrophic risks of the trading business . . . a new way to invest our money.	

© Federal Reserve Bank of Boston.

Computer Game Video Example

The following video script example is by writer Matthew Costello from the opening of the video game classic, *The 11th Hour*. Note how the characters, setting, background story, and key conflicts are set up quickly and visually through the use of the TV news show, the PDA, and Denning's reactions.

```
INTRO-1 INT/DENNING'S COUNTRY HOME—AFTERNOON*

CARL DENNING is watching television. His handsome face is grim and de-
termined, bathed in the flickering light of the TV's images. On the TV
screen, an anchorwoman is reading the evening news.

                         ANCHOR
            State Police have called off the intense search
            for producer Robin Morales of television's CASE
               UNSOLVED.
She continues to speak in voice-over as the screen is filled
with an image of an intelligent-looking woman with compelling beauty.
The words "ROBIN MORALES—CASE UNSOLVED PRODUCER" are superimposed
across the bottom of the screen.
```

                              ANCHOR (V/O)
        Morales was researching a story about the famed
        haunted house in the small town of Harley on
        Hudson—the abandoned mansion of Henry Stauf.

The anchorperson continues to talk over images of old newspaper
stories from the 1920s and mysterious photos of HENRY STAUF and
his ill-fated guests. The screen switches to current images of the
main street of Harley on Hudson.

                              ANCHOR (V/O)
        Police have expressed concern that Morales'
        disappearance may be connected to a series of
        killings that have plagued the Hudson Valley
        this year.

Another IMAGE, a BODY, lying in the grass. Signs of violence,
blood, the skin discolored, leaves and twigs stuck to the body.

                              ANCHOR (V/O)
        So far, four women and three men have been victims
        fitting a pattern of homicide, and several others
        are missing.

Another image of Robin comes onto the screen.

                              ANCHOR (V/O cont'd)
        Robin Morales has been missing for more than three
        weeks and seems to have vanished without a trace.
        The anchorwoman again appears on the screen.

                              ANCHOR
        She is the producer for the very popular and
        flamboyant CASE UNSOLVED reporter Carl Denning.

An image of Denning fills the screen, smiling, confident.

                              ANCHOR (V/O)
        Denning is said to have been in seclusion in
        his country home in Connecticut since Morales'
        disappearance. It's rumored that the two were
        romantically involved before . . .

Denning clicks off the TV with a remote switch. He slumps back in his
chair and massages his temples. He looks up at the sound of a doorbell
ringing, gets out of his chair and crosses the room and opens the door.
A UPS truck is pulling away and a package is on the doorstep.

    Denning crouches down and picks it up and goes back inside. He returns
to his chair and opens the package, revealing a small, portable computer
of some kind. He switches it on, and a game flickers to life on the
machine . . . "Funhouse From Hell". Cartoony images of mayhem, monsters

```
. . . Slowly, the computer game changes to an image of Robin looking
frightened in the basement of an old house. She speaks to him from the
small screen.
                              ROBIN
                Carl . . . help me . . . please! I can't get
                out . . . I . . .
The image of Robin fades away and the video screen goes blank as if
the game has shut itself off. Denning shakes the box and clicks it on
and off but it seems to have died.


                             DENNING
                What is this!?
He sets the game computer on the arm of the chair, gets to his feet
and begins to pace. The game starts beeping. He grabs it and switches
it on. An image of the Stauf mansion appears briefly and fades away and
the game shuts down again.


                             DENNING
                Damn!
Then the screen comes alive for another brief moment: an image of
Robin appears. She mouths the word "Help" but there is no sound and
the picture quickly fades. Denning pulls on a leather windbreaker and
stuffs the game in his pocket as he crosses the room and leaves in a
rush.
```

© Trilobyte Inc.

Conclusion

Although these skills are not needed for every project, a writer who is a master of writing for text, video, and audio will be an asset on an interactive media team. Learning interactive writing tools will make your writing better organized and more productive. Using script formats appropriate to your projects will make your concepts easier to understand. Tools and script formats are covered in the next chapter.

References

Andrew Nelson. Web Writer and Game Designer. Interview with the author

Google Official Blog. https://blog.google/

Nielsen Norman Group. F-Shaped Pattern of Reading on the Web: Misunderstood, But Still Relevant (Even on Mobile)

https://www.nngroup.com/articles/f-shaped-pattern-reading-web-content/

Nielsen Norman Group. How Users Read on the Web https://www.nngroup.com/articles/how-users-read-on-the-web/

O'Meara, Maria. Content Designer. Interview with the author

Usability Guidelines. https://digital.gov/

3 Interactive Writing Tools and Script Formats

Chapter Overview

Interactive media's use of many media and interactivity make the tools for organizing the complex content and clear script formats for presenting the content essential. This chapter will discuss the following tools and script formats:

- Flowcharting and other organizational tools
- Scripting software
- AI based writing tools
- Outlines
- Treatments
- Proposals and design documents
- Single-column scripts
- Multi-column scripts

Interactive Writing Tools

Flowcharting and Other Organizational Software

An interactive writer will use many different types of tools to organize and track project content. Spreadsheets, like Excel and Google Sheets, are definitely useful as are the outline and table features in word processing software for simpler projects. But perhaps the most useful organizational and visualization tool for the interactive writer is flowcharting software.

Flowcharting

Creating a flowchart is perhaps the clearest way to visualize and organize the branching structures of an interactive media program, (Figure 3–1). It is also a useful device to visualize processes, such as the applying for a job online or completing a series of exercises in an e-learning course. Fortunately, software for creating flowcharts is inexpensive and easy to learn.

DOI: 10.4324/9781003430612-5

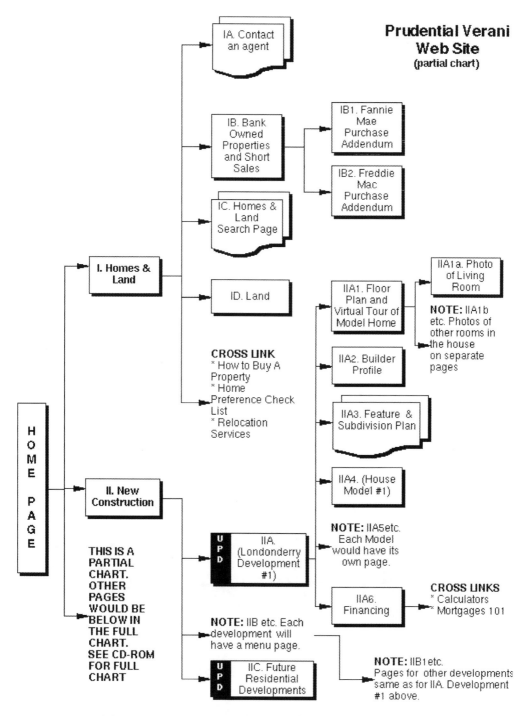

Figure 3–1 Partial flowchart/sitemap for the Verani Realty website

© Verani Realty

Flowchart Functions and Variations

A flowchart can have several functions and variations for the same production:

- To design interactions. Lines with arrows drawn between the labeled boxes on a chart make it possible to understand what links with what and in what way. For example, does the link work in both directions? Is it viewer-initiated or automatic?
- To see the effects of revisions. Continuity is a monstrous issue in interactive media. In linear media, changes in one scene may affect only the scenes immediately following it, but in interactive media, changes in one screen will affect all of the material that is linked to it. It is hard to determine these effects without a chart.
- To chart character development. Some writers create separate charts to track character development, particularly in parallel branching structures where the writers must be sure that the character change is properly set up and consistent in each plot line.
- To present material to clients. A complex interactive script can be inscrutable to a client, particularly one who has no interactive background. A one-page flowchart overview can do wonders to explain a project.
- To communicate with the production team. A production team chart is far more complicated than a client chart, especially a chart for the programmers, in which boxes are labeled with complicated programming code.
- To track large productions. Flowcharts combined with project management software can help chart the progress of a large production, keeping track of what has been accomplished and who is responsible for what lies ahead.
- To form the basis for the user's sitemap. Sometimes the chart itself is the user map, as in Fidelity Investments' retirement counselors' training program, where students can bring up the flowchart at any point and click on a labeled flowchart box to go to that section of the course.

Flowcharting Symbols

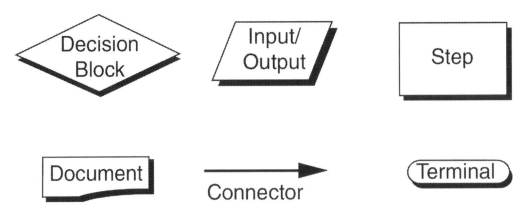

Figure 3–2 Common flowcharting symbols

Flowchart Symbols

There are a number of flowcharting symbols whose meaning is commonly accepted.

- Decision Block: a point where users have to make a choice that sends them to a different branch of the process or information.
- Input/Output: user enters data of some kind, such as a test or a form.
- Step: a single step in a process.
- Document or Page: a single screen or web page, usually contains multiple elements. Particularly on websites, the simple square is also commonly used for this.
- Connector: the link between symbols indicating process or information flow direction.
- Terminal: the beginning and ending points of a process.

Custom Symbols and Labels for a Project

The goal of using flowchart symbols or text labels is to increase clarity, but if there are too many complex symbols, they may add confusion. In my experience, a universal set of symbols has not been totally accepted. Instead, writers and developers seem to adopt symbols and labels that work well for them on a particular project. For example, Aaron Conners of Access Software uses shaded boxes to distinguish characters in his interactive dialogue.

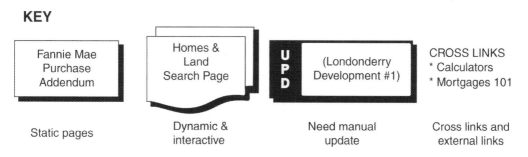

Figure 3–3 Custom flowcharting symbols for a specific project

Flowchart Design Tips

The goal is for the flowchart to be a clear visualization of the project structure. There are a number of techniques that help make it a more useful tool. The following points are illustrated in the Verani flowchart in Figure 3–1.

1. Give every screen of the program a unique number and name. This makes communication with clients and production staff much clearer. Give screens in a specific section of the site the same first number with different second letters. In the flowchart example in Figure 3–1, standard outline conventions were used with numbers and different case letters. For example, the menu page for the Homes and Land section is Roman numeral I. The Contact an Agent Page, which is linked to that page, is page IA, and so on.
2. For ease of printing and presentation to a client or on a review website, run the chart vertically, as in the sample in Figure 3–1, instead of horizontally. If this becomes a problem because your site is more than five levels deep, you may want to reexamine your

information architecture and divide your material into more main categories. If a site has too many levels, it can cause navigation problems.

3. Simplify where you can. If there will be multiple screens that will be designed in the same way, it is OK to say that in a note. No need to draw out all the boxes for repetitive pages. There are several examples of this on the chart in the New Construction section where each housing development will be presented on the site the same way.

4. Make it easier to see the main sections by writing those pages in bold text. See "Homes and Land" and "New Construction" in Figure 3–1.

5. Indicate cross-links (links to screens within the site that are already on the chart) and external links (links to other websites) as text only. This helps make the chart more readable and makes it clearer how many screens have to be produced for this project. If there are multiple cross-links or external links from the same page, use bullets to separate them.

6. Visually indicate the pages that will have special functions. Do not, however, make your chart confusing with too many different types of symbols. Three or four symbols with a simple key at the top are adequate. See the key sample in Figure 3–3.

Flowcharting Software

The key characteristics of a good writer's flowcharting program are that it can:

- Easily and quickly create and edit flowcharts.
- Export the chart in a standard image format, such as PDF.
- Be web based or used cross-platform so everyone on the team can work with your documents.
- Convert the chart into an outline and vice versa. This conversion is useful because:
  - some clients prefer outlines
  - a chart can be converted into an outline, and then that outline can be used as the basis of a script for a program
  - an outline can be imported from another program and then converted to a flowchart.

Software Recommendation

There are lots of tools that you can use to create flowcharts including word processors, draw programs, authoring programs, and presentation software, but like any dedicated task, you are going to be much better off getting software designed specifically for flowcharting.

There are many good flowcharting programs on the market. Depending on your situation, you may not be able to choose the software and will have to use whatever the client or the rest of the production team already uses. Some commonly used flowcharting software are LucidChart, Miro, SmartDraw, and Visio. You can also create flowcharts in any design software. In a pinch, you can use the draw program in Google Docs or MS Word.

Scripting Software

Some types of interactive writing don't have separate script documents at all. This is often the case in UX writing where the primary output might be link text, button labels, and on-screen direction. In this case, the UX Writer may use a simple spreadsheet, text doc, a dedicated UX writing tools, or the same design software used by the designer, allowing the UX Writer to write directly on the design screens. See Figure 3–4 showing a preliminary design

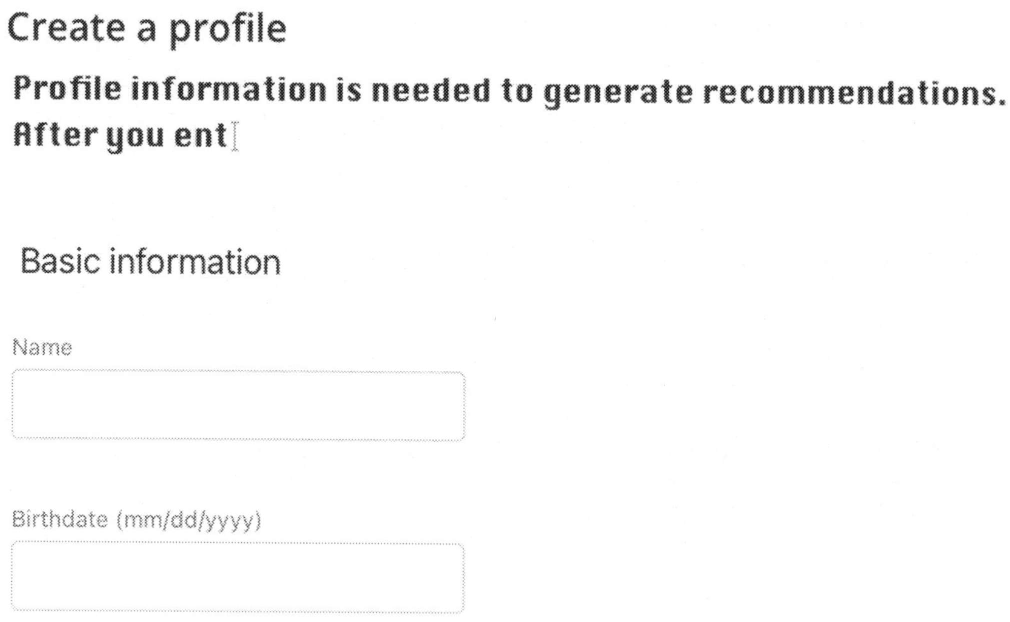

Create a profile

Profile information is needed to generate recommendations. After you ent

Basic information

Name

[   ]

Birthdate (mm/dd/yyyy)

[   ]

Figure 3–4 Design software that allows the writer to enter text directly into the sketch that the designer has created

© Pearson plc

for a nutrition application where the writer enters the text for the application instructions directly into the design. We will talk more about the writing process for UX Writers in Part II of this book.

Unlike UX writing, complex writing projects such as content websites, immersive museum exhibits, training programs, or video games usually have detailed scripts. Some writers use domain specific writing tools, such as Final Draft for video, or custom writing software designed to work with a specific gaming engine. Some of these tools can be real time savers, but before investing in expensive software, it is best to determine what your specific production is using because collaboration is key. You need to be able to easily share your writing with the team, so it is important that everyone has the same software.

For this reason, instead of using dedicated scriptwriting software, some writers use a major word processing program, such as MS Word or Google Docs. Everyone on the team has these tools so your documents can be easily reviewed and edited. The key to script formatting with a word processor is to become skilled with tables and learn how to create macros. Macros allow you to automate certain formatting functions and make writing a script much easier.

AI Based Writing Tools

There are quite a number of writing tools that incorporate AI (Artificial Intelligence). At the low end, these tools can include relatively simple writing assistants that walk the novice writer through the established writing steps, such as research, outline, draft, revisions etc.

At the high end, AI writing tools, such as GPT (Generative Pre-trained Transformer) or its conversational off shoot, ChatGPT, can complete an entire writing assignment based on well written prompts from the human writer. For example, a writer enters into the AI writing tool: "For a history class write an essay on the 5 reasons the South lost the Civil War." The AI tool will reach into its database of information to find information on Civil War history and proper essay format. Based on this information, the AI tool will generate an essay for the student, including citations and bibliography. The quality of the essay will totally depend on how well the models in the AI tool were trained. If highly trained on Civil War history and essay writing, the output might be a reasonable first draft. If the AI tool was not well trained on these topics, the results will be far less impressive and perhaps totally useless.

The example above illustrates the answer to the question: "Will AI writing tools replace the human writer?" The answer is it will depend on what type of writing you are doing. If you are writing in a standardized, well-established format, the answer might be "yes" or "somewhat." One example is a real estate agent who needs to write property descriptions for the company's website. The agent could just enter the unique features of this property, e.g., two bedrooms, on lake, etc., and assuming the AI tool was trained in how to write real estate listing, the tool could churn out a full listing in seconds. The agent might just need to give the listing a quick polish and post it to the site.

On the other hand, if you are writing a more complex work on an unusual topic, such as this book, with many original sources that do not appear elsewhere, the AI tool would be hard pressed to be successful.

AI and Writing for Interactive Media

How AI writing tools will impact writing for interactive media, will depend on the type of writing you are doing and the power of the AI tool you have chosen. If your job is to create a sitemap for a basic ecommerce website, a standard news blog for a corporate site, or a routine celebrity social media post, you can probably find an AI tool to create a draft with effective prompts from the human writer. On the other hand, if the assignment is to flow-chart the interactive dialogue of characters in a computer game or plot out the best way to teach statistic in an e-learning program, the AI writing tool may be less helpful.

The most productive way to think about these AI writing tools is not as a threat, but instead as one more resource in your arsenal as a writer. Pick an AI writing tool that seems to have the capabilities for the writing task at hand. Spend some time to learn how to use the tool effectively. Then use the tool to save time, generate ideas, and compare different ways to approach the project. Be aware where the AI tool may not be useful, e.g., on complex projects with unique topics. Ultimately, you will still need to learn how to be an effective interactive writer yourself, so you can evaluate if your AI writing buddy is giving you gems or junk.

Preliminary Documents: Outlines, Proposals, Treatments, and Design Documents

A project's script or detailed design document includes every word of text, narration, and dialogue; descriptions of all the images, video, and animation; and explanations of the linking and functional elements. Fortunately, projects almost never start with a script. Usually, some sort of preliminary written document is presented to the client and other members of the production teams before the final script is written. This is useful for clients who may have difficulty understanding an interactive script. It also ensures that the basic goals of the project are being achieved before the fine details are worked out in the script. Sometimes the preliminary form itself, such as a website outline, is adequate to get the production green-lighted with the client or business owners. (One preliminary document, the use case, which defines the user's needs, is explained in a later chapter.)

Outlines

Before writing a full text script of all the content on a website or another information heavy program, such as an online course, it is useful to write a content outline and a flowchart to explain the content and navigation to the client and production team.

Flowcharts were discussed in detail earlier in this chapter, but briefly the flowchart illustrates the overall navigation, structure, and size of the site; the outline provides more details about the actual content and functionality of the individual screens. The outline sample that follows is most effectively used with an accompanying flowchart. The client consults the chart for overall structure, and then reads the outline for the details. The structure of each page on the outline below is fairly simple. The outline should be adjusted to match the specific project. The elements include:

- Title: the screen title, which should be the same as what is on the flowchart.
- Image: describes possible images for the page, including animations or video.
- Text: describes on-screen text.
- Links: includes all the links on this page from text within the page and from the navigation bar or menu.
- Navigation: the specific buttons that will have to be created for the navigation bar or menu.
- Functionality: this describes what the user can do on this page besides click and read. For example, if it is a real estate site, as in the example below, can they search for properties or calculate their mortgage?

Partial Outline of the *Verani* Real Estate Website

HOME PAGE

TITLE: VERANI REALTY: The Real Estate and Relocation Resource for Southern NH

IMAGE: Images that demonstrate that Verani is a professional, friendly place. Possible images: logo, friendly Verani staff, Verani office, people enjoying a beautiful home. Might have other images on page to lead user to some of our key features, such as a calculator image for the tools and an E-mail icon for our custom E-mail notification service. Images will be small or designed in such a way that the page will load quickly.

TEXT: Explain that we are a family-owned company with strong roots in Southern New

Hampshire. We have the resources to sell your property effectively and/or make your home search efficient and successful. Also, you should introduce some of the key features of the site, such as our searches, custom E-mail notification tools, extensive information resources, and so on. Near the bottom of the page should be a short disclaimer stating that we have made every effort to make the information on this site accurate but are not liable for any errors or omissions; please see our Terms of Use Policy.

LINKS: Homes & Land, New Construction, Commercial & Industrial, Relocation Services, Verani Mortgage and Title, Real Estate Information & Resources, News & Special Events, Search/Site Map, About Us/Contact. Might also have a link from a calculator image to the tools and calculator section. In text on the bottom of the page and on every page will be links to Terms of Use, Privacy Statements, and a WebMaster Email link.

NAVIGATION BAR: Homes & Land, New Construction, Commercial & Industrial, Relocation Services, Verani Mortgage and Title, Real Estate Information & Resources, News & Special Events, Search/Site Map, About Us/Contact.

I. HOMES & LAND

TITLE: Homes & Land

IMAGE: Small image of attractive house. This could be the same picture all the time or a regularly changing featured house.

TEXT: Briefly explain the range of properties we offer and the area we cover. Direct the user to the search page and other services that will help them in their moving and home buying, such as Relocation Services, the How to Buy a Property Section, Home Preference Check List/Questionnaire, & New Construction.

LINKS: Home, Search, Contact, Relocation Services, the How to Buy a Property Section, Home Preference Check List/Questionnaire, & New Construction.

NAVIGATION BAR: Home, Search, Contact

IA. CONTACT AN AGENT

TITLE: Contact Us

IMAGE: Photo of friendly agent.

TEXT: Phone numbers, addresses, and E-mails for all offices. Plus a form that user can fill out and submit so that we can contact them.

LINKS: Home Page, Search, Contact, Homes & Land.

NAVIGATION BAR: Home Page, Search, Contact, Homes & Land.

FUNCTIONALITY: Users can fill out form with their address and E-mail, click the type of information they want, write a short note and submit it to us. Message will go to different people at Verani depending on what type of information the user requests.

© Verani Realty

Treatments

Although a treatment could be used for a preliminary description of a website, it is more commonly used for media programs, such as a training program. The treatment, a form borrowed from linear film or TV writing, describes the structure and key elements of a project in a form similar to an essay or a short story. Guidelines for treatment writing include:

- Use the third person (e.g., "He shambles," not "I shamble" or "you shamble").
- Use the present tense ("he shambles," not "he shambled").
- Write visually. Be descriptive, but don't call shots if there is video.
- Capitalize:
  - Character names when they first appear.
  - Major sound effects.
  - Technical directions, such as LINK, etc. (but don't use unless necessary).
- Usually summarize on-screen text, dialogue, and narration, although a few bits of dialogue or narration are allowed if they help present the material.
- Usually double-space treatments, although sometimes they are single-spaced, with chapter or section headings in all capitals.

Informational Treatment Sample

The following sample is from the conclusion of the treatment for *The Nauticus Shipbuilding Company*, a multimedia program about shipbuilding presented on a museum kiosk. (The entire treatment may be found under "The Proposal" in Part III of the book in the "Museum Kiosk Case Study: The Nauticus Shipbuilding Company.")

> **Conclusion:** After the last component has been selected, a 3-D animation sequence depicts the launching of the vessel. If the design is suitable for the mission, the visitor will see a depiction of their design successfully carrying out the mission. If the design is fundamentally flawed, the vessel will be shown sinking. Some evaluation will be provided as to the ability of the visitor's design to carry out the selected mission. Finally, the visitor will be given the opportunity to print out their design and evaluation.

© Chedd-Angier Production Company and The National Maritime Center

Narrative Treatment Sample

A narrative interactive treatment is sometimes called a walkthrough. Following is a section of the walkthrough for the video game, *The Pandora Directive*.

> In the introductory conversation with Gordon Fitzpatrick, you learn that he is looking for a Dr. Thomas Malloy, who recently

```
stayed at the Ritz Hotel. Fitzpatrick and Malloy used to work
together (where, unspecified). Fitzpatrick then says he saw
a photograph of Malloy in the Bay City Mirror and found out
that the photograph had been taken at a local university (San
Francisco Tech). Fitzpatrick gives Tex a copy of the photo.
```

© Access Software, Inc.

Proposals and Design Documents

A treatment is usually only one component of the first detailed description of an interactive project. This preliminary description is sometimes called a high-level design document proposal, a design proposal, or just a proposal.

Format for an Informational Design Document Proposal

A proposal can be in many forms. There are several examples in the cases studies. One fairly standard approach includes the following elements. See Chapter 14 for a complete design document following this format.

- Design objective. This is a short description of what the program hopes to accomplish. It is sometimes no more than a paragraph, but it is important because it is the first chance to grab the reader.
- Creative treatment. This is a detailed description of the entire program. It will run for many pages, depending on the size of the project.
- Navigation. This is a description of the interface and how the user will navigate through the program. It often includes a navigation flow chart. The navigation is also described in the treatment.
- Production and marketing. Design documents often have sections dealing with the project schedule or, if it is a mass-market piece, ideas for marketing the program to the public. Biographies of the writer, designer, and other key personnel are sometimes included here.

Format for a Narrative Proposal

A proposal for a multimedia program that includes a story would follow much of the same format as above. It may, however, call the treatment a "story summary." There may also be sections describing the characters.

Final Documents: Scripts

Unlike the preliminary documents discussed above that summarize the key features of a program, the script details every element of a piece. The examples that follow are only a few of the interactive script formats in use, but they present enough options that you should be able to find something that can be adapted for your production.

Be aware that many productions don't use traditional scripts at all and instead use combinations of flowcharts, dialogue lists, walkthroughs, and other types of written material. These materials and other script samples are documented in more detail in the case studies in Part III, "Writing and Structuring Long Form Interactive Information—Websites,

E-Learning, Simulations, and Part IV, Writing and Designing Interactive Narrative—Games, Immersive Experiences."

Linear Screenplay Format

Many approaches to formatting scripts for interactive multimedia use linear screenplay or teleplay format as their basis and then add variations. Also, interactive media such as games or educational programs often have snippets of linear video that are linked in various combinations in the interactive interface. So it is useful to understand the specifics of the linear screenplay format.

Script format is important because the running time of a video is judged by the number of pages. One page, if it is typed in proper format, is roughly, one minute of screen time. There are variations on the example below, such as greater use of double-spacing in television writing, but the example is a standard screenplay format that can readily be adapted to different situations. Note that margins and line spacing are distorted in the example below to allow space for the directions.

The format below includes some technical and camera directions. Be aware that if you a writing a script to hand off to a director or multimedia designer, they may not want such directions included. In that case, you can still use the same format below, but leave out the technical and shot material, such as "Camera Dollies Back."

DIRECTIONS

Top margin = 1". Number pages in upper right-hand corner. No number on page 1.

Slug lines are typed in CAPS at the beginning of each scene, telling whether scene is INT. or EXT. (interior or exterior), location of scene, and day or night.

Scene Description: Left margin 1.5", right margin 1"

Break long descriptions into several short paragraphs. The first time a character's name appears in the scene description, type it in CAPS.

Single-space within scene description or dialogue. Add a blank line space between dialogue passages, scene description paragraphs, and slug lines.

```
THE INTERACTIVE MEDIA WRITER


FADE IN:


INT. ARNOLD'S BEDROOM DAY

The room is a wreck. The floor is
covered with papers and trash,
the bed is unmade, and cigarette
butts litter the desk and
windowsills.

ARNOLD throws the door open and
stumbles into the room. CAMERA
DOLLIES BACK with him. Arnold
is in his early 20s, thin, and
unkempt. His once handsome fea-
tures are contorted in agony.
He clutches what appears to be
a multimedia manuscript in his
hand.

He stumbles to the floor and falls
to his knees, pulling the script
to his bosom. He falls back with
a scream and hits the floor in
agony, dropping the script.
```

Dialogue: left margin = 2.5", right margin = 1.5"

The title of the manuscript is revealed to be The Great American website

                    ARNOLD (OS)*
                    (whispering)

 Why me?

DISSOLVE TO:

EXT. ARNOLD'S APARTMENT DAY LONG SHOT
The door of the apartment swings open and Arnold stumbles out clutching his script.
                    ARNOLD
I keep asking myself: What is the secret?

Name of person speaking dialogue is in CAPS. No space between speaker's name and dialogue. Dialogue speaker: left margin = 3.5"

The booming, powerful, authoritative voice from the unseen NARRATOR of our film is heard.
                    NARRATOR (VO)**
                    (booming)

Dialogue direction is typed in small letters, centered under speaker, and placed in parentheses. Dialogue direction: left margin = 3"

Arnold never did learn the secret. He should have read Tim Garrand's *Writing for Interactive Media*.
THE CAMERA QUICKLY ZOOMS IN TO Arnold. He tosses away his script in the trash and runs off.

Camera movements, such as tilt, pan, track, dolly, and zoom typed in CAPS in the scene description. On right side of page are placed: Fade out and Dissolve to. On left is Fade in. (If you are not the designer or director, you may need to eliminate most of these technical directions.)

Bottom margin = 1". It depends on how dialogue breaks. Don't break dialogue over two pages.

His script sits on the top of the trashcan, its pages fluttering sadly.

FADE OUT.

*(OS) next to the speaker means off-screen. The character is part of the action, but we do not see him or her in this particular shot. A character yelling from the bathroom while the camera focuses on the bedroom is an example of an off-screen voice. Or, as in the example above, the camera could simply be focused on an object in the same room as the character, leaving the character nearby but off-screen.

**(VO) next to the speaker means voice-over. This indicates that the speaker is not a part of the film or video's action. A modern newscaster narrating a World War I documentary is an example of VO.

Single-Column, Simple If-Then Interactive Format

Use: narrative or informational programs with limited interactivity, usually at the scene level. Because it is a single-column script, it would not be well suited to a program with extensive voice-over narration. That usually requires a multi-column script, which is explained later in this chapter under "Double-Column Format" and "Triple-Column Format."

Description: this script is similar to the linear screenplay described above, except that at various points in the script the user is given two or three choices of different scenes. This type of script can be used when the interactivity is fairly simple. The following example is part of an interactive museum piece that was installed at the National Scouting Museum when it was in Irving, Texas. In this story, the characters have to choose whether to search the school, the farm, or the neighborhood for a missing child. The situation is first outlined in a linear fashion, and then the options follow: first the school scene option, then the farm scene option. The neighborhood option is not included in this sample.

BOY SCOUT PATROL THEATER

by Maria O'Meara

```
SCENE 2

TROOP HQ

2-1. WS GROUP

                          ALEX

     Okay. We all know why we're here. Bob has divided the map
     into areas. We're going to use the buddy system to cover each
     one.


                          BOB

Here's a map of the area we're searching.

2-2. MAP GRAPHIC
                     BOB (voice-over)

     This is where she was last seen—the school. Here's where she
     lives. Between the two is the old Wilson Farm.

WHICH PART DO YOU WANT TO SEARCH?
A. THE SCHOOL
B. THE FARM
C. THE GIRL'S NEIGHBORHOOD

IF A. THE SCHOOL
SCENE 2A
2A-1. CU ALEX
```

                              ALEX
        Chas and Don, you guys go see if she's not still hanging
        around the school.
M-1.
TRANSITION MONTAGE TO SCHOOL
1. POV HALLWAY
2. POV SCIENCE ROOM
3. POV POOL
4. POV STAIRS

SCENE 3
3-1.2 SHOT BOYS enter a classroom.

[Scenes have been deleted. The boys search the school and fail to find the girl. They return
to scout headquarters and must choose again.]

WHICH PART DO YOU WANT TO SEARCH?
A. THE SCHOOL
B. THE FARM
C. THE GIRL'S NEIGHBORHOOD

[IF B. THE FARM]
2B-1. 2 SHOT ALEX AND BOB

                              ALEX
              Greg and Hal—search the farm.

M-2.
TRANSITION MONTAGE TO FARM AREA
1. POV WOODS

They happen upon their science teacher who is looking for mushrooms
in a field. He looks very scientific, and has a sample bag, notebook,
magnifying glass, etc. He is humming a little song.

———————————

© National Scouting Museum of the Boy Scouts of America

Single-Column, Complex If-Then Interactive Format

Use: the previous example had fairly simple if-then conditions. For example, if the scout decided to search the farm, then we cut to the farm scene. For many projects the interactivity is far more complex. In such projects, the questions users ask of characters in the program or what action users did previously will affect what new actions, characters, or dialogue will appear on screen. This type of complex if-then interactivity requires a more complex format.

Description: the following sample is from the computer game, *Nancy Drew: Secret of the Old Clock*. This is a highly interactive program where the player gradually accumulates clues and information to solve a mystery. The player gathers the information in a non-linear sequence. So, the game engine needs to keep track of what the player has already discovered in order to reveal the next pertinent bit of information. For example, if the player has already asked a certain character about another character's middle name, they should get a different response than if they had not asked that question previously. In the first line of the sample below, there is an elaborate series of conditions that indicates what the player already knows. "If EV_Saw_Questions = True and EV_EC_Said_Lois = False and EV_JW_Said_Mid_Name = False." This indicated the player does not know the middle name is "Lois" and that the player has not asked this specific character JW about this before. When these conditions are met, the player will be able to click on (ask) the question that follows the conditions tagged with < >, and the character will respond with the line that's in square brackets ([ ]). However, if the conditions are different and JW_Said_Mid_Name = True (see the line below "Go to 1048"), that means the player has asked JW about this before and instead of Scene 1047, Scene 1048 will be used in which the player is sent to another character, Emily. This script format is used in conjunction with a flowchart. There is a more detailed discussion of this script format and this game in Part IV Interactive Narrative.

Scene 1047 Information Check

```
If EV_Saw_Questions = True and EV_EC_Said_Lois = False and EV_JW_
Said_Mid_Name = False

<What was Emily's mom's middle name, do you remember?><NJP47>

['Course I do. It was ... {frustrated}Oh, piffle! It's right on the
tip of my tongue. It was ... it was ...][JWP47]
```

Go to 1048

```
Flag Set: EV_JW_Said_Mid_Name = True
Info Check: No
Bye: No
===========
```

Scene 1048

```
[{with an exasperated sigh}It'll pop into this feeble brain of mine
one of these days. Why don't you just go ask Emily.][JWP48]
Flag Set: None
Info Check: Yes
Bye: Yes
===========
```

Single-Column, Screen-Based Informational Script with Element Labels

Use: this script is best suited to an informational program that has considerable interactivity and a variety of media, such as narration, text, and video. Screen elements are clearly defined in the script by labels.

Description: this script was used in the training program *Vital Signs*, which teaches medical technicians how to perform various tasks. Each script page is one screen of material. The script page has three parts divided by horizontal lines. The top part describes the lesson and topic. The middle part describes the actions. The bottom part describes the feedback (reaction to the actions) and linking.

VITAL SIGNS

Unit: u1
Lesson: Blood Pressure
Topic:
Title:
Screen: u1.4.13p
Type:
Graphic File:

(GRAPHIC/VIDEO: Colette looking apprehensive)
Text:
Meet Colette, age 7. You're going to take her blood pressure.
You've explained the procedure to her. What do you use next?
(CAPTIONS)
Cuff Ball Pump   Valve on cuff Doll

(AUDIO: NARRATOR VO): Now it's your turn. Meet Colette, age 7.
You're going to take her blood pressure. You've explained the
procedure. What do you use next—the cuff, the ball pump, the valve
on the cuff, or the doll? SELECT your choice now.

Feedback: (VO and text)
Cuff, Ball Pump, Valve = (SFX: Little Girl's Voice) **(VO audio ONLY):**
No. I don't want that. It's going to hurt!

NARRATOR (VO): Apparently, Colette didn't buy your
explanation. Try again.

Doll = **NARRATOR (VO):** You're good. That's right. From the look on
her face, you can tell Colette didn't buy your explanation, so you
demonstrate on a doll. (SELECT "GO AHEAD" to continue.)

Branching: u1.4.14p

Special Instructions:

© Harvard Pilgrim Health Plan

Single-Column, Screen-Based Informational Script Table Format

Use: this type of script could be used for a narrative or information piece with a large team, substantial interactivity, and many different types of media.

Description: Houghton Mifflin developed a geology website. The project was quite large, had numerous assets (video, graphics, audio, animations), several content experts, and a number of editors. Developing a coherent script that would clearly describe all these elements and allow all the content people and developers to review was a challenge.

GEOLOGY EXPLORER	
Page Number. **Title Date**	VIII-2b Relative Ages

Screen Text	Now see if you can determine the year in which the car in the center was released. Write your answer in the space provided and then hit "Continue." If you have absolutely no idea, just hit "Continue."
Visual Layout	Layout 2 Text top, Graphic bottom. The graphic consists of the three cars in a row. A text input box labeled "Car Release Date" is above the 1955 Ford.
Screen Action	Input date; hit "Continue."
Feedback	
Links	Correct Answer + Continue ◊ VIII-2b1 Incorrect Answer + Continue. ◊ VIII-2b2.
A: Graphic 1	D1) Model-T Ford
A: Graphic 2	D2) 1955 Ford
A: Graphic 3	D3) 1999 Lexus
A: Animation	
A: Audio	
A: Video	
A: Shockwave	Three pictures are arranged in a horizontal row with a text input box above D2) 1955 Ford.
Assets Notes	
Notes Internal	No need to actually register whether the student is right. We can just give the correct answer.
Notes to Author	
Notes to Vendor	

© Houghton Mifflin Company

Double-Column Format

Use: informational projects with substantial interactivity and voice-over narration.

Description: this format is similar to what is used for documentary video. It has two columns, with images on the left and audio and text on the right. An unusual aspect of this particular script is that it is illustrated, which works very well to present the feel of the completed project. Most double-column scripts do not include images.

This program is displayed in an interactive kiosk at the National Maritime Center in Norfolk, Virginia. This production teaches shipbuilding principles by having the player build a ship. In the following section, users can choose to get information on various hull types and then must pick one of these hulls for the ship they are building. Because there is only a small amount of material on each hull, all the choices are listed sequentially. See Chapter 14 for the full script.

THE NAUTICUS SHIPBUILDING COMPANY

IMAGES   AUDIO & TEXT

"Press a number to learn about a hull"

CHOICES:

1) Air Cushion
-Flat hull rides on cushion of air
-Capable of high speeds
-Needs flat water conditions
-Flat, rectangular deck, easy to load

2) Planing Hull
-V-shaped hull capable of high speeds
-Performs best in flat water conditions
-High stress levels on hull

3) Displacement Hull
-Deep, rounded hull, very stable in
all conditions
-Very large cargo capacity
-Stable platform for large propulsion
systems
-Needs very large propulsion system

4) SWATH (Small Waterplane Area Twin
Hull)
-2 submerged hulls, very stable
-Flat deck provides good work area

After selecting a hull to use,   Loudspeaker VO: "Planing hull being
cut to Design Assembly screen,   moved into position."
animation of hull rollout.

Cut to POV animation moving to   Background sound of motors whirring
propulsion subassembly area.   and machinery clanging. "Next, you'll
                                      need to choose a propulsion system."

Three Column Format with Narration and Text Transcript

Use: informational scripts with substantial interactivity and a variety of media including both audio narration and on-screen text transcripts of that narration.

 Description: this project was for an educational program teaching key math concepts. Often learning programs will have both audio narration and a text transcript on screen of the narration. This helps learners who may prefer to read vs. listen, do not have audio, or who have a disability. The writer cannot just repeat the narration and the text transcript because there will be subtle difference in the narration, which must be listened to (and read aloud by the narrator) and the text transcript which is read silently by the user. Note that the narration column is shaded to clearly identify if for the narrator who must read the text. This format also has a fourth column, which was used for production purposes, such as timing the narration. The animations and graphics are simply described by a file name, which is described in detail on a separate animation page of the script. On the book's website, see the information cases study on "E-Learning: Math and Statistics Online Course" for a more detailed example of this format.

Images, Text, Programming	Narration (Text Transcript)	Narration (Audio Transcript)	Project Note
1)(Title Creating Time Plots			
2)(Main Screen Text) When data are collected over a period of time, they can be represented by a **time plot.**	When data are collected over a period of time, they can be represented by a **time plot.**	When data are collected over a period of time, they can be represented by a **time plot.**	
3)(Definition Box) A time plot is a graph showing data measurements in chronological order.	A time plot is a graph that shows data measurements in chronological order. It is important to note that the interval of time between measurements should be the same. So, if you take a measurement once a week, it should be on the same day every week. Or, if you take a measurement every day, the same time period, such as one-half hour, should be used.	A time plot is a graph that shows data measurements in chronological order. It is important to note that the interval of time between measurements should be the same. So, if you take a measurement once a week, it should be on the same day every week. Or, if you take a measurement every day, the same time period, such as one-half hour, should be used.	
4a)(Procedure Box) Making a Time Plot [il0262m02c01anim01 F1_IW.ai]	To make a time plot, use the following procedure.	To make a time plot, use the following procedure.	

Five Column Format with Live Host, Interactive Media, and Audience Interactivity
(see sample on the next page)

Use: immersive exhibits in museums or complex presentations at major conferences and events that use a combination of live host and interactive before live audiences.

Description: script has five columns for the Host's dialogue, user interaction in this case through a PDA (small handheld computer) attached to each seat, video on big screen, audio and narration, and lighting effects on the audience, and cues for the host who controls the program. A longer example of this script can be read in Chapter 14.

Conclusion

There are useful tools to organize the breaking down of the many bits of interactive content, their relationship to each other, and the content or interaction flow. Besides dedicated tools, the most useful to the writer are spreadsheets and flowcharting software.

Once you have organized your content, there is an even wider variety of ways to present this content to your team. These approaches range from writing directly into the draft designs, outlines, treatment, single and multi-column scripts. There is no one right way to format a script for an interactive media program. The primary requirement is to make sure that whatever format you choose, it is clear to the client/stakeholder and to everyone on your production team.

HOST	VOTE; PDA	VIDEO & LIGHTING	AUDIO, NARRATION & SFX	EFX	CUES
HOST In our first game, we'll be visiting the year 1813 and exploring the beginnings of the textile industry here in New England. Look down at your screen to see how much you have to start with.		Graphic or animation Bank account icon from PDA.		1813 Gobo effect on queue with movie	Host—next at the word screen activates pda info
HOST As you see, you each have $10,000 in your accounts. Remember, that's $10,000 in 1813 dollars. But in that time, just as today, you could earn money ... so let's earn a little more money right now in our Lightning Round.	PDA GRAPHIC on system shows each person how much they have.	MAIN SCREEN Graphic Bank account shows amount of money each person has.			
HOST You'll have a chance to answer 3 questions. For each one you answer correctly, you'll earn		GRAPHIC Lightning Round graphic or animation flashes on main screen. Possible lighting effects	SFXL lightning round theme song plays.	Host spot and blue wash fade out. Gobo Lightning effects	Host—next on the words Lightning Round. Movie starts 30 frames after lights fade out.

Continued

HOST	VOTE; PDA	VIDEO & LIGHTING	AUDIO, NARRATION & SFX	EFX	CUES
$1,000! You'll have 10 seconds after the question to enter your answer. Anyone have any questions? ... Let's start the lightning round.	flash through-out room.			timed to main screen.	
	VISITORS have a pre-set amount of time to answer the questions	GRAPHIC & MAIN SCREEN TEXT BUILD, with graphics What was the relationship between Britain and the United States in 1813? a. They were at war. b. They were allies. c. The US was a British colony. d. Europeans had not yet come to North America.	CHRIS (VO) First question. What was the relationship between Britain and the United States in 1813? a. They were at war. b. They were allies. c. The US was a British colony. d. Europeans had not yet come to North America.		

4   Collaborating with a Team

Chapter Overview

Interactive media is a varied field with a need for many different types of writing skills. This chapter defines the roles of various types of writers ranging from UX Writer to Game Writer to Social Media Specialist.

There are also many different production team members with whom the writer needs to collaborate in order to create impactful content. These team members and their relationship to the writer are also explained.

The Interactive Media Writer

The romantic image of a writer banging away on a keyboard alone in a tiny garret apartment may still be true for writers of novels or spec screenplays, but it is definitely not the way most interactive writers work. Successful interactive writers are effective collaborators with the members of their production and design team. Of course, interactive writers do spend some time alone particularly on longer assignments, but much of the time they contribute to solutions by working with various members of their team. So, if you are used to doing all your writing quietly alone, learning to collaborate will be another challenge you will face as an interactive writer.

Interactive media writers themselves have different titles and perform different tasks. The interactive writer may create: button labels, link text, proposals, outlines, sitemaps, treatments, walkthroughs, design documents, scripts, and all the other written material that is part of an interactive media project. Depending on skill set, a writer may just write the text or may also be involved in developing the information architecture, story structure, characters, and more. Exactly which of these tasks the writer actually does on a specific project depends on the needs of the project, the size of the team, and the skills of the writer. Usually, writers have different titles depending on the tasks they perform. None of these titles and definitions are cast in stone, but they are common understandings of the titles.

Writer

Someone with the title Writer is probably more of a generalist doing a variety of different writing and content tasks, Often the title Writer will be used on smaller teams or projects.

Copywriter

A Copywriter usually works in advertising or marketing coming up with concepts and creating the text for campaigns.

DOI: 10.4324/9781003430612-6

Content Writer

A Content Writer is a broader title that does what the title describes creates larger bodies of content for websites, educational material, or even entertainment. Often also just called a writer.

Technical Writer

In interactive media, a Technical Writer primarily explains how to use complex application software in training and help documentation. Materials, such as FAQs and help articles in an online help center would be written by this writer.

UX Writer/Content Designer

UX writing or user experience writing is one of the fastest growing writing fields in interactive media. The UX Writer primary creates effective bits of text to help a customer use a product, such as a mobile app, website, or learning application. This microcopy can include button labels, link text, on-screen directions, error text, etc. Sometimes the UX Writer may venture into what was formerly the technical writer's domain and write shorter help material, such as FAQs. On smaller projects, the UX Writer may play the role of UX Writer and Technical Writer, possibly Content Writer as well. The UX Writer usually works closely with the UX Designer. The name of this role is gradually changing to Content Designer, but UX Writer is still commonly used. See Chapter 6 for more on UX Writing.

Social Media Specialist/Producer

Although most people write and post to their own social media accounts, writing for social media is also a professional job. The communication channels of media companies and other businesses include social media: Facebook, Instagram, Twitter, TikTok, etc. In addition to writing, social media writers generally prepare other content needed for the social media posts such as photos, graphics, and video. They also often schedule the posts and analyze data to see what posts are successful. See Chapter 7 for more on social media writing.

Game/Narrative Writer

The writers of video games have some of the most varied titles. Game Writer or Narrative Writer are a couple, but you will see others. Game Writers do similar work to that of a film/TV scriptwriter but keeping interactivity in mind. They write the overall story, scenes, dialogue, and create characters. Some Game Writers play a role in the design of the games and earn the title Writer/Designer. See Part IV for more on writing for interactive narrative.

The Interactive Media Team

No matter what the writer's title, understanding who the team members are and how to interact with them can add to the writer's success and ultimately that of the project. Following are some of the key players that an interactive writer might engage with on a project. The team configuration varies on each project. There are other roles not mentioned here. There may also be some overlapping of tasks between roles.

- Content Strategist
- UX/Product Designer
- Content Designer
- Information Architect
- Instructional Designer
- Game Designer
- Subject Matter Expert (SME)
- Business Analyst
- Actors/Voice Talent
- Video/Audio Director
- Product Manager
- Usability Expert

Content Strategist

Content can be presented in a wide variety of ways. Content Strategists determine how the content will be presented through analysis of the users' information needs, technical expertise, favored delivery media, culture, and the products brand position in the market. The strategists also research the current format and organization of the client data and the client's business and branding goals. Based on this research, the content strategist develops a content strategy, which suggests the most effective presentation for each type of content on each communication platform. Strategists will give clear direction to the writer often creating a style guide that the writer and other content creators follow. Sometimes, content strategists may also write content.

UX Designer or Product Designer

The UX Writer collaborates closely with the UX/Product Designer. UX stands for user experience. The UX Designer is in charge of the entire experience of the user on the site or application. The UX Designer organizes the most effective flow for interactions and content presentation so the users can accomplish their goals. The UX Designer explains to the writer what the text needs to accomplish. If there is no information architect, the UX Designer will also organize the content. A Product Designer is usually a senior UX Designer who has a broader understanding of product goals, competitors, and business needs, but sometimes UX Designer and Product Designer refer to the same role.

Information Architect

The Information Architect is the person responsible for the overall structure and navigation of an informational multimedia and web project. The Information Architect is a close cousin to the Instructional Designer and UX Designer, who often have many of the skills of the Information Architect and often also play that role. Dedicated Information Architects mainly work on content rich sites, such as company intranets. Key deliverables for information architecture are sitemaps and navigation flows that break down the content into smaller units and organize the content flow and interaction. Many Information Architects come from the field of library science.

Instructional Designer

This role occurs most commonly in training and e-learning programs where a specific skill or subject is being taught. Drawing from knowledge of the user, content, and instructional design principles, the Instructional Designer carefully structures the information to teach the desired content to the user. Some of the tasks include: breaking information into smaller units, sequencing information units, and determining the approach for interactive elements, such as tests, exercises, feedback, etc.

Game Designer

The Game Designer shares some skills with the UX designer but the focus is on creating an effective gaming experience. On a large computer game, there may be several types of designers, but these categories are sometimes lumped into one title: creative designer, game designer, or just designer. In most cases, a designer's responsibilities include the structure of the game play and often the writing of the content itself. If the designers do not write the content, they work closely with the game writer.

Subject Matter Expert (SME)

Although the writer will often be in charge of doing his or her own research on a subject, if a subject is particularly complex or technical, there will also be a Subject Matter Expert (SME) on a project. This person is crucial to the writer. The SME will often provide reference material, outlines and will review the writer's script for accuracy.

Business Analyst

This Business Analyst has some similarities with the subject matter expert in that the Business Analyst or BA is an expert on business issues. Usually, a Business Analyst has an MBA and some experience in business. This role helps to understand the client's business goals and processes and come up with a way to achieve these goals in the interactive media project. The Business Analyst often writes the user scenarios, which describe typical users and how they might use the product. This is a great resource for writers so they can be sure to slant the writing towards the project's audience and achieve business goals.

Actors/Voice Talent

If a project has audio narration or on-screen actors, then Voice Talent or actors will be part of the team. It is useful for the writer to listen to the actors speaking the lines the writer has written. This can help the writer tune the language so it is better suited for this particular speaker.

Video/Audio Director

The Video Director is in charge of creating video. If roles are not combined, the Audio Director is in charge of developing the original audio for the project, such as narration. The writer's relationship to the director varies with each individual, but in many cases, it is a collaboration that starts with the director commenting on early drafts of the script, and extends into production with the writer performing final rewrites.

Product Manager

The Product Manager (PM) manages the budget, the schedule, the client, and the personnel on the project. Like the Business Analyst, the Product Manager is also an expert on the business goals of the product and a great resource for the writer. On smaller projects, this position might be combined with other positions, such as the designer.

Usability Expert

The Usability Expert makes sure the product is easy to use by the customer while achieving the user's goals. To refine usability, the Usability Expert gets user feedback on products in various ways, including questionnaires, interviews, blind testing, and site visits to the user's location. The Usability Expert also has knowledge of usability best practices and often has an advanced degree in a field such as Human Computer Interaction or Communications. The Usability Expert provides usability test reports, analyzed questionnaire results, interview transcripts, and usability expert analyses. Reviewing this material can help the writer better understand the user and fine tune content that may be unclear. (See "Tips for Writers from Usability Experts" in Chapter 2.)

Conclusion

There are many different types of interactive media writers, each with their own special skills. There are also many different team members that the writer needs to collaborate with. Not all of the individuals discussed above will be on every project. Many projects will have some of these duties combined. Because of the complexity of interactive media, the writers must learn all they can from their team members so that they address business goals and client needs.

Close collaboration and being willing to learn is also an effective way to expand your career. For example, you may start as a writer but by improving your understanding of how to organize and connect content or how to create an effective video game, you may be able to perform the duties of an Information Architect or a Game Designer on a future project.

5 Key Points from Part I: Challenges Writing for Interactive Media

Part I Overview

Part I explains key interactive writing challenges. They include:

- Interactivity
- Writing for the small screen
- Writing for many types of media (text, pictures, video, audio)
- Interactive writing tools
- Interactive writing script formats
- Collaborating with a team

The Challenge of Interactivity (Chapter 1)

Working with interactivity and writing for the small screen are some of the key challenges facing the interactive writer. Although deciding the approach to these challenges are not always under the full control of the writer, the writer must understand these concepts if he or she is to write effectively for interactive media.information.

Writing for Many Media (Chapter 2)

The interactive writer must be expert in a variety of techniques: writing to be read (journalism, copywriting); writing to be heard (radio, narration); writing to be seen (film, video); plus writing for the special demands of the computer screen. This is because interactive media can easily incorporate many types of media in a single production or even a single screen, and interactive media can manipulate these media in ways not before possible.

Interactive Writing Tools and Script Formats (Chapter 3)

There are useful tools to organize the breaking down of the many bits of interactive content, their relationship to each other, and the content or interaction flow. Besides dedicated tools, the most useful to the writer are spreadsheets and flowcharting software.

Once you have organized your content, there is an even wider variety of ways to present this content to your team. These approaches range from writing directly into the draft designs, outlines, treatment, single and multi-column scripts. There is no one right way to format a script for an interactive media program. The primary requirement is to make sure that whatever format you choose, it is clear to the client/stakeholder and to everyone on your production team.

DOI: 10.4324/9781003430612-7

Collaborating with a Team

There are many different types of interactive media writers, each with their own special skills. These types include: copywriter, content writer, technical writer, UX writer, social media specialist/producer, and game/narrative writer.

There are also numerous team members that the writer needs to collaborate with. These team members include: content strategist, UX/product designer, content designer, information architect instructional designer game designer subject matter expert (SME), business analyst, actors/voice talent, video/audio director, product manager, and usability expert.

Not all of the individuals listed will be on every project. Many projects will have smaller teams or have some of these duties combined. Because of the complexity of interactive media, the writers must learn all they can from their team members so that they address business goals and client needs.

Close collaboration and being willing to learn is also an effective way to expand your career. For example, you may start as a writer but by improving your understanding of how to organize and connect content or how to create an effective video game, you may be able to perform the duties of an information architect or a game designer on a future project.

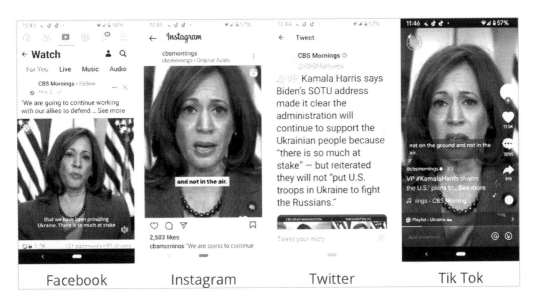

Figure II–1 Various social media platforms covering the same story

Part II

Conversational Writing—UX Writing, Social Media, Mobile

Part II Overview

Part II discusses interactive writing that is conversational, both in the style of the writing and in the way that it responds to users and seeks user input. The writing we will explore includes:

- UX Writing / Content Designer: primarily microcopy in software, applications, and highly interactive websites. Successful UX Writers carefully utilize voice and tone to interact with the user and guide them through the product with carefully crafted labels, direction text, error messages, etc.
- Social Media Writing (Instagram, Twitter, etc.): social media posts created by various types of companies. This type of writing actively seeks user input.
- Writing for Mobile: unlike social media writing and UX Writing, mobile is a viewing platform. Mobile devices are generally hand held, smaller and create a more intimate or conversational experience with the user compared to larger PC screens. Creating a product primarily for mobile requires a more conversational style.

DOI: 10.4324/9781003430612-8

6 UX Writing and Content Design— Software and Applications

Chapter Overview

This chapter discusses UX writing and content design, including

- The Definition of UX Writing and Content Design
- The Work of the UX Writer/Content Designer
- UX Writing Best Practices by Component
- Help and Support Writing
- User Research and Style Guide
- Voice and Tone
- Skills of the UX Writer
- How to Learn the Required Skills

As you read the descriptions in this chapter, look for examples on your laptop or phone to see the concepts in action.

UX Writing and Content Design Defined

The Work of the UX Writer/Content Designer

"UX writing is more than putting words on a screen. You're part of a team designing a software product or website and crafting an experience," said Senior UX Writer Susan Passmore. The UX Writer or content designer creates the voice of a software or website product that guides the user through their journey. In most cases the UX Writer is primarily responsible for micro copy, such as link text, button labels, direction, error messages, in-context help, tool tips, image alt text, and all the other bits of copy that help the user have a successful and positive experience of an interactive product.

Unlike linear media, interactive products, such as those listed above, are really two-way interactions or conversations between the product and the user. The user takes an action, such as selecting a link or button, and the product responds often with accompanying text explaining the next steps in the process or delivering the information the user requested. If the user makes an error, the application comes back with a helpful error message.

At best, the work of the writer is like a friend helping the user through a process with clear, conversational instructions, and feedback. The UX Writer or content designer is generally writing text to be read, but in some devices, particularly mobile, the writer is creating audio that will be read aloud by the device. We will focus on the text-based conversation because that is most common. Creating this conversation makes the writer a "collaborator

DOI: 10.4324/9781003430612-9

with users, helping them through the process," according to Content Designer Justine Hyland. This collaboration with the user requires the UX Writers and Content Designers to adopt a more relaxed conversational style to their writing. In many products, this style is dictated by the Style Guide, which will be discussed later in this chapter.

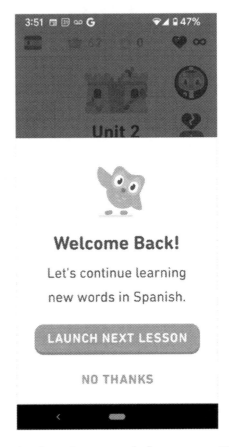

Figure 6–1 Concise, conversational greeting text on the language app, Duolingo
© Duolingo

The team member who does this type of writing has been generally called a UX Writer, but labels continue to evolve and many large companies, such as meta, IBM, and Shopify are starting to use the term content designer. This title change indicates that the content specialist on an interactive product does more than write text, but also collaborates in how the content will be presented in the product. For simplicity, this chapter will use UX Writer when referring to this role.

Just be aware that in some places content designer is synonymous with UX Writer, while in other companies, the title Content Designer, indicates broader responsibilities in terms of design. Content Designer Rachael Hyland said that in past positions with the title UX Writer, the product designer did all the designing, and she just filled in the copy in the designs the product designer had created. In her current role as content designer, she is an equal collaborator with the product designer about the content presentation. Ultimately, what work you will be doing depends on the company, size of product team, and work habits of individual team members. In the ideal world, as UX Writer or content designer, you will be part of a productive collaboration.

The work of the UX Writer can also sometimes blend into other writing roles, such as:

- Copywriter: responsible for large blocks of content or even marketing copy
- Technical Writer or User Assistance Writer: creating help documentation and manuals
- Content Strategist: responsible for the overall approach to content in all media and devices.

So, it is important to be flexible and have a variety of writing skills. The UX writing skills discussed here provide a solid foundation for other types of interactive writing. Many of which are covered later in this book.

Even if the UX Writer and technical writer roles are distinct, there is close coordination between the two roles because the content experience for the user should feel the same. So, the two roles usually follow similar product terminology, word usage, voice and tone, and other writing style guidance.

Value of the UX Writer

UX Writers and content designers are in high demand. A quick job search on LinkedIn for these job titles finds thousands of open positions. Software, website, and other product owners realize that effective microcopy, such as labels, directions, errors messages, etc. is key for users to have a positive experience with their product. In addition to helping users successfully use a product, the product content also helps create the product's personality, such as a serious, knowledgeable banking site, or fun, lively learning software for children.

UX Writing Best Practices by Components

As Principal UX Writer Laura Wixted points out, the UX Writer has to keep in mind that the user is often task oriented. They are using your product to accomplish a goal, whether it is to check their bank account balance or order groceries. The goal of your writing is to help the user be successful.

To help the user be successful, the UX writing discipline has identified best practices for key components used in your product. These principles may vary somewhat from product to product and will be described in detail in your product style guide.

Common software interface components are described below along with UX writing best practices for each component. Keep in mind that there are many more components and principles than those listed below. The goal here is to give an introduction to key concepts of UX writing and how they are applied.

Key UX Writing Principles

- Concise

   Make sure every word and punctuation mark adds to the meaning. Remove filler words, such as "that" and punctuation, such as periods in lists, that do not add meaning. As we noted earlier, space is limited, particularly in mobile, and users are task oriented. They want to quickly accomplish their goals, not read pages of your text, not matter how beautiful your writing may be.

- Clear

   Writing concisely is important, but clarity is even more important. If users do not understand your pithy one-word button labels, then you may have to add additional text to make your label meaningful. As Principal UX Writer, Laura Wixted said, "Start with concise, but land on clarity."
- Sentence case

   Write multi-word labels in sentence case. For example, "Shared with me" not "Shared With Me" or "SHARED WITH ME." Title case and all caps are hard to read.
- Active voice

   Active voice focuses on the doer and the action. It is clear and energetic, for example: "Select cart icon to purchase." Passive voice focuses on the object of the action. Tends to be longer and harder to understand, for example: "The cart icon should be selected when ready to purchase." Main exception for passive voice is error messages, so the user isn't blamed, for example, "The form has errors" is less scolding than, "You entered errors in the form."

Applying UX Writing Principles to Software Components

There are many components on a software or website screen. A product's style guide will have a pattern for each component, describing exactly how each one should be utilized. Some of the most important components are listed below, but keep in mind this is not the complete list of all possible components. The principles described above should be applied to the writing of each of these components. The writers interviewed, also added some additional component specific writing tips. (See Figure 6–2 to visualize components.)

Page Title

Page titles are crucial for users to decide if they are in the right location. Page titles also appear in search results. So, it is important to be concise and meaningful in your titles, for example "Create profile" tells me exactly what I can to on a screen. By starting the title with the main action, "Create," a user can quickly understand the purpose of the page. Eliminating extra word "a" (Create a profile) adds to brevity without hurting clarity.

Headings

A screen broken down into sections with clear headings is far easier to scan than one big wall of text or fields. For example, a create profile page, might have several subheadings, such as "Personal information," "Address," and "Payment method." If the heads have multiple words be sure to put most important one first, such as "Payment." Easier to quickly grasp than "Method of payment."

Calls to Action (CTAs)

Calls to Action or CTAs indicate the next action step the user can perform on a screen, they could be links, button, icons etc. The CTA labels should start with a verb and be very specific as to what the button does, "Create new profile" is better than just "Create." Never write "Click here" as an inline text link. Instead tell where that link will take you or the information it will provide, such as "<u>Accepted photo formats</u>."

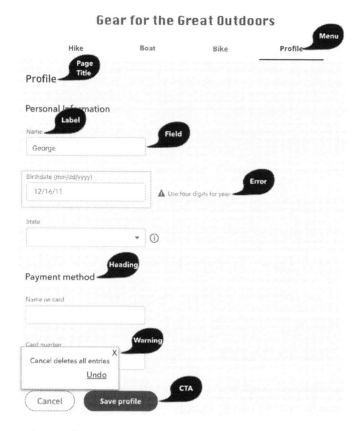

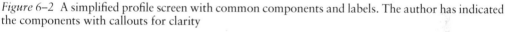

Figure 6–2 A simplified profile screen with common components and labels. The author has indicated the components with callouts for clarity

Created by the author

Limit the number of CTAs on a single screen, or the user may be unsure what to do next with too many choices. If there are multiple CTAs, headings discussed above, can help by grouping them with the appropriate sections of the screen.

Error Messages

Everyone makes mistakes, such as filling out a profile form where you might enter the wrong date format or forget to complete a field. The resulting error message should be clear, friendly, specific and give instructions how to fix the error. Be careful not to blame the user and be positive, "Use four digits for year" not "You entered the wrong date format." Ideally, the error message is shown at the point of error, such as next to the field where the error occurred and not in a list at the bottom of the page.

Field Labels

Fields are input components that allow the user to enter data. Examples include text boxes, dropdown lists, etc. Each input field should have an effective label so the user is clear what data the field is calling for. These field labels should be concise, scannable, and be quickly understood. They should be written to limit cognitive load on users. There shouldn't be any puzzling over a field label. Consistency is also hugely important within a product. The label for the same time of input should be consistent throughout.

Menu Names and Links

Your product menu and other links allow your user to move around your site and discover what you have to offer. Be sure your menu names are familiar to your users and descriptive. If you have long menus or lots of navigation, break them down into meaningful categories. For example, on an outdoor sports gear site, do not use general menu categories like "Adventure" or "Water." These names are too vague. Instead, be more specific, such as "Hike" and "Bike." Specific labels let users know what content they will find by following those links. To give your users a smooth ride through your product be sure the page title of your menu item matches the label on the menu. For example, a menu item labeled "Hike" should lead to a screen titled "Hike" not "Boots and trekking poles."

With links within text content, follow the same concept introduced earlier that the important content should come first not in the middle of your sentence. "The <u>variety of athletics</u> offered is one of our best features." Not "One of our best features are our <u>athletics</u>, which offer great variety."

Success, Confirmation, and Warning Messages (Modals and Toasts)

Confirmations, warnings, and success messages are types of user notifications. These notifications usually appear in a modal of varying sizes and onscreen positions depending on the importance of the message. The most urgent messages usually appear in larger modals mid screen, while a simple confirmation might be in a small banner called a toast near the bottom of a screen.

An important part of writing a notification is to make it abundantly clear what response you expect from the user, if any. The success message is the simplest message. It simply lets the user know their action has been successful, for example, "Profile saved." It's important not to overuse success messages, which can disrupt the user.

In terms of notification interaction demands, the next step up from a success message, is the confirmation message. This occurs when the user has taken a serious action that should be confirmed. For example, "Your payment method has been deleted." Confirmation messages require actions from users such as an "Undo" link or a way to dismiss the notification to confirm the action. If it is not obvious how to address the error, that needs to be added to the message.

Warning messages are usually more important and might suggest that you are about to exceed a character limit or your battery will soon die. Often warning messages are larger than confirmation and success messages and are in a more obvious place on the screen. Warning messages need to be clear but not alarming, and should give users a way to address the impending issue.

Empty States

Empty states occur in a product when there is no obvious action to take or content to display, so the screen is essentially empty. The most common examples are a screen not found error, a wait screen until a process completes, or the first start of an application, such as a new social media account without any of your content or connections. A well written empty state message often appears similar to an error message and will provide positive clear communication, tell the user what is happening, why it is happening, and what needs to be done to populate the screen. Depending on the product, the empty state could be engaging in some way, such as using humor, and not just a boring blank page (See Figure 6–3).

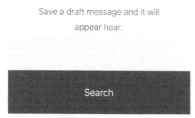

Figure 6–3 Empty state example showing humor
© Anna Cywinska

Help and Support Writing

Although writing microcopy for various components as discussed above is the primary work of the UX Writer, the writer may on occasions be asked to help create the help and support content for the product.

Integrated Help

Writing help and support content has historically been the domain of the Technical Writer. This writer created print manuals in the past and the content in the online help centers that are more common today.

The latest trend in help writing is a small snippet of help content integrated into the user interface at the point of need—just in time help. This type of writing needs to be concise and action oriented. It often becomes the responsibility of the UX Writer because it is closely related to the design of specific screens. This help content often requires a click or hover to access, and is usually text but small images or short videos are also used.

Conversational Copywriting

Another approach for providing help content is through conversation using audio or more commonly message-based interactions. Chatbots are a common example of this. They offer an interface similar to a message app and use AI (Artificial Intelligence) to provide information to the user in a conversational style, as if the user is using a messaging app. These tools generally respond to user questions, but using AI, they can also identify patterns of user interactions that indicate a problem. Once the pattern is recognized, the chatbot spontaneously offers tips to start a conversation or help the user complete the current task.

These chatbots have mixed success. In responding to user questions, chatbots have a limited amount of content that they can provide. Unless the user needs something fairly simple, it is easy to get to a dead end.

The AI tools that spontaneously offer help also have issues. The most common is that a user feels bothered by these unsolicited offers of help. This was the case with the infamous Clippy that Microsoft Office launched a number of years ago. If you are not familiar with Clippy, it was an animated paper clip that appeared on the screen and constantly offered assistance. "Looks like you are writing a letter. Do you want help with formatting?"

Despite their problems, these conversational type tools are probably here to stay and will require the UX Writer to have some understanding of conversational copywriting. Conversational copywriting requires writing as if you were chatting with a friend. This includes use of contractions, simple language, and avoiding third person, while always keeping your brand style guidelines in mind.

User Research and Style Guide

Knowing the user and creating a style guide are two ways to create and present a consistent and engaging personality for your product.

Know the User

Whatever type of writing the UX Writer creates, it must meet the needs of the target users and create a supportive conversation that helps them have a successful experience with the product. Most established companies have already done considerable research into their users. This information is often distilled into personas/user profiles, user stories, and process flows/journey maps. Some important users may not be customers, but instead internal users, such as customer support people who are using your content to answer user questions.

Personas and User Profiles

Personas identify user characteristics, such as information needs, technological sophistication, education levels, age, common pains, software used etc. Personas may be part

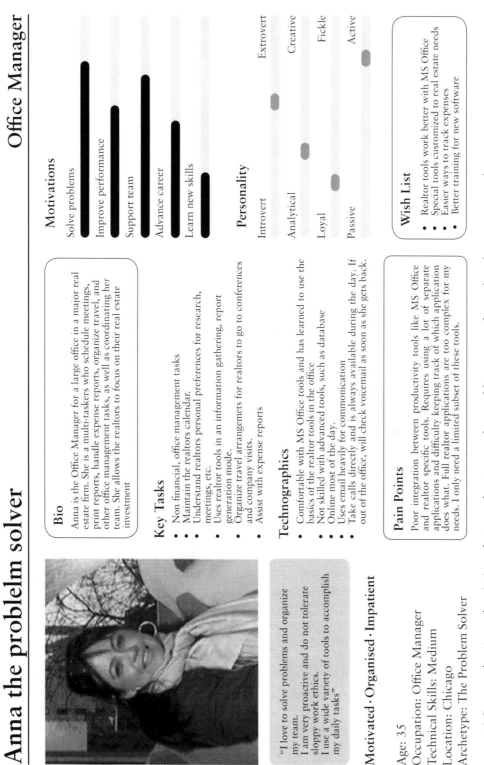

Figure 6–4 Persona showing a description of a type of customer who would use your software based on user research

Created by the author from template courtesy Wladislav Glad on SketchApp Resources

of the company style guide. A lighter version of a persona is called a user profile, which focuses on just the key use characteristics without the narrative that often accompanies a persona.

Responding to the user profiles or personas for your product helps refine your writing style for this product. A persona helps makes the user into a real person and enables a conversational writing style suited to them, just as you would speak differently to a colleague than you would to a child. As we have indicated earlier, usually writing for interactive media should be succinct and to the point, but sometimes the opposite style is required.

Content Designer Justine Hyland once worked for a company that created a very technical product and whose main audience was engineers and developers. These customers were happy with lengthy explanations with as much detail as she could provide. The opposite end of the user spectrum could be something like a supermarket website that has a broad audience from all different age levels. In this case, the text has to be simple, clear, and easy to understand with a recommended reading level of Grade 6. (The average reading level in the United States is Grade 8.) If you are working on a product with customers who use English as a second language, you need to keep that in mind as well and avoid content that relies on cultural context. (See Localization later in this chapter.)

As noted above, most companies will already have done significant research into their users, but if they have not, the UX Writer will have to team with a UX researcher to do some of this research themselves. This includes research before writing, such as user interviews and testing your completed copy as part of usability testing. In usability testing, content issues are identified when user are asked to accomplish their tasks with your product.

User Stories

At its simplest form, a user story is a common task that the user wants to perform in your product. The user story builds from the work on personas and user profiles and follows this standard format.

> As a < type of user >, I want < some goal > so that < some reason >.

For example, in an educational program, user stories might be:

> As a professor, I want to email students directly from my online gradebook, so that I can quickly alert them of issues with their grade.
> As a student, I want an average of my current grades in the online gradebook, so that I can evaluate my success in the course.

User stories help the writers and designers ensure that users can successfully achieve their key tasks.

Process Flows and Journey Maps

Process flows basically link together a series of user stories showing how the user completes an entire process. A journey map takes this process flow a step further by evaluating users' emotions, needs, and expectations at each step of the flow.

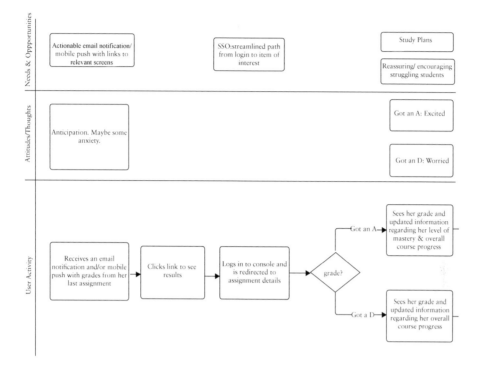

Figure 6–5 A section of a simple journey map showing user activity, attitudes/thoughts, and design opportunities at top. Maps help writer adopt correct tone for each stage of a user journey

© Pearson llc

The journey map helps the writer to decide what tone to use in each stage of the customer's journey. For example, if the user successfully completes a long process, the writing tone could be celebratory. Conversely, if the system made an error, the tone might be apologetic. The nuances of tone depend on the user and the product voice. Voice and Tone will be discussed in more detail later in this chapter.

Style Guide

According to Principal UX Writer, Laura Wixted, "UX Writers write short-form writing, meaning that they concern themselves with small screens and very short attention spans. Because of this, the UX writing guidelines are unique and take into account usability above all else." Research into the product users provide the foundation for these guidelines. Senior UX Writer Susan Passmore said the style guide, "includes UX writing basics, content guidelines for components, specific rules for your organization (such as preferred abbreviations), and brand voice and tone."

The style guide typically can either be a standalone reference or as part of a design system site. If the guide is part of a design system, the style guide will cover all aspects of the product not just the text because understanding the relationship between the visual style and the text style are important to have a coherent and effective overall presentation. For example, a product that had a serious message, but used pastel pinks and blues in their design like a candy store would be a failure. The style guide will be most important in a product company that is trying to communicate the personality of an external product in a consistent way.

The style guide also promotes consistency across a company's products. For example, it is less confusing for the user if all products use the same name for the same item, and consistency in data, such as date formats is essential. A word list of some kind is part of most style guides. Some software, such as Acrolinx, allows the integration of your style guide into your writing/design tools. This allows you to access guidelines from your main authoring tool without having to refer to another document. In larger companies or on more complex products, there may be multiple writing style guides for different types of writing, such as marketing copywriting, tech writing, and UX writing.

A well-developed style guide governs many characteristics of the writing including:

- Writing standards: e.g., simplicity, reading level, punctuation, etc.
- Structure and presentations: e.g., avoid long blocks of text, start with a main point.
- When to use and how to write components, e.g., error messages, tool tips, link labels.
- Voice and tone.
- Language usage, e.g., when to use courtesy language, please, thank you, sorry.

Many companies or design systems make their style guides publicly available, check out Shopify, Adobe Spectrum, and Google Material Design for examples. If you don't have a style guide, reviewing existing style guides will provide some basic principles as a starting point.

Voice and Tone

Most of the standards in a style guide are concrete instructions and easy to understand, e.g., be succinct, don't use passive voice, or use second person. Voice and tone might be a little harder to grasp as they define the desired subjective experience or personality of your product.

Voice

The Voice of a product is consistent across the product, just as your own demeanor and way of communicating stays consistent with your personality. For example, the voice of a banking website might be: serious and knowledgeable. These basic principles never really change. A well-defined voice ensures the user has a consistent experience and helps build a relationship with your product.

Although voice is consistent within a company's writing, between companies there can be great variation. The ticket selling app, Today's Tix uses fun colorful language "Let the spectacle surround you. GoodRx uses plain, straightforward language because it is about a serious subject, prescription drugs. ". . . will help you pay less than the cash price for your prescriptions."

Tone

The Tone of communication does change, it depends on what the user is experiencing. Just as in real life, your tone will be quite different if you won the lottery or if someone stole your car. In the case of the bank website example, the tone will be different if users just qualified for a special offer or if they bounced a check. The first example should be celebratory and the second should be serious, maybe firm if the customer is a repeat offender. The variations in tone, of course, have to keep within the parameters of the products defined voice. Your success message on a banking site will be more restrained than that on a site selling toys.

Skills of the UX Writer

A UX Writer or content designer needs a wide variety of skills to be successful.

Writing Clearly and Concisely

A key skill is the ability to write clearly and succinctly in the required styles. Clarity is ultimately more important than brevity. Principal UX Writer, Laura Wixted, said, "A common mistake for beginning UX Writers is focusing on conciseness over clarity." Minimal words are a worthwhile goal, but the primary requirement is that the user understands your label or message.

Design Thinking

In addition to writing skills, the writer has to be able to define effective solutions. The most common software approach to problem solving is called Design Thinking. Design thinking is a multi-step problem solving approach that starts with a deep understanding of the user. Among many other uses, it is also an effective way to find the best content for digital products, e.g., software, websites, etc.

The d.school at Stanford University defines a popular model of Design Thinking:

1. Empathize with your users: user research to clearly understand user needs.
2. Define user needs: the problem, goals, constraints.
3. Brainstorm: possible solution ideas, challenge assumptions.
4. Prototype: create versions of the solution, e.g., paper sketches, simple software etc.
5. Test the solutions: put your solution in front of users.

Repeat. Based on your test results, you usually need to go back and revisit any or all of the steps above in any order that helps refine the solution. But the core of the process is to develop a deep understanding of the user's needs so that you are solving the right problem. Wherever you work as a UX Writer, you will find some variations of this process.

Research and Listening

In order to be a successful practitioner of design thinking, the writer has to be able to understand user research and possibly help create it in order to really know the audience. According to Content Designer, Justine Hyland, in order to understand the user, the writer needs great listening and interviewing skills, and be able to talk to all different types of people and understand their needs. Having empathy and experiencing a product through the users' eyes will help you anticipate the needed content and approach. Empathy includes the product users as well as team members and stakeholders (see Collaboration below).

In addition to user research, it is also valuable to perform competitive research to see how other writers are approaching similar problems to yours. One approach is to search your problem topic with an image search on Google. This allows you to see how other products solved your problem.

Another use of a web search is to help decide the best words for a label. You can search a couple possibilities and note how many search results each word has. Popularity is one indication of what term is in common usage, but you still need to verify that this popular term is the right one for your specific users.

Collaboration and Persuasion

UX Writers do not work alone, they collaborate with other team members. The most common partnership is with the UX or product designer. The nature of this collaboration can vary. Sometimes, the product designer designs the primary interactions, screen layouts, and the flow from screen to screen. The product designer will indicate the goal of each element and interaction, and then collaborate with the writer to create the content to help achieve that goal. In other cases, the UX Writer or content designer takes a larger role and collaborates with the product designer earlier in the process. This is ideal because then the writer gets to be a part of the initial user research, stakeholder discussions etc. This allows the writer to make informed decisions about the content design and contribute to the overall UX design. One of the challenges of the UX Writer is to advocate for the role of UX Writer or content designer as a design partner. If the UX writing is centralized at a company, the UX Writer will report to a content manager or some kind who will help the writer become a full design partner. If UX writing is decentralized, then the writer will report to one of the product leads, such as the UX Lead or the Project Manager. If this is the case, it will fall to the writer to advocate for equal design status. A way to do this and to collaborate effectively is to clearly and persuasively present your ideas, give and receive feedback, and iterate new content versions based on the design discussions.

The writer and designer or Content Strategist may collaborate on planning and evaluating content using tools like content inventories, which document all the content in a product, and content audits, which evaluate the value and quality of existing content and identify gaps where new content is needed.

The UX Writer also collaborates with other team members including the Product Manager, UX Researcher, and the Developers. (See Chapter 4 for more on collaboration.)

Accessibility

Accessible writing and design ensure that users of all different abilities can use your product. This includes users who have issues with hearing, seeing, movement, etc. Many of the interactive media writing principles we have already discussed also help make UX writing accessible. These principles include writing that is concise, clear, descriptive, and action oriented. This style of writing is particularly helpful to users who rely on screen readers to read interface text aloud. This includes both the visible text, such as button labels, link text etc., but also invisible text that a user cannot view without a special reader, such as JAWS, TalkBack, or VoiceOver.

This invisible text is referred to as alt text. All visual elements need alt text if a product is to be accessible to all users. Alt text is only for images so no need to write "image of" in your alt text. Alt text should be a short, descriptive phrase as if you were describing the image to a blind person. Long phrases slow down the screen reader as it moves through a screen. Screen readers cannot read text embedded in an image, so if that information is important, include it in alt text.

Screen readers also read every UI element aloud so for these elements, it is important to add short action labels that describe what the element does, such as "print" or "search." Similar to the image alt text, there is no need to define each type of UI element because the screen reader does that automatically. For example, when a reader encounters a search field, the reader first identifies it as an "input field," so the writer's element label is simply "search."

Localization and Inclusion

Localization

If your software, website or other product has a multicultural following either in your home market or internationally, you need to accommodate users who do not speak English as their primary language and for different cultural references. Although, there are companies that specialize in localizing software for each country, it helps your writing to be aware of some of the basic issues. For localization, you need to view the world through the lens of a different language and culture. Some of the things you need to be aware of are:

- Slang
  Should generally be avoided in all your writing but is a particular problem with different cultures. For example, in English, quitting "cold turkey" means to stop something abruptly. In other languages, it could mean chilled poultry.
- Culture specific phrases and references
  Some phrases common in English do not translate directly into another culture. For example, in American English to "plead the fifth" is a reference to the US Bill of Rights 5th Amendment and means in general conversation that you don't want to discuss something that might get you in trouble. In other languages, it is meaningless.
- Space considerations
  You can't base your content placement and spacing on English alone. Some languages, such as German, use much longer words than the same word in English. Short English words translated to German:

  - Sale = Sonderangebot
  - Mall = Einkaufszentrum

- Many languages, including English, are read from left to right, but some major languages, such as Arabic and Farsi, are read from right to left. Make sure your content designs will accommodate both directions.

Inclusion

Localization includes users from different cultures, but there are many other types of users that you need to be aware of when you write. A few examples:

- Gender: use neutral, not gender specific words

  - they, not he/she
  - police officer, not policeman

- LGBTQ: don't assume two genders, use latest accepted LGBTQ terms

  - students, not boys and girls
  - gay or lesbian, not homosexual
  - cross dresser, not transvestite

- Illness: don't use actual illnesses to describe temporary states

  - sad, not depressed
  - mercurial, not bipolar

- Disabilities: focus on the person, avoid negative language
  - a person with a disability, not a disabled person
  - accessible parking, not handicapped parking

Attention to Detail While Understanding Context

The team relies on the writer as the word person, so you need to be meticulous in your copy to make sure the information is exactly correct, in line with the product voice, and of course have no punctuation, spelling, or other basic writing mistakes. But Content Designer Rachael Hyland warns that the focus on small details should be balanced with an ability to see the big picture and think strategically about how your copy fits into the overall experience.

UX Design

If you want more control of how your content is presented in the product and a better understanding of the overall design process, it is not a bad idea to get some background in UX Design. This will give you better understanding of the relationship between Content Design and UX Design and make you a more informed collaborator.

Software Skills

One of the areas where you will need to be most flexible is learning new software. The type of software used will vary from company to company and even between products.

- Word Processors

  For early-stage writing, any word processor, such Google Docs or MS Word, can be used, as long as the tool allows online sharing, commenting, and some sort of version control. The downside of using a separate word processor is that at some point, someone will have to copy and paste this content into the designs.
- Spreadsheets

  Spreadsheets, such as Google Sheets and Microsoft Excel, are sometimes used for writing related tasks, such as content inventories, where the writer details all the content in a product, and for content audits, where the writer evaluates content quality and looks for gaps. Spreadsheets can also be used to track all the bits of microcopy that goes into a product. Spreadsheets have similar problems to word processors in that the content eventually needs to be entered into the design or development system.
- Design Tools

  Modern design tools, such as Sketch and Figma, incorporate text capabilities. The writer can enter content directly into the design software that the designer uses. In this case, the content is already placed in the designs by the writer, so it does not have to be transferred at some later point. This approach also allows the writer to show how the content will work in the context of the design and become a full design partner. Some writers take this a step and learn the design tools so that they can present alternative content designs for considerations. This approach relies on a highly collaborative product designer. These design files with content are shared with all the team members.

  According to Principal UX Writer, Laura Wixted, one drawback to using current design tools for writing is that there is no easy way to update strings of text in designs so that all team members get those updates or to track and analyze strings of text to validate they are following the style guide. Design tools, however, continue to evolve and hopefully these limitations will be addressed in the near future.

- Writing assistants

    Some software fine-tunes your writing, making it more concise and correcting common errors. Examples include: Wordtune, Hemingway app, Ditto, and Grammarly. Some of these assistants, such as Ditto, have plugins to integrate them with the design tools discussed above.

- Technical content authoring and publishing

    Software, such as MadCap Flare and Adobe FrameMaker, are primarily used for creating help systems for a complex product or website. These are heavy duty enterprise writing tools that have careful versioning controls, built in styles etc.

- Collaboration and conceptualizing tools

    Although many of the top design tools have collaboration capabilities built in, some writers like to use more dedicated tools for this purpose, such as Miro, Mural, and even Airtable.

So be prepared to learn something new when you start a new project. The good news is that there are a lot of similarities with different design and writing software, so once you learn one, it is relatively easy to learn a new one.

How to Get the Skills of a UX Writer

There are many ways to get the skills needed to become a UX Writer. This will be discussed more in the last part of the book on careers. Resources to consider include:

Books

There are books that are focused on UX writing and content design. Some good ones include:

- *Content Design* by Sarah Richards (2017)
- *Conversational Design* by Erika Hall (A Book Apart, 2018)
- *Microcopy: The Complete Guide* by Kinneret Yifrah (Nemala, 2017).
- *Nicely Said: Writing for the Web with Style and Purpose* by Nicole Fenton and Kate Kiefer Lee (Peachpit Press, 2014)
- *Strategic Writing for UX* by Torrey Podmajersky (O'Reilly Media, 2019).

Colleges and Online Learning Sites

There are many colleges and universities that offer courses in UX Writing, Technical Writing, and UX Design both online and in person. They range from your local community college to major universities. Research them and find the best fit for your needs. Examples include:

- Cornell University
- University of Michigan
- University of California San Diego
- Georgia Institute of Technology
- Carnegie Mellon University.

There are also a number of online learning sites, that offer courses and certification programs in these fields, such as:

- Daily UX Writing
- SVC (School of Visual Concepts)
- Career Foundry
- UX Writing Hub
- Coursera
- LinkedIn Learning
- General Assembly
- Udemy
- Springboard
- Google Career Certificates.

If you can't find a course precisely in UX Writing or Content Design, you can benefit from related courses such as:

- UX Design
- Content Strategy
- Technical Writing.

Communities, Articles, Training, Discussions

There are a number of UX writing communities and information hubs that collect articles, discussions, and sometimes host writing events:

- *UX Content Collective*
- *Content + UX*
- *Daily UX Writing*
- *UX Writing Hub*
- *UX Writers Collective* (Medium)
- *Writers in Tech* (Spotify)
- *Readability Guidelines* (Content Design London)
- *Writing for the Web* (Nielsen Normal Group)
- *The Massive List of Content Design & UX Writing Resources.*

UX Writing Mentors

Another way to learn is to connect with a mentor. Senior writers in a variety of online communities offer their time to new writers to guide your learning process. There are many variations of mentorship in terms of time, commitment, and cost. Search for some of the sites below and find the best match for you:

- *UX.Coffee.Hours*
- *UXWritingHub*
- *Design Buddies*
- *ADPList.*

UX Writing Conferences

Another way to meet more experienced writers and to get a big dose of ideas about UX writing and content design is to go to a conference. Some good ones include:

- *Button: The content design conference*
- *Confab: The content strategy conference.*

Hands-on Learning

All the theory is great but ultimately you have to put what you have learned into practice. Writing internships are a great way to get some experience. Many companies offer them. They are usually available through the internship program at your school.

If internships are not available in your area, you can get practice and build a portfolio by rewriting existing sites or applications. You need to show the improvements you made and rationale for the changes.

If you need a little push to practice, try *Daily UX Writing*, this group will email you a writing challenge every day to keep you writing.

Conclusion

This chapter has given an overview of the type of work and some of the skills needed to be a top UX Writer or content designer. You are not expected to have all this knowledge and skills on the first day of the job. UX Writers and content designers come from all different career paths. The key requirement for a successful UX Writer is to be a solid writer, a voracious learner, and a passionate advocate for the user.

References

Balawender, Carole. Senior UX Writer. Interview with the author
Conversational Design by Erika Hall (A Book Apart)
Design Thinking. https://dschool.stanford.edu
Hyland, Justine. Content Designer. Interview with the author
Hyland, Rachael. Content Designer. Interview with the author
Localization. https://www.lionbridge.com/
Material design writing guidelines. https://material.io/design/communication/writing.html
Passmore, Susan. Senior UX Writer. Interview with the author
Readability Guidelines. https://readabilityguidelines.co.uk/content-design/
Strategic Writing for UX by Torrey Podmajersky (O'Reilly Media)
Wixted, Laura. Principal UX Writer. Interview with the author

7   Social Media Writing—Twitter, Facebook, Instagram, TikTok

Chapter Overview

This chapter discusses social media writing, including:

- Commercial Social Media Defined
- Social Media Writer/Producer Skills
- How to Get the Required Skills
- Best Practices by Social Media Platform
- Social Media Style Guide
- Coping with Constant Change in Social Media

As you read the descriptions in this chapter, look for examples on your laptop or phone to see the concepts in action.

Commercial Social Media Defined

Social media usage is huge with monthly active users measured in the billions for the most popular application, such as Facebook, Instagram, and TikTok. The user base is not only immense but it is engaged, which is after all what makes it social media. Users can create their own content, but they also interact with the content provided by others, through likes, retweets, commenting and other means. This provides an opportunity for companies to connect closely and have a conversation with their customers. Most social media writing/producing jobs are with one of the following types of companies.

News Organizations

- Mainstream news, such as CBS, NBC, and CNN.
- Niche news, such as *theSkimm* (women), *Politico* (politics).
- Government news and information, such NASA and FEMA (Federal Emergency Management Agency).

Brand Marketing

- Promoting company products for sale and creating excitement about a brand, such as *Nike* or *Starbucks*.
- Brand marketing on social is more about creating awareness than directly selling a product. You want to make users aware that your company is launching a show, service, or product.

DOI: 10.4324/9781003430612-10

- Providing information on more complex products and enhancing an existing user base, such as banks and investment companies like Chase and Mastercard.
- Celebrities, promoting individuals or lifestyles, such as Kim Kardashian and Taylor Swift. Some celebrity brands blend into the next category of influencers.
- Employer brand and recruitment marketing involves promoting a company as a great place to work to bring in top recruits. LinkedIn is the preferred platform for this niche area of brand marketing. A brand marketer writes posts about a company's events and other initiatives, giving potential candidates an inside view of the company's culture and people.

Influencers

- Social media influencers are individuals or groups, are people who have built a reputation for their fame and expertise on a specific topic, such as music, film and TV, sports, beauty, etc.
- Influencers, who build up an audience to get high engagements, need metrics and followers to sell ads and sponsor content.
- Major influencers have teams of social media writers to maintain their accounts.
- Influencers come from many different backgrounds, such as Tory Dunlap posting on women's finance, Kim Kardashian on lifestyle and beauty, and former president Barack Obama on politics and social issues.
- Although influencers come in all ages, the very top influencers are dominated by Millennials with Gen X, a distant second.
- Instagram is the biggest platform for a majority of the top social media influencers.

Social Media Writer/Producer Skills

Social media posts often have images, text, video, and audio. Because of this, the social media writer is often called a social media producer or social media coordinator. To keep with the book's focus on writing, social media writer will be used here, but keep in mind that this position may have different names as indicated above.

Writing Skills

Even though the job title may usually be social media producer, strong social writing techniques are essential to engage your users with your posts. Many of the important social media writing skills are common to other types of media writing, including:

- Writing quickly and accurately.
- Editing longer documents for shorter social media posts, for example from a news feed like AP or Reuters.
- Knowing effective journalism techniques, such as the inverted pyramid which always places the important content first.
- Mastering good grammar and punctuation, many companies use the AP Style Guide.
- Have a large vocabulary. A social writer will create a lot of posts every day. You need different ways to describe things so each post feels unique.
- Ability to multitask, you will usually be working on multiple different platforms.

Other techniques, such as those listed below, are more specifically related to writing for social media.

Focus Post on Key Emotion

Manager of Social Media, Sophie Lewis, said the key skill for a social media writer is "to narrow down a story to the key emotion." In social, there is only a few seconds to capture a user's attention so it is essential to trim larger stories to a post that can be consumed quickly and that engages the user with a primal emotion, such as anger or joy.

When you focus down your post, it still needs to stand on its own without requiring the user to read all the captions or have a large body of knowledge.

Senior Social Media Producer, Danielle Garrand, adds that "complicated topics are hard to break down. If the topic is too complex, don't cover it on social. You can't provide enough context for complicated topics in the limited content expected in most social posts."

Create Curiosity Gap

Don't give the entire story in the post's headline. Give just enough to get the user interested so they click or tap. Too much info and users may not feel the need to learn more. Too little info and users might just be confused.

This example may have too little information:

```
"If you're going to do one thing . . ."
```

Too vague. One thing about what?
This has too much:

```
"Name, picture of Putin's lover scrubbed from Russian media website."
```

Seems like the whole story, why engage further?
This example has the right amount of information to create the curiosity gap:

```
"Tom Brady was very close to officially joining the . . ."
```

If readers are curious about Tom Brady, they want to discover what he was going to join. Closely related to this approach is the Fill-in-the-Blank:

```
"One thing I am proud about is ___"
```

Lead with a Question

Asking a question is another user engagement technique.

```
"Will the U.S. Send Reaper Drones into Ukraine?"
```

If readers are interested in the topic, they will want to see the answer to the question.

Use a Numbered List

According to Senior Social Media Producer, Danielle Garrand, "People like numbered list because they are super digestible." The numbered list approach clearly indicates the scope of the post. Three to five is the sweet spot for the number of items on the list. Less obtuse than other titles.

```
"Three Factors That Could Increase Your Chances of an IRS Audit"
```

Combine Videos and Text

Videos and video thumbnails combined with text are also good clickbait. For example, show an exciting video clip of a movie with the caption:

```
"Why is Pixar's Turning Red Making History?"
```

On certain platforms, such as TikTok, POV videos can be successful. A POV video shows an experience from a participant's point of view, pretending you are experiencing it, such as navigating a new hot bar.

Manage CTAs

CTAs are Calls to Action. This is a way to get your users to not just view your content but interact with it. There are many types of CTAs. Some are just for fun, others lead to more information or to an opportunity to purchase.

```
"Give a round of applause."
```

Means use clap emoji.

```
"Tag a friend and let them know?"
"Send this photo to a friend you got drunk with."
"Select our bio to get more details."
```

Probably the one general rule is that you don't want too many CTAs on one post. One to two per post is ideal. The amount of effort the CTA can require also varies by platform, with Facebook users willing to engage in the more complex interactions, TikTok the least.

Avoid Clickbait

Clickbait is a title or caption that is exaggerated. "Best Ever Car to Buy" is clickbait. "Will Smith's Secret Life" is clickbait if all the story delivers are commonly available facts about his college years. Title and captions should always be honest and match the content that you are delivering. Otherwise, users don't trust your brand in future and will not click at all.

Include Key Words

For many social media platforms search is important so writers need to use key words particularly in title. For example, "Best Pizza Spots in NYC" or "Top Coachella Moments 2023. These are straight to point and what people are searching for looking for.

From an SEO (Search Engine Optimization) perspective, consider what popular elements in your post you can honestly foreground in the title or caption, so your post appears high on search results.

Media and Analytical Skills

In addition to effective writing techniques, a social media writer needs to have a variety of other skills. How many of these skills and how expert you need to be in each skill depends on the size of the organization and team structure. For example, a niche news organization may want most of these skills, whereas a large corporate branding operation may let you focus more on writing.

Strategy, Planning, Posting

Social media writers need to be able to determine what is trending and what should be covered on various platforms, using their analysis of news, Twitter posts, and social monitoring platforms, such as CrowdTangle, Chartbeat, and Later. These monitoring platforms display the types of posts you are interested in based on topic or location filters. What is hot on each platform suggests that topic is trending. Look to Twitter for news trends, whereas TikTok popular posts indicate what the youngest social audience is into. You can also find trending articles in mainstream news and translate them to social. Keep tabs on what your main competitors are doing. If they are jumping on a topic, consider if you should be doing the same.

Prioritize trending content for immediate posting. Evergreen content can be posted later in the day or even the next day if necessary. Evergreen content is not time sensitive and has value whenever posted., such as anxiety treatment or diet tips. It's always good to have a few evergreen posts ready in case it is a slow news day.

Actual posting is not done natively in the social platform, as you are used to doing in your personal accounts. Most companies use some sort of social media management platform, such as Dash Hudson, Falcon.io, or Sprinklr. These tools allow the team to manage the cadence of the posts for the team. Cadence is how often you post. Different platforms have different requirements for posting cadence. For example, Facebook and Twitter should have at least 20 minutes between posts. In general, give some time between each post. If you send posts out at the same time, some social platforms will tend to favor one, and the other could get minimal exposure. Also try to be consistent in your cadence, posting about the same intervals every day, for example every 20 minutes or every hour.

Keep in mind what is going on in the news. You don't want to send out a silly meme or a product promotion in the middle of a disaster, such as the famous example of Epicurious that posted their scone recipes on Twitter right after the Boston Marathon bombing.

Know Your Audience

You have to know your audience and give them what they want. For example, a niche news company like theSkimm might use humor and turn news into a meme. A meme is a super shareable somewhat humorous post. Usually, text and graphics but can be video or animation. A straight news company like NBC news would use more straightforward reporting.

One of the big pluses of social media is that you get immediate responses from your users. Track the engagement with your posts: likes, views, saves, comments, impressions (number of users who see posts), and reach (how many times the platform presented the post to users). You can increase engagement and get further insights into the audience by responding to user comments. Figure out why a particular post is popular and build on that. If a post has low engagement, don't repeat something similar.

Figure 7–1 Viral Success Kid meme using humor promoting a product
© Metaweb

Another audience factor to consider in social is that, the audience for your post may not be limited to your company's pages. For example, crossposting is popular on Facebook. A crossposting relationship is a mutual agreement between you and another company that allows crossposting between your pages, without requiring case-by-case approval. For example, a large national news organization will have cross posting agreements with many smaller, local media outlets who can cross post content from the national news page. It is useful for writers to be aware that they are interacting with other brands. In the news example above, if you are writing for national news account, you should be aware of your potential local news audience as well.

Another social media audience twist is the availability of paid media. With paid media, a content provider can pay the platform to show a post to a specific segment of the audience, such as dog lovers. So, the writer can create a more focused version of the post for that particular audience.

Manu companies have specific goals for their social media activity, such as to get their social users to link back to the parent website, where the main content and financial engagement is. But generally, the goal is to engage a company's current audience and grow the user base. The ultimate goal is to go viral.

Know Your Company and Competitors

Social Media Manager, Stephanie Orozco, said that when she is hiring a new social media writer, she creates a social media writing practice test. She gives the applicant an assignment for video ideas and some caption drafts. The key thing she needs to know is that the person has looked at what is out there already for social or similar companies. She wants to see how the applicant has taken what is already out there but adds their own creativity.

It is essential to know the brand or product at the place you want to work. She said that lots of people deliver samples that have nothing to do with the company they are applying for. Social media writers should know their brand/products and competitive brands as well.

Understand Major Social Media Platforms

An aspiring social media writer should have a clear understanding of the characteristics of the main social media platforms. For example, the Facebook audience is older and likes more detailed content. Most Facebookers are not visual natives. Conversely, don't post older content on Instagram. Review more information on the various platforms below in the section, Best Practices by Platform.

Graphic and Video Skills

Because most social media posts have some sort of a visual element to them, it is helpful to have an understanding of basic graphic and video design concepts. You can learn these from a course or by grabbing one of the many books on the topic. You are even more competitive if you can express these design concepts with photo and video editing on the latest software being used in the social field.

How to Get Required Skills

Self-taught and On-the-job

Most of the social media writers that I talked to were primarily self-taught or learned on the job. Social media writing has less formal learning opportunities in place than UX Writing as discussed in the last chapter, but the big advantage with social media is that you can easily create your own social media posts on any platform to learn and practice your skills. Creating your own content for social media helps you understand the basics of how social works and the characteristics of each platform. One of the writers I interviewed got her start in social by creating her own beauty platform that gained 20,000 users. Another writer freelanced articles for blogs and sites like Today.com to show her writing chops.

In addition, software for related skills, such as video and image editing, is often available for free within the social platform. If not, needed software can be accessed for little or no cost, allowing practice in these areas as well. Sometimes expensive software has free trials. If there are no free trials, there are also usually cheaper alternatives that are good for practices. For example, Photoshop is the industry standard for graphics editing, but it is expensive. However, the basic version of Canva graphics software is free. Other software that is good to be familiar with includes Premiere, After Effects, Watch It, and for basic productivity, the Google Workspace suite of tools, such as Google docs, Gmail, and Sheets.

Colleges and Online Learning Sites

Some writers feel that studying journalism or communications in college gave them a solid foundation to succeed in the social media field. It helped them understand the big picture of the communications field and honed their writing skills. Another advantage of the college experience is the possibility to get real experience by working on the student newspaper, college social accounts, or other media opportunities.

When you actually get your first social job, you will get significant training in the voice of that particular organization and often assigned a mentor who will help you prosper in the world of social. An employee also gets access to more advanced social software, such as analytics tools. While you have access to these tools, practice them as much as you can to gain new skills.

There are many colleges and universities that offer courses in Communications, Journalism, Digital Media, and even Social Media. These schools range from your local community college to major universities. Research them and find the best fit for your needs. Examples include:

- Carnegie Mellon University
- Georgia Institute of Technology
- MIT
- Savannah College of Art and Design
- Florida State University
- Arizona State University

There are also a number of online learning sites, that offer courses and certification programs, such as:

- Google Digital Garage
- Coursera
- General Assembly
- LinkedIn Learning

Best Practices by Social Media Platform

In addition to having a variety of skills as described previously, a social media writer also needs to understand the different audiences and characteristics of the major social media platforms. Although there are many social media platforms, the major platforms currently used by news organizations, brand marketing, and influencers include:

- Facebook

- Instagram
- Twitter
- TikTok

The key characteristics to be aware of for each platform are:

- Audience demographics: which age generations tend to use your target platforms?
- Localization: if your audience is international, how does the platform demographics and usage vary by country?
- Space limitations: does your platform have space limitations? For example, Twitter only allows 280 characters per post.
- Platform algorithms: what are the current algorithms used by your platform to determine which posts to display often and prominently? An algorithm is a group rules based on usage data that determines the type of content users typically want to see on a particular platform. Each platform has their own algorithms that change on a regular basis.

Table 7.1 Generation breakdowns with favorite social media platform. Other platforms are still used just not as much as the favorite platforms.

Generation	Boomers	Gen X	Millennials	Gen Z	Gen Alpha
Dates Born	1946–1964	1965–1980	1981–1995	1996–2010	2011–2025
Favorite Social Media	Facebook	Facebook	Facebook Twitter Instagram TikTok	Twitter Instagram TikTok	Instagram TikTok

Facebook

Facebook is one of the older social platforms and remains one of the most popular with billions of users. Its users tend to be older than newer platforms, such as TikTok. The major users of Facebook are Baby Boomers, followed closely by Gen X and Millennials. Younger users tend not to use Facebook and, as its core audience ages, Facebook has seen a decrease in growth.

- Facebook likes more personal stories with strong emotions that can be longer and more complicated than other platforms. Adding a lot of quotes can make a story more personal and build the emotional impact.
- Facebook posts are not usually time or event dependent.
- On Facebook, it is often a good idea to include an all caps headline to get users' attention and let them know what the post is about, such as RECALL ALERT or ATTENTION PARENTS.
- Facebook wants to keep people on their platform, so writers have to be discreet if including a crosslink to send a user somewhere else.
- Live events coverage is a special type of coverage of an event while it is occurring. It is most common on Facebook and Twitter. For breaking news like a mass shooting, it is hard to plan coverage. The social team goes live on Facebook and Twitter and posts

events as they happen. Scripted live events like the Oscars can be planned somewhat because you have a basic outline of what they are doing. In this kind of coverage, it's good to have some possible stories sketched out so you can be quick to post, for example the historic firsts that might happen at the event.

Samples of company content that might work well on Facebook include: product news, brand marketing, events, media mentions, and evergreen content. Evergreen content is content that can be used at any time and is not time or season dependent, such as a story about how not to kill houseplants.

Instagram

Instagram trends to a younger audience than Facebook and is very popular with Gen Z and Millennials but less so with Boomers and Gen X.

- Instagram content tends to be less personal than Facebook and less complex with shorter stories.
- Instagram may feed out content several days old so not the best site for breaking news.
- At this writing, the algorithm prioritizes faces. So, if you want Instagram to display your post prominently and often, give them some faces.
- The algo is also favoring Instagram Reels and Stories over Feeds.

  - Feeds are like your home page on Instagram where your main content is stored.
  - Stories are video, photos, text and only remain online for 24 hours and limited to 15 seconds. They give a quick view of what you are up to now.
  - Reels are video only with a maximum length of 30 seconds. They stay online as long as you want. They are good for showing more details about your brand. Reels are a reaction to TikTok, which has a younger, less serious audience than Instagram. If you want to reuse TikTok videos, they may take some editing to appeal to the Instagram audience.

- Instagram Collabs allow you to invite someone to collaborate on a Feed or Reel, so they can share the content directly with their followers. Essentially, you co-author content with a fellow Instagram user, and the post will show up on both of your accounts. Good tool to use if you have strong synergy with another brand or news organization.
- Shorter captions are helpful to get people to click and expand. Longer captions, keep the audience.
- On Instagram, write in a more personal voice, rather than a straight company or news style. Use more personal story telling which is different from the more formal style on Twitter.
- A great Instagram tool for collaboration or creating immediacy is the Takeover. In a Takeover, a field news correspondent might create a post in their own voice. For brands, it is a great way to cross-promote products, letting another brand post on your site.

Samples of company content that might work well on Instagram include: outtakes, cool office visitors, life at the company, cool stuff we make. Instagram is the behind the scenes, more personal voice of a brand.

Twitter

Although Twitter is not as popular as Instagram or Facebook, it is important because it is the platform that many users look to for news and current updates. Less popular with Boomers but roughly the same level of popularity with the other generations.

- Because Twitter is more timely, breaking news content might perform better here.
- Although, it has a 280-character text limit per post, there is usually more text in Twitter than on Instagram or TikTok.
- Twitter stories tend to be less personal than those on Facebook or TikTok.
- Live tweeting is a useful feature to cover breaking events, such as a natural disaster or an awards show, like the Oscars. With live tweeting, the writer is posting immediately and frequently on one event. Many other platforms do not encourage that much posting at one time.
- Social Media Manager, Sophie Lewis, feels that Twitter is a "good place to go back and forth with a conversation. It's easier for the audience to read the interaction because it will show in same panel." With Twitter, you can engage with lots of different accounts in the same conversation.
- A Retweet is usually someone else's tweet that you reshare with your followers. This is a great way to share news and engage with other accounts. Sometimes a writer may decide to retweet one of their own older tweets if it is relevant. You can also add your own comments to a retweet, making it into a Quote Tweet.
- Hashtags are used a lot with Twitter. Hashtags are a hash sign (#) followed by a word or phrase to connect your content to a topic, such as #president or #oscars. This helps users who follow that hashtag to find your content. Creating your own hashtag for a brand usually doesn't work because users may not know what it means. It's easier to connect your post with an existing hashtag.

Content appropriate to Twitter could be similar to what is good for Facebook but with more of an emphasis on current and breaking news.

TikTok

TikTok is the newest platform on this list, but in has grown quickly in popularity, particularly for the younger Millennial and Gen Z groups. Compared to older platforms like Facebook, TikTok it is one of the least popular for Boomers and has the youngest audience of all the major social platforms. For much of the TikTok audience, it is the only social platform that they use.

- TikTok is limited to short videos that tend to be very personal.
- If it is promoting a brand, it might be a behind the scenes look.
- News stories tend to be more personal stories, not major breaking events.
- Expect to write very conversationally, use first person a lot even if a brand.
- Be very specific and to the point.
- Memes were defined earlier in this chapter as popular online content that gets copied and altered numerous times. Memes in TikTok are always short videos. Also popular on TikTok are Trends, which is like a fragmentary meme—a sound, hashtag, dance etc. that goes viral and appears in many TikTok videos. A writer can use popular trends to hook an audience.

- TikTok also has micro communities that sometimes evolve from trends with names like MoneyTalk, CrimeTalk, or BabyTalk. These micro communities are good for brands and niche news because they have an audience focused on a topic.

The type of content on TikTok is similar to Instagram content listed above but more personal and immediate.

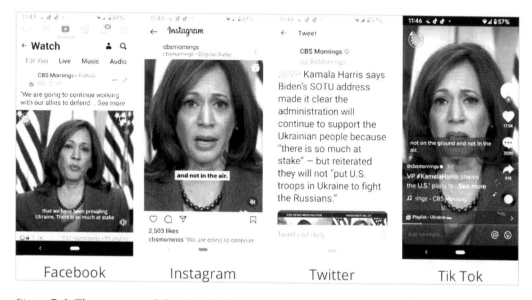

| Facebook | Instagram | Twitter | Tik Tok |

Figure 7–2 The same speech by Kamala Harris covered on Facebook, Instagram, Twitter, and Tik Tok, illustrating the differences between the platforms

© CBS News

Style Guide

In addition to needing to adjust to the guidelines from the various platforms. A social media writer also has to be aware of the social media guidelines for their company. If you joined a new company, you will have rigorous training on voice and tone and usually have to follow their style guide. Many straight news organizations follow standard journalism style guides like AP Style, but most other companies develop a unique style guide as in the example below.

Social Media Style Guide Example—Mailchimp

The purpose of this example is to illustrate what you might see in a social style guide and give a possible starting point for your own style guide if you decide to create one. Mailchimp is an email marketing company with a well establish and unique brand which is maintained by a detailed style guide for all content including social media.

The guide sums up their voice as, "We impart our expertise with clarity, empathy, and wit." It also recommends specific grammar and word usage including use active voice, avoid slang and jargon, and write positively.

Like most major companies, Mailchimp, has a social media presence to build relationships with their customers and promote their products and services. The guide has additional specific tips for social media as illustrated in the excerpt below.

Write short, but smart
Some social media platforms have a character limit; others don't. But for the most part, we keep our social media copy short.

- Twitter: 280 characters.
- Facebook: no limit, but aim for 1-2 short sentences.
- Instagram: no limit, but try to keep it to 1 sentence or a short phrase. Feel free to throw in an emoji.

To write short, simplify your ideas or reduce the amount of information you're sharing. . .

Engagement
. . . When appropriate, you can tag the subject of your post on Twitter or Facebook. But avoid directly tweeting at or otherwise publicly tagging a post subject with messages like, "Hey, we wrote about you!" Never ask for retweets, likes, or favorites . . .

Hashtags
We employ hashtags rarely and deliberately. We may use them to promote an event or connect with users at a conference. Do not use current event or trending hashtags to promote Mailchimp.

Style Guide Sample, courtesy Mailchimp. © Mailchimp
https://styleguide.mailchimp.com/writing-for-social-media/

Voice

Voice and tone are discussed in detail in the previous chapter on UX Writing, refer back to that chapter for details. Basically, voice is the personality of a company's communications. It is the way your posts will sound to the user, just like every person has a single voice or way they present themselves. Tone varies depending on the situation or type of content, just as your tone is different depending on the situation, but the basic voice is constant.

Voice and tone may be even more important in social media than in UX writing because social media is generally more personal communication. If you are hired as a social media writer, you will be trained carefully in that particular company's voice and usually have a style guide to follow as well.

Even in the same general subject area, the voice of a product can be quite different. For example, *The Cut*, *theSkimm*, and *Bitches Get Riches* are all companies that focus on news and information for women, but their voices are quite different. *The Cut* voice is a bit like the older sister, more serious, with more in-depth content. *theSkimm* is lighter, pleasant, more humor, can be silly at times. *Bitches Get Riches* is sassy, rough, and more political. Visit the social accounts of these companies and look for the differences on similar posts.

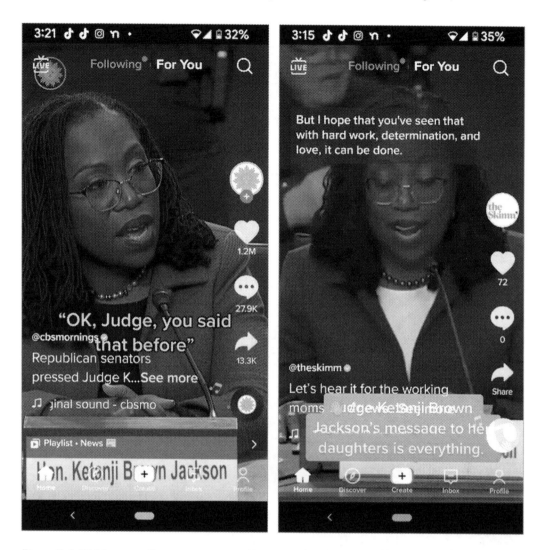

Figure 7–3 Writing tone. Supreme court nominee senate hearing covered by the women's online news magazine *theSkimm*. *theSkimm* focuses on the smiling Judge's message to her daughters. The commentary in the green box strengthens the lighter tone

© *theSkimm*

Conclusion: Coping with Constant Change in Social Media

The guidelines above illustrate the types of things you need to keep in mind when posting to various social media platforms, but these guidelines are not carved in stone. Senior Social Media Producer, Danielle Garrand, said, "The one constant about Social Media is change." The company you are working for and especially the social media platforms will be continually tweaking their approaches to get the best fit for their users. For example, a few years ago TikTok would not be on this list, and most posts would be graphics and text, as opposed to video which is currently popular. Platforms continue to fine tune their algorithm, prioritizing different types of content based on usage data. Unfortunately, writers will have to chase the changing algorithm if they want their posts to be shown prominently and often. So, if you become a social media writer be prepared to continually learn new ways to post as you adjust to changes in company style guides, current social media platforms, or to the appearance of totally new platforms.

References

Bitches Get Riches. https://www.bitchesgetriches.com/
Garrand, Danielle. Senior Social Media Producer. Interview with the author
Kim, Dasle. Senior Manager, Employer Brand & Recruitment Marketing, Daily Pay, Interview with the author
Mailchimp. https://styleguide.mailchimp.com/writing-for-social-media/
Lewis, Sophie. Social Media Manager. Interview with the author
Orozco, Stephanie. Social Media Manager. Interview with the author
The Cut. https://www.thecut.com/
theSkimm. https://www.theskimm.com/

8 Writing for Mobile—Phones, Tablets, Readers

Chapter Overview

This chapter discusses the special challenges of writing for mobile devices, including:

- Writing for Mobile as Conversational Writing
- Mobile Writing Tips Shared with Other Types of Interactive Writing
- Writing Tips Unique to Mobile
- Writing Responsive Websites
- The Importance of Testing Your Mobile Content in Multiple Screen Sizes and Operating Systems

As you read the descriptions in this chapter, look for examples on your laptop or phone to see the concepts in action.

Writing for Mobile as Conversational Writing

The two previous chapters discussed writing for social media and writing for UX, which are two types of writing that have an intimate and conversational relationship with the user. Writing for mobile is not a type of writing but a device (phone, table, etc.) for presenting writing and other content. For example, UX writing and social media writing are often presented on mobile devices. Mobile is included in the discussion of conversational writing because the way that people consume content on a mobile device is more intimate than a larger desktop device. The mobile device is usually hand held and much closer to the user. Many of the ways to improve writing for mobile are shared with other types of interactive writing and some are unique to mobile.

Mobile Writing Tips Shared with Other Types of Interactive Writing

Many of the writing tips shared earlier for other types of interactive writing can also help improve writing for mobile. Because of mobile's smaller screen space, each of these tips need to be followed even more stringently than if you were writing for larger screens, such as desktop computers. These tips include:

- Start with a strong lead. Keep it short and above the fold (viewable area).
- Cut filler words. Write tight.
- Short clear sentences. Leave complicated structures like interjections and appositives behind.

DOI: 10.4324/9781003430612-11

- Short paragraphs to complement your short sentences. Ideally paragraphs short enough to fit on a small screen.
- Subheads. Subheads are secondary headings that identify sections of content, making it easier for users to scan to the desired section.
- Hate the text wall; love the bullet point. If your find yourself writing a long list in a sentence see if it can be broken into more digestible bulleted text.
- Read good online mobile content. Find a major content producer such as a major news organization and read their posts. To write strong content, you need to read strong content.

Writing Tips Unique to Mobile

There are other writing techniques that are particularly important when designing content for a mobile device.

Avoid Desktop-specific Language

- Don't say "click on this." On mobile devices, users tap. If you are writing for a responsive website, you have to accommodate both types of users, so a general word, such as "select" works better than "click" or "tap."
- If you are a fan of hover text and tool tips in your writing for desktop, you will need to find an alternative on mobile. Mobile devices don't display text if you simply hover your finger over a location. There are several workarounds for this, but it is usually best to just put the supplemental information on a sub-screen that the user can tap to view.
- Similarly, there is no right click on mobile. So don't rely on that if you are building menus. You can usually access right click content on mobile but holding your finger on a screen target for several seconds. You can also follow a similar solution mentioned about hover text above and put the content on a secondary screen.

Images

- Dump the decorative images. If it is not central to your content, there is no room for that daisy border on a small mobile screen.
- An added problem with images is that they draw the user's attention away from your text, so they better be meaningful.
- Meaningful images should be small and help identify content, such as the icons that highlight a paragraph on finding ways to save money by showing a dollar sign in a magnifying glass.

Widows, Orphans, and Waifs

- Be aware of widows, orphans, and waifs. Not the human type but lost words and phrases.
  - Widow: the last line of a paragraph that is cut off by the screen fold and appears by itself on the next page.
  - Orphan: the opposite problem. An opening line for the next paragraph that appears by itself at the bottom of a screen, cut off from the rest of its content.

- Waif: a single word sitting on a line by itself at the end of the paragraph.

These issues can be less of a problem with a longer scrolling screen, but you should still be aware of them because the small mobile screens force many more page breaks. One further challenge is that different operating systems, such as Android and iOS, handle these problems differently. As you write keep the paragraphs short and work with your designer to decide on a strategy to deal with these issues if they come up.

CTAs (Calls to Action)

Calls to action, such as "Share with a friend with big feet," or "Buy now, 20% off ends tomorrow!" Should be high on the screen. If possible, put them at the top of the content. Never below the fold. Important navigation should be treated in a similar way.

CTAs should also be on the right of a phone screen because most people are right-handed and will tap the phone with their thumb as they hold it in their hand. If the CTA is on the left that will be challenging.

Chunking Content or Scrolling Content

Another challenge is the small amount of content that can fit on a small mobile screen. Users are willing to scroll to access some types of longer cohesive content, such as a news article, short story, or a list of products.

Many other types of content are smaller discreet pieces of information, such as those in the e-commerce apps. This type of content may have to be chunked or grouped into smaller units. Key content will show on the primary screen, but the secondary content will be relegated to separate screens one level down. This means a higher level of interactivity may be required than on a larger screen where more content can be viewed at once on the landing page.

In this situation, the writer has to identify what content is primary and what is less important. The primary content that will appear on your first screen has to succinctly explain what the site or application is about and why it is important to the user. The writer working with the designer or information architect will have to decide what secondary content links to the primary content directly or can be relegated to a deeper level. Typically, this content is organized by order of importance but sometimes a logical progression makes better sense, such as when completing an application or making a purchase.

Labels

The limited space for content on a smaller screen increases the need for effective interaction design and for the writer to create highly descriptive navigation and other labels. The link and button labels should clearly help the user understand where the link is taking them and what actions the button performs. The labels need to be short to fit on the small screen, but as we noted in the UX Writing chapter, clarity trumps brevity. So, if the short label is confusing, add the extra word if you must.

Phone Usage

The way phones are used emphasizes the need to be extremely clear and to the point. Users are generally on the go when using a phone, not sitting at a desk. Because of this, there is often lots of distractions, such as noise, movement, and interruptions. Users are also often in a rush when performing tasks on a phone, such as checking stocks, paying a bill, reading news. They have no time to figure out wordy text or vague labels. Keep your content short and clear.

Writing Responsive Websites

Writing for small mobile screens is hard enough, but if you are writing for a responsive website, you have a set of additional challenges. A mobile app is specifically designed to only display on a small screen, but a responsive website is designed to be viewed effectively on a range of screen sizes from a large desktop monitor all the way down to a phone screen.

Figure 8–1 Home page of *the Skimm* website, showing laptop and tablet view in responsive design. The content display and organization are quite different between the larger and smaller screens

© *theSkimm*

To accommodate all these different screen sizes, the content on the screen has to move around and be reprioritized as the site is viewed in different size displays. This means that for each screen size or breakpoint, choices have to be made as to what content will display, how it relates to other content, what needs to be minimized, and what will be completely hidden.

One technique to ensure that the content will fit on the smaller screens is to write mobile first. Start by writing for the smallest screen. Decide how you will fit the necessary content there, and then add content as you move up to the larger screen sizes. This is more effective than writing for the large desktop screen first and then trying to cut your content down.

The responsive content choices will be made collaboratively with the designer or information architect, but the writer will help find an effective solution. Fortunately, responsive designers will have a set series of screen sizes that need to be accommodated, including the smallest and largest screen that will be supported. So, the writer does not have to plan for an infinite number of screen sizes.

Conclusion: Test Early and Often

Writing for mobile apps and responsive websites has created new challenges for the interactive writer. With mobile usage continually growing and diversifying, these challenges will continue to grow and get more complex.

The only way to be sure that your content displays as desired on your mobile screen or responsive site is to test early and often. Testing should include viewing content on different screen sizes and different operating systems (iOS, android, etc.) because they all handle content a little differently. Before testing. it is crucial to know what screen sizes and operating systems your product will support so you can focus your testing efforts. The writer will usually collaborate with the designer and researcher on product testing.

References

How to Optimize Your Writing for Mobile Devices by Laura Mondragon. https://medium.com/swlh/how-to-optimize-your-writing-for-mobile-devices-8bd549d243bf

How to Write Content That Engages Mobile Readers by Neil Patel. https://contentmarketinginstitute.com/2015/04/content-engages-mobile-readers/

Hyland, Rachael. Content Designer. Interview with the author

7 fast, effective ways to write for mobile by Davis & Company. https://www.davisandco.com/tip/7-fast-effective-ways-write-mobile

9 Key Points from Part II: Conversational Writing—UX Writing, Social Media, Mobile

Part II Overview

Part II discusses interactive writing that is conversational, both in the style of the writing and in the way that it responds to users and seeks user input. The writing we discussed in the Part included:

- UX Writing: primarily microcopy in software, applications, and highly interactive websites. Successful UX writers carefully utilize voice and tone to interact with the user and guide them through the product with carefully crafted labels, direction text, error messages, etc.
- Social Media Writing (Instagram, Twitter, etc.): social media posts created by various types of companies. This type of writing actively seeks user input.
- Writing for Mobile: unlike social media writing and UX writing, mobile is a device for presenting content. Mobile devices are generally hand held, smaller and create a more intimate or conversational experience with the use compared to larger PC screens. Creating a product primarily for mobile requires special techniques.

The Work of the UX Writer/Content Designer (Chapter 6)

The UX writer or content designer creates the voice of a software or website product that guides the user through their journey. In most cases the UX Writer is primarily responsible for micro copy, such as link text, button labels, direction, error messages, in-context help, tool tips, image alt text, and all the other bits of copy that help the user have a successful and positive experience of an interactive product.

UX Writing Best Practices (Chapter 6)

- Concise
  Make sure every word and punctuation mark adds to the meaning. Remove filler words, such as "that" and punctuation, such as periods in lists, that do not add meaning.
- Clear
  Writing concisely is important, but clarity is even more important. If users do not understand your pithy one-word button labels, then you may have to add additional text to make your label meaningful.
- Sentence case
  Write multi-word labels in sentence case. For example, "Shared with me" not "Shared With Me" or "SHARED WITH ME."

DOI: 10.4324/9781003430612-12

- Active voice
  Active voice focuses on the doer and the action. It is clear and energetic, for example: "Select cart icon to purchase."

Help and Support Writing (Chapter 6)

The UX Writer, the writer may on occasions be asked to help create the help and support content for the product. The latest trend in help writing is a small snippet of help content integrated into the user interface at the point of need—just in time help. This type of writing needs to be concise and action oriented. It often becomes the responsibility of the UX Writer because it is closely related to the design of specific screens.

User Research and Style Guide (Chapter 6)

Knowing the user and creating a style guide are two ways to create and present a consistent and engaging personality for your product. The writer uses various methods to capture the user's key characteristics and product goals including personas, user profiles, user stories, process flows, and journey maps. The recommended writing style plus voice and tone of a particular product is captured in a style guide.

Skills of the UX Writer (Chapter 6)

The writing related skills of the UX Writer include expertise in writing clearly and concisely, design thinking, research and listening, collaboration and persuasion, accessibility and localization and inclusion. Additional skills not directly related to writing such as UX design and a broad range of software skills are also useful.

How to Get the Skills of a UX Writer (Chapter 6)

There are various resources to learn the skills needed to become a successful UX Writer, for example: books, colleges and online learning sites, communities, articles, training, discussions, mentors, conferences, and hands on learning.

Commercial Social Media Defined (Chapter 7)

Social media usage is huge with monthly active users measured in the billions for the most popular application, such as Facebook, Instagram, and TikTok. The user base is not only immense but it is engaged, which is after all what makes it social media. This provides an opportunity for companies to connect closely and have a conversation with their customers. Most social media writing/producing jobs are with one of the following types of companies: news organizations, brand marketing, and social media influencers.

Social Media Writer Writing Skills (Chapter 7)

Social media posts often have images, text, video, and audio. Because of this, the social media writer is also often called a social media producer or social media coordinator. The person in this position needs a wide variety of writing relating skills: writing quickly and accurately, editing longer documents into shorter social media posts, using good grammar and punctuation, possess a large vocabulary, and have the ability to work on many projects at once. In addition to these general writing skills there are also a number techniques specific to social media: focus post on a key emotion, create a curiosity gap, lead with a question, use a numbered list, combine video and text, and manage CTAs.

Social Media Writer Media and Analytical Skills (Chapter 7)

A social media writer also needs to have a variety of other skills, such as strategy, planning, production, audience research, understanding of major social media platforms, and graphic/video skills. There are various ways to gain the needed skills for this position including: self-taught, colleges, and online learning sites.

Best Practices by Social Media Platform (Chapter 7)

In addition to having a variety of skills as described previously, a social media writer also needs to understand the different audiences and characteristics of the major social media platforms. Although there are many social media platforms, the major platforms currently used by news organizations, brand marketing, and influencers include:

- Facebook
- Instagram
- Twitter
- TikTok

The key characteristics to be aware of for each platform are: audience demographics, platform space limitations for content, and platform algorithms used to determine which posts to display often and prominently. These characteristics determine the type of content that you want to post for each platform or if you want to use certain platforms at all.

Style Guide (Chapter 7)

A social media writer also has to be aware of the social media guidelines for their company. If you joined a new company, you will have rigorous training on voice and tone and usually have to follow their style guide.

Coping with Constant Change in Social Media (Chapter 7)

Senior Social Media Producer, Danielle Garrand, said, "The one constant about Social Media is change." The company you are working for and especially the social media platforms will be continually tweaking their approaches to get the best fit for their users. If you become a social media writer, be prepared to continually learn new ways to post as you adjust to changes in company style guides, current social media platforms, or to the appearance of totally new platforms.

Writing for Mobile as Conversational Writing (Chapter 8)

Writing for mobile is not a type of writing but a device (phone, table, etc.) for presenting writing and other content. Mobile is included in the Part II discussion of conversational writing because the way that people consume content on a mobile device is more intimate than a larger desktop device. The mobile device is usually hand held and much closer to the user.

Mobile Writing Tips Shared with Other Types of Interactive Writing (Chapter 8)

Because of mobile's smaller screen space, each of these tips need to be followed even more stringently than if you were writing for larger screens, such as desktop computers. these tips include: start with a strong lead, cut filler words, short clear sentences, short paragraphs, effective subheads, and bulleted lists vs. text walls.

Writing Tips Unique to Mobile (Chapter 8)

There are other writing techniques that are particularly important when designing content for a mobile device such as avoid desktop computer specific language, find alternatives to hover text and right click content, eliminate decorative images, be aware of widow and orphan text, keep CTAs on top right, and create descriptive labels.

Writing Responsive Websites (Chapter 8)

Writing for small mobile screens is hard enough, but if you are writing for a responsive website, you have a set of additional challenges. A responsive website is designed to be viewed effectively on a range of screen sizes from a large desktop monitor all the way down to a phone screen. This means that for each screen size, choices have to be made as to what content will display, how it relates to other content, what needs to be minimized, and what will be completely hidden. To ensure that the content will fit on the smaller screens write mobile first.

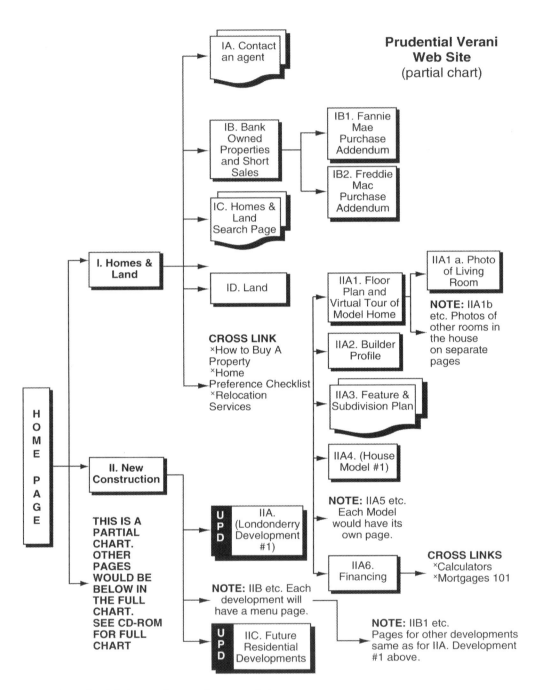

Figure III–1 Partial sitemap for a real estate website

© Verani Realty

Part III

Writing and Structuring Long Form Interactive Information—Websites, E-Learning, Simulations

Part III Overview

Part II discussed short forms of interactive writing, such as writing for software or social media, where the writing may be just a word, phrase, or a few sentences.

Part III discusses longer interactive informational writing that appears on most websites, learning programs, and interactive exhibits in museums and theme parks. This part includes an introduction to this type of writing and three case studies:

Ch. 10 Defining and Achieving Goals for Interactive Information Projects
Ch. 11 Information and Interactive Architecture Patterns
Ch. 12 Marketing Website
Ch. 13 Online Feature Story
Ch. 14 Educational Simulation

DOI: 10.4324/9781003430612-13

10 Defining and Achieving Goals for Interactive Information Projects

Chapter Overview

This chapter introduces interactive information writing that communicate information without using fictional storytelling techniques. The aspects of interactive information examined in this chapter include:

- Definitions of interactive information writing.
- How to define your project goal by considering business context, data, and users.
- Techniques to achieve common interactive information communication goals.

Interactive Information Writing Defined

Most interactive information writing is designed to communicate information or to allow users to perform information-based tasks. This type of writing is found in marketing and customer service websites, e-learning courses, corporate training programs, museum and theme park exhibits, and other interactive media.

If the information being presented is about something concrete, such as a person or a place, interactive informational programs generally follow the documentary tradition of presenting its information through the actual locations and individuals studied. For example, Compton's Interactive Encyclopedia shows a video of Babe Ruth hitting a home run in the Yankee Stadium, as opposed to having an actor portray Ruth in a studio. The Harlem Renaissance website (see Chapter 15) has photos and video of Harlem in the 1920s.

If the information is more abstract, such as the process of buying a home, the material can be explained through text; visualizations, such as charts; and even interactive devices, such as calculators. See the case study in Chapter 12, "Marketing Website: Verani Realty."

There would be nothing wrong with an informational program that used an actor to play Babe Ruth, and many informational programs are created using narrative fiction. Examples include character-driven training programs in which an actor takes on the role of a typical employee or dramatic re-creations of historical events, such as the videos of New England History in the *New England Economic Adventure* profiled in Chapter 19. Narrative fiction and informational programs using narrative have special concerns of their own and will be dealt with later in Part IV, "Writing and Designing Interactive Narrative." The focus of this Part of the book is interactive informational programs that do not use fictional storytelling techniques.

DOI: 10.4324/9781003430612-14

Defining the Goal: Business Context, Data, and Users

Before you can start building an informational project you need to clearly define your user and your goal for the project. Defining the user is actually one of the three components of defining the project's goals. These elements are listed in the table below.

Components of Project Goal Definition		
Business Context	Data	Users
• Corporate Goals • Resources • Brand	• Document types • Formats	• Information needs • Research modes • Expertise • Technology • Culture & Language
Business Context + Data + Users = Project Goals		

Business Context

The business context is the needs and resources of the client or the entity that is funding the project.

- Corporate Goals
  What does the client think that they need to get out of the project? For example, do they want to build a website to sell more real estate, such as Verani Realty profiled in Chapter 12. Does the client also have secondary goals?
- Resources
  Where are the resources that the client can commit to this project? This includes overall budget, development staff, subject matter experts, and staff to maintain the project after it is completed.
- Brand
  What is the company's brand? How is the company perceived by potential customers or how do they want to be perceived? For example, T. Rowe Price whose website is profiled on the book's website is a financial investment company. Their brand is that they are knowledgeable, reliable, and serious about taking care of your money. There will be little that is light or funny on their site.

Data

- Document types
  What type of information does the client already have? Is there adequate product information? Is there information about the company? What areas of information are lacking?
- Formats
  What is the format of the data? Is it in a database, print brochures, videos, or just in the heads of key company personnel?

Users

Information programs are usually focused tightly to a specific group of potential users. For example, the Verani Realty site (Chapter 12) wants to serve people interested in buying homes, lands, or commercial property in New Hampshire and northern Massachusetts. The training program *Vital Signs* on the book's website wants to teach medical assistants how to take a patient's temperature, blood pressure, and other vital signs. Because users are so well defined for most informational programs, it is essential to understand the user before coming up with a program's goal.

Depending on the amount of detail, this user definition is called a user profile or a persona. A persona is more detailed and usually creates a fictional character representing a type of user, such as Harry the Nervous Home Buyer. User profiles are less detailed and do not create characters, instead focusing on the key user characteristics that affects the experience of your website or other interactive project.

- Information needs
  What information or activities do the users want from your project? For example, on a real estate site, are they going to just want lists of houses for sale or also mortgage calculators and other tools? Will they need to perform any online transactions, such as buying a product?
- Research modes
  How does your targeted user typically look for information? Do they like to search or browse? Do they need an online advisor tool that will allow the user to write answers to a series of questions and get advice? How will they want the information organized? What are their key information categories?
- Expertise
  What does the typical user already know about the product or topic? Does there need to be a lot of background information or can we move right into the main content?
- Technology
  How will users generally access your information? Will they use a smart phone, tablet, desktop computer, etc.? Are the users sophisticated with technology to allow advanced features or are they novices who will be easily confused by highly sophisticated technical approaches?
- Culture & Language
  What is the dominant culture and language of your users? Is there a significant minority of users from another culture? If so, you may need to have separate programs or at least sections of your programs in another language. Adapting a project to another culture and language is called localization and is a complicated process usually handled by specialist localization companies. It involves more than just translation and needs to consider cultural differences that affect communication. For example, in India, red represents purity. Indian brides often wear red gowns. In the West, brides wear white for purity, and would never wear red, which symbolizes passion and sexuality in the West.

User Stories, User Scenarios, and Use Cases

One of the ways that interactive programs try to understand their users is in the writing of user stories and user scenarios. A user story is a way to capture the step-by-step information or action needs of a specific user of a software program or website. A single user story will have a description of a type of user and a specific task they need to perform to achieve a goal. For example, "As an editor, I want to review content before it is published so that I can assure it is optimized with correct grammar and tone." A user scenario is a little more complex, combining several user stories. A use case is the most complex used by developers and QA. It describes the steps a user will take using the program and how the system should respond to meet user needs and achieve the client's business goals. Whether you need a user story, user scenario, or use case depends on the complexity of your project and the needs of your collaborators, but the bottom line is that you need to know the key tasks that users are trying to achieve using your program.

Use cases can be very detailed, include extensive research, and fill many pages answering all the questions posed in the previous section about users. There are also many formats for writing use cases. Some follow narrative prose similar to the treatment format outlined in Chapter 3, others are in outline or table form such as the sample below. To write an effective use case requires researching the users of a program. This can involve user surveys, interviews, and site visits to the user's location to watch them use a product. Often secondary sources that know the user, such as the sales team, are also helpful. Usually, a product owner, business analyst, product designer, or an instructional designer will write the use case. A writer should request these documents or user stories to help inform the writer how the user utilizes the website or other program. Sometimes, particularly on smaller projects, the writer may be required to write the user stories or scenarios. If you are on a project and there is no documentation like this, it is something you might suggest.

The sample below is a simple use case for an online chemistry course. Notice the description of the user, the activity, and the sequence of the user's actions. This use case attempts to put the writer in the head of the user and thus allows the writer to provide the content that the user needs to complete a task.

Brief Use Case Sample

Chemistry Online Course
Use Case 6: Instructor Reviews Grades

Description of User

- Instructor reviewing grades
- Viewing in office (broadband connection)
- Computer quality and speed range = very good
- Technically somewhat sophisticated

Activity

- Login to course already begun
- Navigates to grades
- Checks answers and grades then logouts
- Logout

Description of Steps/User Actions	Notes
• Each cell below = a screen • Popup screen text is in italics and separated from main text by lines	Explanation of screen view and user actions
1. Instructor logs on to Blackboard	
2. This leads to Welcome page. Instructor clicks on course link under My Courses	
3. This links to announcements page. Instructor clicks on control panel on announcements page in left menu	

4. On control panel page, user clicks on Gradebook in Assessments area of control panel	Other options in Assessment area of control panel: • Test Manager • Survey Manager • Pool Manager • Gradebook • Course Statistics
5. This leads to View Spreadsheet screen of Gradebook, which shows all students in course and a summary of their grades by exercise. The instructor clicks on a grade of a particular student	Other Major options on View Spreadsheet page include • Add Item • Manage Items • Gradebook Settings • Weight Grades • Download Grades • Upload Grades
6. On the View Grades/Modify Grade page that results, instructor clicks on the View button at the right of the desired exercise listing that the instructor wishes to view.	[NOTE: The screen title of this page is View Grades, but the sequence menu at the top of the page calls it Modify Grade.]
7. The Modify Grade page shows the entire quiz with the question, the correct answer, and the student answer. The instructor also has the option of getting the Teacher Answer Instructor reviews student work. Making notes offline.	• This screen will display student and correct answers to the questions, but not the answers to the hints. • The Teacher Answer consists of the worked-out solution and sometimes some additional notes to the instructor. When the Assignment is an algorithmic one, the solution should use the variables rather than a single numerical value. But the instructor also needs to see the numerical answer for a given instance of the algorithm. (Please note that this Teacher Answer does not include placing the algorithm used by the computer to determine the answer on the screen.) • In Blackboard, if desired, instructor can clear student attempt or change the weighting of each question in the exercise. • Instructor makes notes offline because there is no notes column in the Gradebook
8. Instructor logs out and returns to original login page.	

The use case sample courtesy of Houghton Mifflin Company. © Houghton Mifflin.

Example of Defining the Goal

Once you have answered all the questions listed in the previous section and have a clear understanding of business context, data, and users, you can define your informational project's goals. Goals should be clearly defined, measurable, and limited in number.

An example is probably the best way to understand how this process of goal definition works. Although the Verani Realty site will be discussed in more detail in Chapter 12, we will focus on the goal definition of this project here.

Verani Business Context

Verani Realty is a large regional company and was willing to commit resources to make their website the dominant real estate site in their market. The Verani family has lived and worked in the New Hampshire real estate market for three generations. Even though they are a fairly large organization, their brand is that of a friendly, local company. One of their slogans is "We're not just your realtor, we're your neighbor." They originally had multiple business goals for this website:

1. Better attract and serve customers (buyers)
2. Better attract and serve clients (sellers)
3. Sell properties more effectively
4. Help agents and staff make the most effective use of their time

Verani Data

Verani Realty main document types were descriptions of real estate listings. These were in a database that was not searchable online. They also had information in print material about the company, the real estate selling and buying process, mortgages, and other related information. Last, there was quite a bit of real estate related knowledge in the heads of their top agents and managers.

Verani Users

The potential users of the Verani site were primarily English speaking and middle-class New Englanders. Southern New Hampshire and Northern Massachusetts is an area with lots of high-tech businesses, so many of the potential users are sophisticated users of the technology. Because buying a property is something most users do infrequently, their knowledge of current real estate practice is limited. The primary information need was to search for a property, but users also had significant secondary information needs about the real estate selling and buying process and related issues, such as radon, lead, and relocation assistance.

Verani Website Goals

The Verani Realty website goals were defined by analyzing the information described above on business context, data, and users. The goal decided for the new site was to make it an information resource for sellers and buyers of real estate. Much of the information that was currently in print was made accessible online. This included information, such as school reports, town reports, lists of home inspectors, etc., and tools such as mortgage calculators, interactive check lists, and email updates of current properties. This greatly increased traffic to the site. Users came to the site for real estate information and tools. This well-presented online information helped the agents deliver information to clients more effectively and demonstrated that Verani is a well-run, knowledgeable, friendly company. This encouraged users to consider them when they are buying or selling a property. To support this primary business goal, all properties were easily searchable by users, according to multiple criteria, and new homes had their own section with substantial graphics and virtual tours.

As much as possible, the information was presented in such a way that the user made a connection with the realtor. For example, after a site visitor used the mortgage calculator, he/she had the option of viewing Verani properties in that price range or to connect him/her to an agent. The end result was a website that achieved both business and users' goals and made effective use of the existing data.

Techniques to Achieve Common Informational Goals

The goals for the Verani Realty site as described above are the specific goals for just one type of informational program and audience. But as mentioned in the beginning of this chapter, informational programs cover a wide range of information including general reference, infotainment, education, interactive magazines and news, sales and marketing, training, public relations, customer support and much more. The good news for the writer trying to grasp the techniques used to create this wide array of informational programming is that most of these productions have one or more of the following general goals, each of which have their own techniques for execution:

1. To persuade
2. To entertain
3. To enable transactions
4. To create a sense of community
5. To inform
6. To teach

Of the above goals, the two most fundamental to informational programs are the last two: to inform and to teach. (Inform about real estate was one of the major goals of the Verani Realty site.) Inform and teach are also the goals that are of the most concern for the writer and that are at the core of most other goals. Because of this, I will only briefly discuss goals 1 through 4 and devote the rest of the chapter to a detailed analysis of how to use interactive media to achieve goals 5 and 6: to inform and to teach.

Goal #1: To Persuade

Persuasion is a meta-goal that most informational media share. Advertising sells products. Non-fiction book writers try to persuade us to accept their view of the world. Marketing websites want to convince us that their company is the best. Because this is such a universal goal, extensive material has already been written about persuasion technique so this topic will not be discussed in detail here. Aristotle was the first to point out the three time-tested modes of persuasion to change hearts and minds:

- Ethical: if your viewer believes the speaker, they will believe the speech. (*Ethos* means speaker in Greek.) This is the reason that we have to listen to all those highly trained athletes tell us that they love sugary soft drinks. A second meaning of ethical is to align your message with the beliefs or ethics of your audience. Many Americans are concerned about the environment. Hence the growth of "green" advertisements that seek to show that a product is as beloved by the little forest creatures as is Snow White.

- Logical: logical simply means convincing us with facts. Show us why this is a better built toothbrush.
- Emotional: connect to our emotions. "I am going to be one sexy dude if I wear those blue jeans." This is one of the most popular approaches used by advertisers.

Goal #2: To Entertain

Entertainment as a goal will be discussed in more detail in the book's Part IV, "Writing Interactive Narrative," but one point worth mentioning about entertaining the audience is that all programs must entertain or engage to some degree. Even if a program had the greatest information, it would have limited communication value if it was absolutely boring. A project can be viewed on a continuum, with a plain listing of information at one end, to a program that is pure entertainment at the other end. But most pieces do not exist at either end of this continuum; rather they fall somewhere along the line, embracing elements of both entertainment and information. Where a specific project sits on this continuum is an important consideration for the writer.

Goal #3: To Enable Transactions

The goal "to enable transactions" is important to e-commerce and other retail sites, for activities, such as buying a book from Amazon.com or opening a bank account at BankofAmerica.com. In transactional sites, such as these, the writer is still teaching the user information. In this case, how to perform the transaction. Many of the principles we will discuss concerning the goal "to teach" will apply to writing for transactional sites. Online transactions and activities do, however, put special demands on the writer who must teach the user about the product and how to perform the transaction in the most efficient way possible. If it takes the user too long to get the information they need to perform the transaction, they simply won't do it. The actual designing of online applications that enable transactions is a topic worthy of detailed study but it is more the responsibility of the product designer than it is the job of the writer.

Goal #4: To Create a Sense of Community

Many information websites try to create a sense of community among their users. For example, many major software companies such as Adobe and Macromedia have online user forums on their websites, where users of the same software tools can discuss tips and tricks with the software and get to know each other. Social media sites, such as Facebook and Instagram, allow users to share their ideas, photos, and other media. This sharing can make a user feel as if they belong to a group of like-minded individuals. Physical communities, such as towns or cities, can use similar techniques on their websites to get their citizens involved and make them feel a part of their community. The writer's job for such sites involves informing the user about their community, its values, and common assumptions.

Goal #5: To Inform

A writer whose goal is to inform wants to provide users with access to a large body of information. This could be an online encyclopedia, a magazine site, or a comprehensive product information site, such as the websites profiled in Chapters 12 and 13 of this book. The viewers need not and usually are not expected to access all of the information. Instead, they simply take what they need. The information is usually presented clearly and is structured into discreet units so users can find precise answers to their questions.

Approaches: Creating Access to Loosely Related Body of Material

The major challenge with a large body of loosely related data is to organize the information in a way that allows users to easily access the information that they want. There are a number of ways to do this.

GROUPING BY CATEGORIES

The simplest way is to group by categories, that is, putting all the same types of items together. For example, a movie site might group movie listings, biographies, awards, and media. The media category includes the subgroups of movie stills, portraits, dialogue, music, and film clips. A common designer or information architect technique for grouping by category is the card sort method. Users first break the content into separate small units or chunks. Write this information on cards (paper or electronic) then sort the cards into the appropriate categories or bins.

Content categories are the most obvious grouping, but material can be organized according to numerous criteria, such as place, time, or theme. For example, a movie site could have a feature that allows searching by place so a user could search for all the material that originated in New York. A search by time could include all material before 1930. By theme, it could include all material involved with crime.

Even more useful is to combine categories into what is called a complex query. Combine the movie criterion with the place criterion and get all the movies made in New York. Add the time criterion and get all the movies made in New York before 1930. Add the crime theme criterion and get all the movies made in New York before 1930 that deal with crime.

The limitation of this category approach is that the categories that the writer comes up with may not be the ones that the user would come up with. The ideal program would help users create their own categories and customize the content for their use.

CONCEPT MAPS

Concept maps are a way to visualize categories in a loosely related body of content according to a visual image or map. A simple concept map is the tabbed navigation used on many websites that try to make the website look like a file drawer with tabbed file folders that can be sorted through. The museum and journey approach are other common images. The museum approach allows users to enter a virtual museum, enter exhibit rooms in their area of interest, and view exhibits about a particular subject. The journey allows users to travel along a certain road, path, or timeline.

A danger with concept maps is combining incompatible maps. An early draft of the program *Sky High* attempted to combine the temporal map of journeying along a time line with the spatial map of the stars and planets. These two different types of maps did not work smoothly together and had to be abandoned.

See the book's website for the "Educational Multimedia Case Study: Sky High," to read a full discussion of this issue.

CUSTOMIZED AND PERSONALIZED INFORMATION

Another excellent approach is to presort the content to only present the user the information that they need. To do this, the website has to first collect the user's information preferences. There are two basic ways this can be done: customization and personalization.

Customization involves the user consciously inputting their preferences into the computer program. This is usually done by filling out a form or clicking answers on a questionnaire. Once the user's preferences are noted, then just the information that interests them can be presented. For example, on a financial services site, users can define what mutual funds they want data on. Next time they log on to the site, only those funds will be presented. Learning programs can also be customized by allowing the user to choose which sections they want to study and in what order.

Personalization's main difference from customization is that the user generally does not provide conscious input about their preferences. Instead, the computer program learns the user's preferences by previous activity on the program. Personalization is most commonly used in transactional websites that are trying to match their products with the user. The best-known example is Amazon that tracks the items you bought in the past and recommends new purchases based on your previous activity. Amazon will also try to guess your preferences by associating you with other customers. If you bought books about angels, and several other customers who bought books about angels also bought books about devils, then Amazon might suggest some devil books to you on your next visit. Personalization can also be used on learning programs that can track the user's progress through the program and adapt the type and difficulty of material it will present based on the user's previous performance. One popular college math program will offer review exercises and additional information on earlier material if the student gets several problems with this material wrong.

SEARCH

Search is perhaps the most useful tools when accessing a large body of loosely related or unrelated information. The web itself fits that category and tools, such as Google, devise every more sophisticated ways for the user to find exactly what they want. Any website of any size usually has a search tool as part of it. Designing the search is not usually the writer's job, but a few things a writer can recommend are make sure search results are in a usable form and design search around the terms users commonly use. One warning, don't automatically add search to your website if you don't have the content to support it. Users get frustrated when they search and don't get desired results because of lack of content. So, for smaller sites, a browsable content organization might be better.

GUIDES AND AGENTS

Another approach to make a large body of content accessible is by creating guides or agents to lead users through the material. These guides could be software creations that are part of the program. For example, a family health program includes an on-screen character who introduces material and helps to guide users in the direction that they want. This type of a guide is limited by the material that was written for the screen character to present, but it can help make a program more accessible. A common use of software agents on the web are those used on job sites, such as Monster and LinkedIn. A job seeker enters the criteria for the type of job he/she is interested in and then the job websites will email the user when jobs that match the criteria appear in their database.

Avoiding Cognitive Overload by Controlling Complexity

Guides, agents, and customized information are some ways to keep users who are browsing a vast collection of information from getting confused by the diversity and complexity of the unsequenced material they encounter, but cognitive overload is still a problem. Browsing a website is a quite different experience from reading a textbook, where the information is carefully explained and structured to build understanding of an overall topic gradually. In any loosely structured collection of material, the opposite to understanding can occur. Topics of varying degrees of difficulty can be encountered and only partially understood by the student. For example, search engines will often drop you into a middle page of a website and you may have to back track to the home page to get your bearings. To facilitate learning this cognitive load needs to be controlled.

Cognitive load can be reduced in a number of ways, for example:

- Reduce the number of choices available on the screen at any one time. Some experts feel it should be less than ten.
- Reduce the level of difficulty available to the student at any different time. Students must have viewed crucial introductory material before they are allowed to access advanced concepts.
- Build a note-taking function into the program so students can track their progress and note partially understood concepts. Note-taking should include text and pictures.
- Give students the opportunity to "bookmark" a section of the program that they can return to later.
- Build in a clear orientation so students can understand where they are and that the various pieces of information are connected. Navigation maps and consistent interface design helps with this.

Goal #6: To Teach

In a large collection of varied information, such as discussed above, what information the user accesses and learns is up to the individual. In a teaching program, however, the information is more tightly structured and the writer has a clearer goal of what information he or she wants the user to take away from the program. For example, Fidelity Investments' training program for retirement counselors is focused on teaching how to advise clients about retirement. Houghton Mifflin's *Geology Explorer* website teaches key concepts about geology.

Instructional theory is a complicated subject that must be studied in depth if one is to become an instructional designer, but it is important to be at least familiar with some of the basic concepts of instructional design before writing educational or training programs.

Interactive Instruction as Interpersonal Instruction

An effective interactive media instruction program should include the characteristics of interpersonal instruction: immediacy of response, information that adapts to user's learning needs, feedback, two-way communication, and ability to alter the flow of information.

IMMEDIACY OF RESPONSE

In practical terms, this means that an action the learner takes should get a response immediately. It is psychologically important for the learner to feel connected. For example, when a student clicks on an answer in a quiz, he or she should get some sort of response even if it is just a sound. Similarly, if there is going to be a wait after a student clicks an icon to access a large file, something should be happening on the screen—preferably something more interesting and tied to the program than an hourglass or a watch. Wait-state and other responses should be in tune with the program. Rodney's Wonder Window, a humorous children's educational program, has funny wait-state text messages, such as "Please wait, Rodney is putting on clean underwear," and visual images, such as the heads on the character icons spinning around or their hair curling.

FEEDBACK

Immediacy of response does not mean complex feedback to every action. Deciding what kind of feedback to give and when to give it to the learner is a difficult question. There is no consensus on this subject. There is even disagreement on simple types of feedback. For example, some writers provide only a minimal response, such as "Correct," to correctly answered test questions, and reserve complex feedback for questions answered incorrectly. Others include detailed feedback for correct answers as well, to reinforce the message and to guard against students' guessing the right answers and not learning the material.

TWO-WAY COMMUNICATION

Clearly related to immediacy of response and feedback is two-way communication and ability to alter the flow of information. A well-designed learning program gives the user ample opportunity to communicate with the program as well as for the program to communicate with the user. This includes letting the learner communicate through various methods, including typing text, manipulating images, and sound. This is essential if maximum learning is going to happen for the maximum number of students, because studies have proved that we all learn in different ways—some by watching, others by doing, and yet others by analyzing. Thus, it is important to present the content in a variety of approaches.

ABILITY TO ALTER THE FLOW OF INFORMATION

Students should be able to interrupt the program at any point and go in the direction that is useful for them. They should, for example, be able to return easily to earlier material for review. If they feel comfortable with the material, they should be able to jump ahead to a more advanced part of the program.

Programs that do not allow this movement can be frustrating. For example, an otherwise excellent education program on video production, requires that students complete a series of quizzes on video production techniques before they are allowed to create a video in the program's studio. This defeats the purpose of interactive media and incorporates the drawback of linear media and classroom instruction where all levels of students must progress through the material in the same way.

HELP

Excellent help programs are now included in basic productivity programs, such as word processors, but a surprising number of educational programs or complex websites do not provide a constant helping hand. Help features are particularly important with complex online processes, such as opening a bank account online. It is important to build the help function into the interface design from the beginning as well as into the writer's schedule. Writing help pages can be extremely time-consuming.

PERSONALIZING INSTRUCTION: NONSEQUENTIAL ACCESS TO INFORMATION,
ADAPTABILITY, AND OPTIONS

Interactive media's ability to access information in the order that the user finds most useful allows a writer to personalize or customize a program and make it adaptable to the user. Many programs allow users to customize the program at the beginning by filling out a user profile based on such criteria as educational level, job, and familiarity with the subject. Once entered into the computer, this profile might cause the program to take the user down a completely different path, or just alter the text on certain screens, or offer different product suggestions.

Personalization can also occur without the user's conscious involvement. Transactional websites, such as Amazon, track what products you have purchased and use this activity to determine what products to show you in the future. Whatever the approach, personalizing the program continues beyond the beginning by tracking the user's progress and adapting to his or her needs. For example, a learner who consistently has difficulties in a certain area might be directed to special remedial sections geared to that particular problem. The program might also alter the way it presents the instructional material in the rest of the lesson. If the student learned best from the video segments, the video might be increased and text minimized.

A simple way to customize a media piece is to allow students to choose the level of difficulty and thus advance at their own rate. Another adaptation is the degree of control allowed to the student over the learning material.

The way subject matter is approached also customizes a program. Someone learning marketing should be able to choose various contexts designed into the program in which to practice their new skills, such as marketing a virtual baseball team, restaurant, or rock group.

Conclusion

By clearly defining your user and goals, you can then use the most effective techniques to achieve those goals. Likewise, poorly defined or contradictory goals are impossible to execute. The time spent in the early planning stages of a project will radically improve your chances of success.

11 Information and Interactive Architecture Patterns

Chapter Overview

Informational interactive media programs and websites have a variety of possible structures and ways of interacting with the content. This structure and interaction design is called information architecture and interactive architecture. A key question the writer must ask when developing a piece is which approach will best achieve the communication goals. As discussed in *Chapter 3, Interactive Writing Tools and Script Formats*, information architecture is often planned with flowcharts and outlines. Every possible interactive architecture is not listed here, merely those that are most commonly used by the writer and designer of informational interactive media programs.

Examples of Information Architecture

Linear Structure

Defined

Linear structure has no linking or interactivity. Linear structure can be compared to a desert highway with no crossroads. It is the structure of most motion pictures and television programs.

Use

Linear structure makes it possible to integrate into interactive media some of the standard linear informational structures, such as the problem-solution structure and the dialectical structure. The problem-solution structure is used by setting up a problem linearly and then asking the user to solve it interactively. Dialectical structure, a favorite of the TV news magazines, sets up a dialogue between two different points of view. First, we hear from the Army general who wants to spend billions on a bomber; then we hear from the peace activist who doesn't want to spend any more money on new weapons. This A/B, love/hate pattern is repeated until a conclusion emerges or we can draw our own conclusion. A simpler use of linear structure in interactive media is the presentation of key information that should not be interrupted. This is often used for introductory material. For example, *The New England Economic Adventure* (Chapter 19) introduces each new section with a linear video on the historical background of the period.

DOI: 10.4324/9781003430612-15

Linear Structure with Scene or Section Branching

Defined

Linear structure with scene or section branching is basically a linear structure with a few limited choices as to how certain scenes will play out. This structure can be compared to a desert highway that has a few detours (see Figure 8–1). The detours, however, always return the traveler to the same highway.

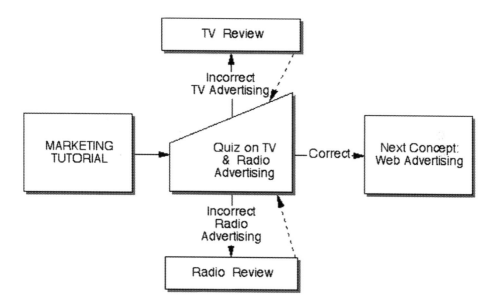

Figure 11–1 Linear structure with scene or section branching for part of a marketing tutorial

Use

This is sometimes used in training pieces that are explaining a step-by-step concept by following a linear structure. There is often an option of detouring from the step-by-step instruction for a review of the concept or for additional material, but after the detour, the user is returned to the screen that he or she had left. Another example is software's introductory screen that explains how to use the company's product. The basic step-by-step instruction is brief, but users have the option to link to the help pages in each section for additional background material. Sometimes a program will actually force the user to link to different sections. In the marketing tutorial charted in Figure 11–1, the student who answers information incorrectly on radio or television advertising is sent back to the radio and television content to review before proceeding forward in the tutorial.

Hierarchical Branching

Defined

In hierarchical branching, information is organized according to categories and subcategories, so users can click an information category, and then a subcategory to find the information that they want. This approach could be compared to going to a mall looking for an Italian cookbook. At the first fork in the mall, you can choose left for the department store, straight ahead for the bookshop, or right for the cooking shop. You want a cookbook, so you choose straight and go to the bookshop. In the store, you must choose between nonfiction, fiction, and magazines. You choose nonfiction, which includes many choices, ranging from biography to cookbooks to zoology. You choose cookbooks. The cookbook section has many types of cooking, including French, Indian, and Italian. You choose Italian and, phew, you are finally done.

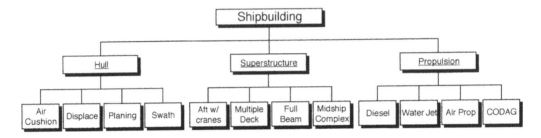

Figure 11–2 Hierarchical structure for a website on shipbuilding

Use

Hierarchical branching in an interactive media program works like the mall shopping example with a hierarchy of ever-narrowing choices, except your finger does the clicking instead of your heels. See Figure 11–2 for a diagram of hierarchical structure for a program about shipbuilding. The user can click various categories to drill down to the level that has the information they need.

Although hierarchical is one of the most popular interactive media structures, it has several potential pitfalls. One is branching explosion, which means creating too many user options. Too many options are created because increasing the number of decision points or the number of choices at each decision point means that the total number of possible branches increases exponentially. In Figure 11–2, the options quickly jump from 3, to 12, and, by adding one more level, to 48. The amount of material quickly expands to a volume difficult for a writer to create and a user to navigate.

For the user, the danger with hierarchical branching is that if there are too many levels of information, the user can get lost and find it difficult to make connections with material on the same level, such as 48 subcategories on level four of a shipbuilding program. There is also a practical limitation to the number of choices at any one branching level (some studies say that five to seven choices are the most people can easily comprehend).

Branching explosion is kept under control by limiting categories at a level, segmenting the audience at the top of the hierarchy, and by allowing alternate access to information on the site, such as search and site maps. See Figure 11–3 for an example of how the T. Rowe Price financial site segments their audience at the top level by key users, such as Individual Investor and Institutional Investor. This is an alternative to using subject categories, such as mutual funds that might apply to multiple user groups. This allows each major section to be less dense with information and categories because it focuses on the needs of just one group. In general, most effective websites do not go very deep—not more than three or four sub-categories.

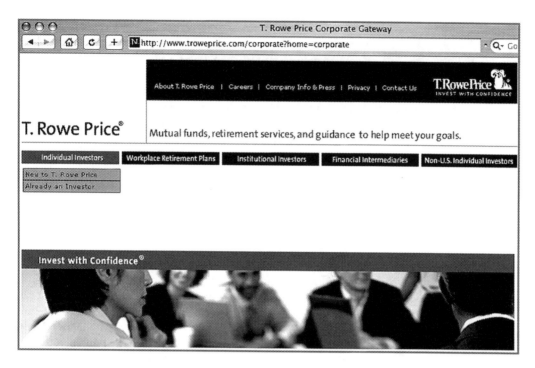

Figure 11–3 Segmenting audience to reduce branching explosion. Home Page from the T. Rowe Price
website

© T. Rowe Price Associates, Inc.

Effectively done, hierarchical branching can be a useful and economical way to present
information, which is why it is the structure of many websites or other informational programs. This does not mean it is the best structure for all types of information. Alternatives
are presented in this remainder of this chapter.

Single-Level Linking

Defined

There is no hierarchy in this approach. Usually, the user is presented with a problem and
given a number of possible resources for solving the problem that can be accessed in any
order. As opposed to hierarchical branching, which looks like a well-organized mall, single-
level branching is like wandering into a chaotic flea market. At a flea market you can go any
number of places and talk to anyone in any order.

Use

In the interactive documentary *A Right to Die: The Case of Dax Cowart*, Dax Cowart has
a serious illness. He wants to refuse treatment and die. His doctors and others feel differently. The user of this program can access video interviews, text, and other material about
this case in order to answer the question: does Cowart have the right to choose his death?
(The irony of this piece is that Dax was not allowed to choose his death; the therapy was

successful, and he went on to live a happy life.) Although single-level linking structure is useful, it is fairly rare on a complete program because it must be limited to a focused topic with limited options. If there are too many options, then a hierarchical structure or another approach has to be used to organize the material.

Single-level linking is more common in small parts of programs. A section of the *Geology Explorer* e-learning program examines the formation of a cross-section of land. Within each part of the program, students have the option of looking at screens dealing with a description of a layer, an animation showing the process of layer formation, an explanation of the geologic event that caused the layer to be formed, or a quiz. Because it is useful for the student to compare all these elements, they have the option of accessing and reviewing this material in the order that makes most sense to them.

Parallel Path or Multi-Path Architecture

Defined

This approach is borrowed from interactive narrative where one of the main structures is parallel path stories. See Figure 17–4 in the middle of Chapter 17, "Elements of Interactive Narrative." In a parallel paths story, the writer lays out three or more possible versions of the same basic story. Depending on the players' choices as they move through the game, they move back and forth between the different story versions. This will be explained in more detail in the narrative section of the book. When applied to an informational program, this approach creates three or more distinct paths the user can travel through a specific body of information. In the physical world this could be compared to a traveler having three or more possible distinct routes that would lead towards the same destination or slightly different destinations.

Use

One of the most effective uses of this approach is with online transactions or other activities where the user is trying to accomplish a specific goal. One example would be users who wanted to open a bank account online at a bank website. The challenge for the writer is that these users are a heterogeneous group. Some are web savvy; others are newbies. Some know a lot about banking products; others need lots of explanations. Some want banking accounts; others may want investing accounts.

To accommodate this variety of user needs, the writer can prepare multiple information paths through the online account opening application. One of the ways this can be achieved is through good interface design, such as putting the essential information and activities on the left side of the page and putting the secondary product information on the right side of page, perhaps in a box to indicate that it is secondary. Context-sensitive help should also be available on every page. Another approach would be to allow users to customize the transaction by choosing their knowledge and skill level at the beginning of the process.

With structure, such as these, the web savvy user who knows banking products can move quickly down one path performing only the essential activities. The web savvy user who needs product information could take a slower path moving to the product information and then to the essential activities. The user most in need of help could move through the help feature, to the product information, and finally the essential transactional activities.

This approach is different from a hierarchical structure because the user can easily move from one information path to the other and does not have to navigate up or down through multiple subcategories.

Dynamically Generated Database Driven Sites and Apps

Defined

This is not a separate structure, but the way most informational interactive programs are assembled for the user. Most programs do not have static pages of information on their servers. Instead, they have a more or less blank framework or template for different sections of the site or mobile app. The actual content that fills that framework is drawn in small chunks from a database and the pages are dynamically assembled to be viewed on your computer or phone screen. What this means for writers is that they have to be particularly skilled in the technique we discussed earlier of being able to write small units of information that can stand alone, but also work in conjunction with other information if need be. In terms of structure, from the user's point of view, a dynamically generated program will appear to follow one of the basic structures above. For example, if you drill down the category menus on Amazon the structure is hierarchical.

Use

Most sophisticated transactional sites or mobile apps are dynamically generated. For example, the home page of a site selling products, could have a page template arranged like the example below.

Header and Global Navigation: Your Store, Your Account, Cart, etc.		
Long Menu of Different Product Categories	Center Content Area Listing Products and Special Offers Separated by Headers	Small Block Advertising Featured Product Small Block Advertising Featured Product More Small Blocks
Bottom Links: Customer, Support, International Sites, etc.		

What goes into each section of the template will change depending on your shopping habits and if you have been to this site before. If you have ordered toys before, the advertisements and products offered will show ads and links for toys. If you have never bought products before, then different more general ads will be shown. This is called personalization. The site is adjusted to you by the server software. These individual ads and product information are in chunks on the server and they are delivered to the template and displayed on your browser based on your shopping or browsing habits.

As mentioned above, the key point of this discussion for the writer is that most web or app pages are not "pages" at all, but rather snippets of information assembled on the fly to display in your browser as if they were a single page.

Passive vs. Active Information Delivery

Passive Information Delivery

Many interactive informational writers use the structures previously discussed in this chapter and deliver their content in a way that requires no user action beyond click-and-read. For example, users on a website might click a series of menu items and read the linked content. This is a functional way to access information, but it keeps viewers at a distance by not making them use or think about the information. For example, Figure 11–2 in the discussion of hierarchical branching, shows the structure of a click-and-read approach to an educational project about shipbuilding. In this case, the writer simply organized the information according to categories and subcategories, so users can click an information category and view material about it. This information is presented in a clear manner, but it is not very engaging.

Active Information Delivery

Active or dynamic information delivery demands more of the user than simply click-and-read. For example, the same shipbuilding program charted in Figure 11–2 could be developed as a program that involves the user interactively. Figure 11–4 charts the structure of an actual museum kiosk program on this subject called *The Nauticus Shipbuilding Company*. In this program, the user plays the role of a shipbuilder. The user is first asked to choose between three different types of ships that need to be built: transatlantic cargo ship, cross-channel ferry, and oceanographic research vessel. The user is then asked to assemble one of these ships by choosing from a variety of components for the hull, propulsion, and superstructure. At the end of the program, the completed ship is evaluated. As it leaves the dock, it floats or it sinks. This approach teaches the same information as the click-and-read hierarchical approach illustrated in Figure 11–2, but it does so in a more engaging fashion. The answer to getting beyond click-and-read is to involve the user in some way. This is, after all, interactive media.

Using Click-and-Read

Active information delivery is not appropriate for every type of project. Passive information delivery is actually much more common. For example, if you want to present product information on a simple product or answers to customer support questions, click-and-read is perfectly fine. It is also generally less expensive than active information programs. But if your goal is to engage the user to fully experience and learn your topic, then active delivery should be considered.

Getting Beyond Click-and-Read: Simulations, Worlds, Role Playing

The following approaches, simulations, worlds structure, and role-playing are only a few of the many approaches and techniques that can fully engage the user and present information actively. The correct approach should emerge from understanding the information to be presented and the intended audience.

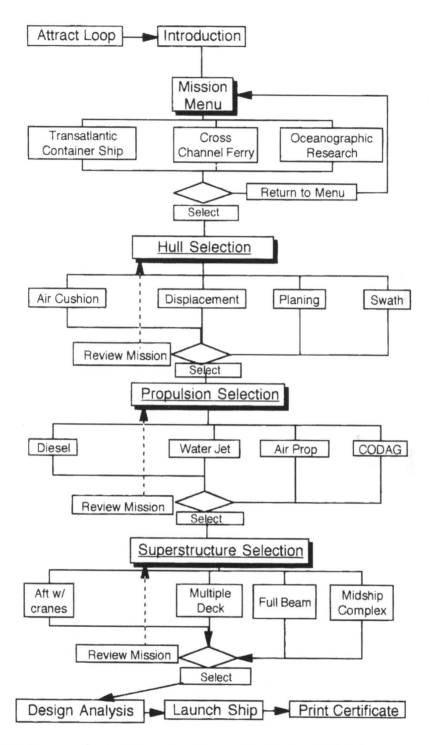

Figure 11–4 Structure of active information delivery—*The Nauticus Shipbuilding Company.* Courtesy Chedd-Angier Production Company

Simulation

Defined

In a simulation, an experience or activity is recreated virtually on screen. The activity can be driving a car, flying a plane, snowboarding (Chapter 20), or building an entire city. The structure is dictated by the activity.

Use—Problem Solver

Educational simulations that have extensive need of writers are usually more complex than simply flying a plane or driving a car. For educational programs, the simulations usually involve a problem for the user to solve or task to accomplish. For example, the classic *Sim City* programs give the user the power to build a city by altering the landscape, adding parks, schools, railroads, power plants, and other components, but it must be done within budget and the user must cope with disasters, such as flood, fire, and alien invasion.

The Nauticus Shipbuilding Company, which was discussed earlier in this chapter and illustrated in Figure 11–4, is another example of a problem solver simulation. In this case the problem to solve is building a ship.

Use—Gamer

In this approach, the user takes on the role of a player in a game. Not all games are simulations. Interactive media versions of crossword and word search are not. But if the player actively takes on the role of a character in the game, they generally are. This is somewhat similar to the problem-solver approach, except that it usually operates with more clearly defined game rules. For example, Houghton Mifflin's World Languages program has a "Words in Space" game (Figure 11–5). The player takes on the role of a defender of the home planet. At the beginning of the game, it is announced that the planet is being attacked by spaceships from a planet whose name is a certain category of words, such as vegetables or as illustrated in Figure 11–5: Numbers Greater Than 50. All the spaceships are labeled, some have numbers greater than 50 in the foreign language; others are friendly ships labeled with words for lower numbers. The player has to translate the names of the ships and shoot them. If the player shoots the wrong ship, the player is shot by the enemy ships. Three enemy hits on the player, and it's game over. Time to go study more vocabulary.

Use—Explorer, Worlds Structure

As an explorer, the user takes on the role of an explorer or traveler who explores an entire world of information. There is no set problem to be solved or sequence of actions to be accomplished as in the previous uses (gamer and problem solver). The worlds structure organizes the options available to the viewer not in a linear fashion or in a hierarchy but in a graphic spatial representation. This approach is most useful if there is a large body of information that can be incorporated in a location. It does not have to be a physical location that we normally visit. The museum interactive piece *Into the Cell* allows viewers to take a

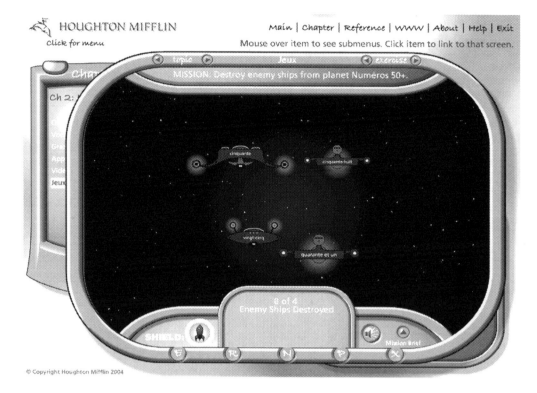

Figure 11–5 Words in Space game for French teaching program *Mais Oui!* Courtesy Houghton Mifflin Company

© Houghton Mifflin Company

fantastic voyage into a living cell. A writer approaches a project like this by first deciding on a list of locations in the virtual world that he or she is creating, then determining what will happen in each location, and finally how the user will be able to discover these events. A flowchart is not that useful here. More useful is a graphical illustration of the world, a list of the locations, and descriptions of the events that will occur in each location. This is explained further in the following section.

Writing a Simulation

To write a simulation, start defining the players roles and the locations. Then the interactive objects within each location, including each object's attributes and rules of behavior.

In *The Nauticus Shipbuilding Company*, the attributes of the air cushion hull are that it is capable of high speeds, needs flat water conditions, and has a flat deck that is easy to load. Its behavior, if chosen for the oceanographic research vessel, is that it will sink because it can't withstand the rough seas off New England.

Attributes and Behavior of the Hulls in *The Nauticus Shipbuilding Company Simulation*

ATTRIBUTES AND BEHAVIOR OF HULLS IF USED FOR OCEANOGRAPHIC RESEARCH VESSEL

ATTRIBUTES	BEHAVIOR OF HULLS IF USED FOR OCEANOGRAPHIC RESEARCH VESSEL
Air Cushion: • Flat hull rides on cushion of air • Capable of high speeds • Needs flat water conditions • Flat, rectangular deck easy to load	Nonfunctional • Can't withstand rough seas
Planing Hull: • V-shaped hull capable of high speeds • Performs best in flat water conditions • High stress levels on hull	Functional • Capable of high speeds • Not very stable in rough seas • Limited work and living space
Displacement Hull: • Deep, rounded hull very stable in all conditions • Very large cargo capacity • Stable platform for large propulsion systems • Needs very large propulsion system	Functional • Stable in rough seas • Plenty of work and living space • Deep draft limits access to shore areas
SWATH (Small Waterplane Area Twin Hull): • Two submerged hulls very stable • Flat deck provides good work area	Optimal • Very stable in rough seas • Plenty of protected work and living space • Shallower draft provides access to shore areas

Sample Courtesy Chedd-Angier Production Company © Chedd-Angier Production Company.

Other Approaches to Active Information Delivery

Simulations, role-playing, and worlds structures are among the more popular techniques for active information delivery, but there are other options, ultimately only limited by your imagination.

Reporter

A number of educational programs, including *Sky High*, allow users to report on their interactive media experience by using a virtual camera and a word processor to write a journal. This is probably not a true simulation because, although you are playing a role, your actions don't affect what happens in the program. But being a reporter is at least more engaging than a simple click-and-read approach.

Tools

Allowing the user to work with the information by giving them functioning tools in your program is another way to get users engaged. For example, the Verani Realty website profiled in Chapter 12 has dynamic information elements such as calculators, rent vs. buy estimators, and interactive checklists.

Virtual Advisors

Virtual advisors are online forms that ask the user a series of questions. After the user has filled out the form, the online advisor suggests the proper product to buy or action to take. This is commonly used for more complex products, such as opening a bank account online. Many major banks have some sort of online advisor on their websites to help users choose the type of account that is right for them. Sometimes these take the form of AI chatbots.

Active Information Delivery as Part of Larger Passive Information Delivery Program

In the programs described above, *Sim City* and *The Nauticus Shipbuilding Company*, the complete programs are simulations. It is also perfectly good technique to add a simulation or other type of active information delivery to an otherwise click-and-read program. For example, in Houghton Mifflin's *Geology Explorer* educational program, the users are asked to chart the location and magnitude of an earthquake using interactive animation tools. Another exercise in the same program allows users to date the geologic layers of a cross-section of land.

Benefits of Active Information Delivery: Learning to Learn

An additional benefit of an active information delivery, particularly simulations, is that in addition to teaching a specific skill or subject matter, this type of interactive media is also very successful at teaching students how to learn. A couple generations ago, the standard structure for most school classrooms was a sea of student desks in neat rows with teachers standing in front of the class delivering knowledge from their information-packed brain to those of the empty-headed students.

A visit to many classrooms today would find a different structure. The sea of desks is gone. Students are grouped in fours or fives around smaller tables and are engaged in activities. The teacher moves about the room, facilitating their learning. This different structure reflects current learning theory, which rejects the concept of empty heads waiting to be filled and replaces it with the goal of teaching students how to learn.

A big reason for this major change is the rapid explosion in knowledge. A hundred years ago, the body of knowledge was relatively stable. Individuals could learn a trade and successfully perform that trade until retirement. Today, information is expanding so rapidly that education has become a lifelong pursuit. Students have no assurance that the information they are learning will be valid in a few years or even that the careers they are training for will exist after graduation. To thrive in this type of a world, students must be excellent learners and have a full bag of learning tools to take with them for the rest of their lives.

Teaching Toolmakers with Interactivity: Playing as If

One of the best ways to develop these tools—to learn how to learn—is through hands-on learning, an opportunity to interact with the subject under study. One way to do this is through interactive media programs. For virtual hands-on experience to be an effective learning experience, it needs to include reliable feedback and give the learner the ability to reconstruct the experience. There should be some way to reconstruct and replay the learning experience in a safe environment. The major way learners incorporate new material is not through the experience itself but through the ability to recreate the material in some fashion, thus making it their own. This allows for the creation of interaction models or plans that can be used with similar real-world interactions.

In an interactive media program, this construction of models can range from trying out different marketing techniques in a virtual business case study to building an entire city in one of the *Sim City* games. Simulations become crucial in situations that are difficult to recreate in the real world. For example, NASA uses simulations to train their astronauts for work in outer space. Interactive programs like these, allow users to explore "what" will happen "if" they try various options.

Conclusion

Whether you use active or passive information delivery, it is important to pick the type of structure and approach to your material that will best fulfill your goals as discussed in the previous chapter. The user's needs, business context, and type of data will all have a major effect on your final decision. For example, creating a simulation will generally be more expensive than a click-and-read approach and may not be appropriate for a low budget project.

In larger projects also, keep in mind the possibility of linking all of the structures described in this chapter in one unlimited information experience. A user might start at one section that is hierarchical, link to another with a linear video, and yet another that involves the user in a simulation. A graph of this would look like a mad combination of all of the examples in the chapter.

This chapter concludes the introductory informational interactive media material. Beginning with the next chapter, informational interactive media programs will be examined in depth to better understand how the principles we have been exploring are applied on actual projects.

12 Writing a Marketing Website from Proposal to Documentation
Realty

Summary

Name of Production: Verani Realty Website
Writer: Timothy Garrand
Developers: InterWrite
Audience: Commercial and Residential Real Estate Customers, General Public
Medium: Website
Location: Where realty sites are viewed, mostly home
Subject: Real estate
Goals: Inform, teach, transact
Information architecture: Branching, hierarchical branching, dynamic database generated

The text samples, flowcharts, and illustrations used in this chapter are courtesy of Verani Realty. © Verani Realty.

Scope of This Chapter

This chapter studies the different types of writing that can be required to develop a commercial website, with an explanation of the goals of each document and some tips for achieving those goals. Although a writer's efforts are sometimes limited to the content of a site, the writer may be also called upon to write the initial proposals, planning documents, maintenance instructions, and online marketing writing, such as meta tags. The writer playing these roles needs to understand organizational tools, such as flowcharting software; how writing affects the site's online marketing efforts; and the capabilities of the latest web technology to communicate information effectively. This chapter is different from the later case studies that will focus primarily on writing the project's content.

Program Description and Background

Program Description

The Verani Realty Website is a marketing and content website designed for Verani Realty, one of the largest real estate companies in New England. The goals of the site are to:

- Attract buyers of commercial and residential real estate
- Attract real estate sellers to list their properties with Verani

DOI: 10.4324/9781003430612-16

- Attract customers for other Verani services, such as relocation and mortgages
- Present a positive image for the Verani company
- Recruit new agents to join the company
- Present useful real estate information

The site includes extensive searchable information about Verani properties, descriptions of Verani services, general real estate information, and numerous interactive tools, such as calculators, checklists, maps, and email updates.

Note that this is only one approach to creating a website. Other sites might concentrate less on content and more on visual elements, video, and interactive tools. This example was chosen because it provides a good introduction to common types of writing on a content heavy site.

Site Version

The website profiled here is an earlier version of the Verani Realty Website. This chapter focuses on this earlier site version because it gives us a rare opportunity to examine the complete site development process from concept to maintenance documentation and the writer's role in each stage of the process. Take a look at the current site, compare it to the version described here, evaluate the changes, and discuss whether or not they have moved the site closer to its goals with the new version.

Planning the Verani Realty Website

Key to a successful website is adequate planning. Adequate planning ensures that a website achieves its goal and communicates its intended message for the least possible cost. A clear plan on paper allows a client to discuss options and make revisions for far less cost than it does to make revisions on a completed site.

Scoping the Project

The first stage of developing the site was to better define the project. This is accomplished through researching similar sites (competitor analysis), meeting with the client, and digesting all of the client's existing marketing material. Some of the key questions that have to be answered and discussed with the client are:

1. What are the client's goals for this site? For example, is the primary purpose informational, marketing, content, or transactional—selling products online?
2. What is the client's wish list (stakeholder research)? What elements does the client think would be great for the site? Why would these elements be effective in achieving the client's goals? Can the client rate the wish list items in order of importance?
3. Who is the audience for this site? What are their demographics? What information about the product are they most interested in? What information do they already have? How sophisticated are they with using the web? Are the users likely to view the site on their phones? If so, the site may need to be responsive. What are the key use cases? (Use cases are the most common ways visitors will use the site.) Important to talk to users directly and test early version of the site with them to determine their needs (user research). Create personas or user profiles describing the most common user types to help keep them in mind as you create the site.

4. Who are the client's competitors? What are their websites like? What techniques do they use? (Competitor research).

5. What are the elements in existing company material that the client likes or that seem particularly effective? What digital resources already exist, such as pictures or videos? Is this material useful for the website?

6. What are the branding issues? Are there guidelines for a specific way material needs to be presented?

7. Is a website the correct medium to present all the material, achieve the client's goals, and reach the intended audience? Would a mobile app, a video, or a brochure be more appropriate for some of the material?

8. What form does the intended information take? Is it numbers and statistics? Video? Graphics? Text?

9. How often and how extensively does this information need to be updated? Does the client have adequate staff and planning to do the updating?

10. Are there ways that we can present this information that are customizable for the user?

11. Will this project need to pay for itself, for example by incorporating advertising?

12. What are the ways this site can be marketed to drive traffic to it?

The Proposal for the Verani Website

Once the project has been defined by answering the above questions, it is time to write the proposal. For this version of the Verani site, the designer created a proposal that outlined the goals of the site and possible approaches to achieving those goals.

The purpose of proposal writing is to present options to the client clearly, succinctly, and appealingly. This should not be a hard-sell document, but it should point out the advantages of the work being suggested. This is only one approach to proposal writing. For large projects, companies request so many details that proposals will be many pages long.

```
Section of Verani Website Content Proposal
Goals of an Improved Website

1. Better attract and serve customers (buyers)
2. Better attract and serve clients (sellers)
3. Sell properties more effectively
4. Help agents and staff make the most effective use of their time
5. Improve cooperation with business partners
```

```
Suggested Content Revision: Make Verani the Real Estate and Relocation
Information Source for New Hampshire

Your current site tells the user about your company and your
properties. An alternative is also to make your site an information
resource for sellers and buyers of real estate. This would greatly
increase traffic to your site.

Users would come to your site for information. This well-
presented information would demonstrate that you are a well-run,
knowledgeable company. This would encourage users to use you when they
```

are considering buying or selling a home. The site would also of course continue to fulfill its current functions of presenting your properties and company.

Types of information that could be included are:

- Mortgage calculator
- School reports
- Town reports
- Relocation information
- List of home inspectors
- Interactive tutorials on how to buy a property.

This material would be presented in such a way that the user makes a positive connection with your agency. For example, after a site visitor uses our mortgage amount, then we would offer to show the visitor Verani properties in that price range.

This is only part of the proposal. Full proposal is much longer.

Scope of Work

The proposal was discussed with key members of the Verani team and eventually the scope of work of the project was clearly defined. This scope is an important document because it can be the basis of your contractual agreement with the client. The writing needs to be very clear and unambiguous. There is no need for salesmanship here. Do not promise anything you cannot deliver, and make it clear what work is not your responsibility. Many of the elements in the scope of work have been refined and simplified from the original proposal.

REVISION PLAN/SCOPE OF WORK FOR THE VERANI WEBSITE

1. Content Structure

The first stage of designing the website is to clearly define the site content in an outline and flowchart. The flowchart will consist of a visual plan of the site, illustrating every internal page in the site and each page's place in the overall site architecture.

2. Content Revision Scope

The current site presents your properties, company, and agents. We will create new material and build on the existing material to make this presentation more effective. We will add new material about the company that is not on the current site, such as a new mortgage and title section and an easily updateable Special Events page for announcing open houses or special meetings.

This is a fragment of the scope of work. The complete scope defines every content element that will be created for the site.

Gathering and Grouping Site Material

Once the scope of work is accepted by the client, the next step is for the website designer and the writer to gather as much information as they can about the client's products and services. This information can come from existing information collateral, such as brochures, advertisements, older websites, even marketing videos if they exist. But the source for the most current information will be the client themselves. In the case of this site, a number of the top executives and agents at Verani Realty were interviewed.

It is also a good idea to examine the user scenarios. User scenarios describe exactly how users will use the site. User scenarios will discuss where each type of user might enter the site, what information they will be looking for, and step by step how they will move through the site to get to that information. For example, someone looking to buy a commercial warehouse and get a mortgage will need different information and travel a different path through the site than would someone buying their first home with cash. It's crucial to make sure the information each user wants is where they expect it to be on the site and in the proper sequence.

In addition to grouping the content by following user scenarios, another common method is the card sort. Sometimes actual physical paper cards are used, but I prefer electronic "cards" that can be sorted on the computer. The first step is to determine the "bins" or main categories, such as "Homes and Land" and subcategories if the site is big enough, such as "New Construction." Then all the possible information on the site is broken down into discreet units or chunks, such as "Radon and Lead Information." Then, working with the client, these information units are sorted to the proper bins. A variation with a large group of stakeholders is to place the bin categories on the wall and give each user a sticky label with each content chunk. The stakeholders can then vote by placing a sticky under each bin category on the wall. If the majority of the "Radon and Lead" stickies are placed under the "Homes and Land" category, then that is probably where that information should be placed on the actual site.

If using the card sort method, it is important to make sure that the content arrangement supports the user scenarios. You may have to rearrange some content or create cross-links to make sure that users can accomplish their goals. As with any major change, when you have settled on an initial site structure it is a good idea to verify it with potential site users.

Sitemap

Once the content grouping has been approved by the client, the next step is usually the development of a sitemap of the site. The sitemap, usually in a flowchart, should indicate

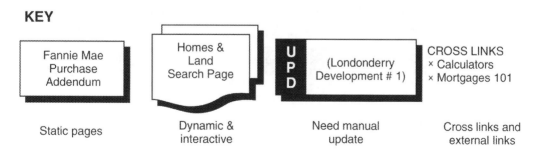

Figure 12–1 Symbol key for Verani website sitemap

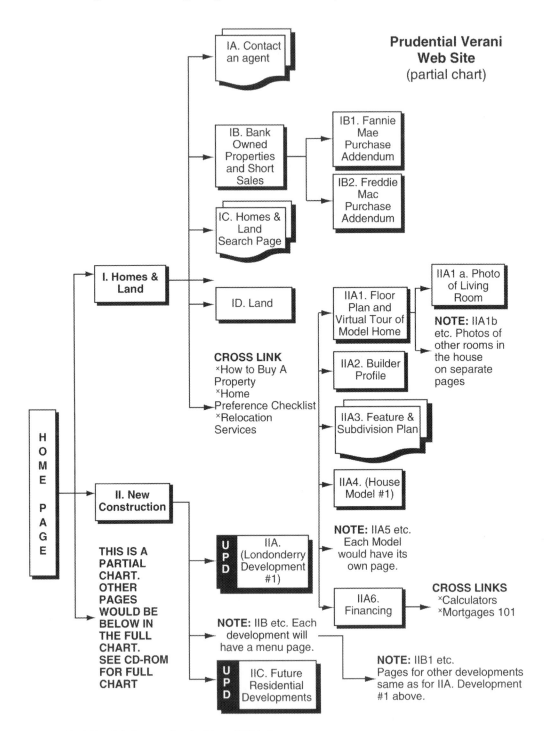

Figure 12–2 Partial sitemap for the Verani Website

every page of the site. The goal is for the flowchart to be a clear visualization of site structure. See Chapter 3, "Interactive Writing Tools and Script Formats," for a detailed discussion of flowcharting and flowchart software. As discussed in Chapter 3, there are a number of techniques that help make the sitemap a more useful tool, including:

1. Give every page of the site a unique number and name.
2. For ease of printing and presentation, run the chart vertically as in Figure 12–2 instead of horizontally.
3. Simplify where you can. If there will be multiple sections that will be designed in the same way, it is OK to say that in a note. No need to draw out all the boxes for repetitive pages.
4. It can make it easier to see the main sections of the website by writing those pages in bold with drop shadows.
5. Indicate cross-links (links to pages within the site that are already on the chart) and external links (links to other websites) as text only.
6. Visually indicate pages that will have special functions. For example, pages that will have interactive elements (see Figure 12–2).

Content Outline

As discussed in Chapter 3, the sitemap illustrates the overall navigation, structure, and size of the site; the outline provides more details about the actual content and functionality of the individual screens. The flowchart and outline that follow are most effective when used together. The client consults the chart for overall structure, then reads the outline for the details. Not all sites use outlines, but they are particularly useful for information heavy sites and to explain content groupings to non-technical clients.

The structure of each page on the outline below is fairly simple. The outline should be adjusted to match the specific project. The elements include:

- Title: the page title, which should be the same as what is on the sitemap.
- Image: describes possible images for the page.
- Text: describes onscreen text.
- Links: includes all the links on this page from text within the page and from the graphical navigation bar.
- Navigation bar: the specific buttons that will have to be created for the navigation bar.
- Functionality: this describes what the user can do on this page besides click-and-read. For example, can they search for properties or calculate their mortgage.

Partial Outline of the Verani Website

Home Page

Title: Verani Realty

The Real Estate and Relocation Resource for Southern NH

IMAGE: Images which demonstrate that Verani is a professional, friendly place. Possible images: Friendly Verani staff, Verani office, people enjoying a beautiful home. Might have other images on page to lead user to some of the key features, such as a calculator image for the tools and an email icon for our custom email notification service.

TEXT: Explain that we are one of the largest real estate companies in New Hampshire, but also a family-owned business with strong roots in southern NH. We have the resources to sell your property effectively and/or make your home search efficient and successful. Also introduce some of the key features of the site, such as our searches, custom email notification tools, extensive information resources, etc. Near the bottom of the page should be a short disclaimer stating that we have made every effort to make the information on this site accurate but are not liable for any errors or omissions; please see our Terms of Use Policy.

LINKS: Homes and Land, New Construction, Commercial and Industrial, Relocation Services, Verani Mortgage and Title, Real Estate Information and Resources, News and Special Events, Search/Site Map, About Us/Contact.
  Might also have a link from a calculator image to the tools and calculator section. In text on the bottom of the page and every page will be links to Terms of Use, Privacy Statement, and webmaster.

NAVIGATION BAR: Homes and Land, New Construction, Commercial and Industrial, Relocation Services, Verani Mortgage and Title, Real Estate Information and Resources, News and Special Events, Search/Site Map, About Us/Contact.

I. Homes and Land

TITLE: Homes and Land

IMAGE: Small image of attractive house. This could be the same picture all the time, or a regularly changing featured house.

TEXT: Briefly explain the range of properties we offer and the area we cover. Direct the user to the search page and other services that will help them in their moving and home buying, such as Relocation Services, the How to Buy a Property Section, Home Preference Check List/Questionnaire, and New Construction.

LINKS: Home, Search, Contact, Relocation Services, the How to Buy a Property Section, Home Preference Check List/Questionnaire, and New Construction.

NAVIGATION BAR: Home, Search, Contact.

IA. Contact an Agent

TITLE: Contact Us

IMAGE: Photo of friendly agent.

TEXT: Phone numbers, addresses, and emails for all offices, plus a form
that user can fill out and submit so that we can contact them.

LINKS: Home Page, Search, Contact, Homes and Land.

NAVIGATION BAR: Home Page, Search, Contact, Homes and Land.

FUNCTIONALITY: Users can fill out a form with their address and email,
click the type of information they want, write a short note, and submit
it to us. Message will go to different people at Verani, depending on
what type of information the user requests.

Writing the Website

Online Writing Style Tips

With an approved sitemap and outline, the content for the website can be written.

As discussed in Chapter 2, "Writing for Many Media," strong writing for interactive
media follows many of the principles of good journalism, including:

- Strong lead sentences that summarize content.
- Inverted pyramid style: put most important content first.
- Simple sentence construction.
- Concrete words: nouns and verbs, avoid adjectives and adverbs.
- Active not passive voice verbs.

As also discussed in Chapter 2, "Writing for Many Media," there are also a number of
writing techniques that are specific to writing for the web. Please refer to Chapter 2 for the
full discussion, following are just a few of the main points:

- highlighted keywords
- meaningful subheadings (not "clever" ones)
- bulleted lists
- one idea per paragraph
- half the word count (or less) than conventional writing

(Nielsen, *The Alertbox: How Users Read on the Web*)

These concepts are particularly true on the first couple of levels of a website where the
user is trying to find the information they want. Once they have located their information
deeper in the site, users may be content to read longer material.

These general style techniques apply to most online writing, but specific types of pages
make unique demands on the writer. Examples of special types of pages on the Verani site
include:

- Home page
- Section menu/introduction pages
- Static content pages
- Interactive content pages.

Each of these page types will be discussed in detail in the remainder of this chapter. A special aspect of writing for the web is search engine optimization. This involves creating content that will help search engines find your site. This is often done by specialists and will not be covered here, but it is worth being aware of if this task falls to you. You will find numerous resources online if you search for "writing for seo."

The Home Page

The home page is the most important page of a website. If this page does not accomplish its goals, then the user may go no further and the site can fail. There is a heavy burden on the home page. It must:

1. Hook the user's interest.
2. Communicate the basic message and tone of the site.
3. Introduce key site elements and lure the user deeper into the site.
4. Provide the correct keywords and frequency of keywords to help search engine placement.
5. Address legal issues.

The writer shares some of the above duties with the graphic and interface designers, but good writing is a major component of the success of any home page. It is important for the writer to work with the graphic designer when creating the page so that the designer's images support and expand on the writer's content.

The Title

Word for word, the title is probably the most important text on your home page. The page title and the main heading are frequently confused. The page title is not the heading that appears immediately above the text. On the Verani home page (Figure 12–3), the main heading is "We're not just your real estate company . . . we're your neighbor." The title on the Verani page appears in the bar at the very top of the browser: "New Hampshire Real Estate: Specializing in Southern NH Homes, Land, and Commercial Properties."

   The functions of the title are to:

1. Identify a web page for the user.
2. Identify the site in search engine and directory lists.
3. Identify the site in bookmark lists.

The title in the first draft of the home page:

```
"Welcome to Verani Realty,"
```

identifies the business and is a common sort of title on the web. However, the second draft title is much more descriptive of the Verani services. It also contains many keywords that will help determine search engine placement with search engines that track keywords. The second draft title is:

```
New Hampshire Real Estate: Specializing in Southern NH
Real Estate, Homes, Land, and Commercial Properties.
```

Figure 12–3 The home page for Verani Realty

In addition to describing your content, another key function of your title is to identify your website in search engine and directory lists. Remember that, unlike the title of a newspaper story, a website title often must stand alone in a search engine or directory list. So be sure that your title is effective on its own. Don't use a teaser or trick title that has little independent meaning. Stick with something that is clear and descriptive of your site.

The Main Menu

The main menu on the home page is the clickable list of the main sections of the site. Its key functions are to:

1. Provide a brief outline of the site, giving the user a sense of what lies within.
2. Serve as a main navigational tool.

The titles in the main menu should be descriptive and brief. Many designers also believe that they should be limited in number. Other designers, however, like to give their sites a portal look with dozens of links. This approach requires careful text design, but it can still overwhelm the user who is looking for quick information. Yet another alternative is to rely less on long menus and put bits of content and images on "cards" to draw the user into the site.

The first draft menu titles on the site discussed in this chapter are:

- Residential
- New Construction
- Commercial/Industrial
- Relocation Services
- Mortgage and Title
- News and Special Events
- Search/Sitemap
- About Us/Contact
- Resources

The only change with the second draft was to use more descriptive language for two of the titles: "Residential" was changed to "Homes and Land"; "Resources" was changed to "Tools and Information: Calculators, Maps, and More."

Links to Exciting Elements

In addition to the main menu links on the home page, it is also a good idea to have links to any areas of your site that the user might find particularly exciting or interactive. The goal is to:

1. Lure the user deeper into your site.
2. Get the user interacting with your site. If you can get a user doing things on your site besides reading, you have taken a good first step to getting them to explore the site. Designers often call this making the site "sticky." On this site the links to interactive elements include:

- Search for Properties
- Calculate your Mortgage
- Get Email Updates

As you can see, these links are brief, descriptive, and written in terms of actions. They address some of a user's key interests for visiting a real estate site, and they encourage the user to do something.

Slogans/Headings

A slogan can help express the personality of the company.
   The slogan for this page is:

We're not just your real estate company . . . we're your neighbor.

Each of the two parts of the slogan is centered over the paragraph that relates to it. There is not much text on this home page, but web pages that do have more text should break the text into sections and have clear, descriptive headings at the top of each section of text. This helps the user scan your information more quickly.

Body Text

The body text is the main text on the page. Its functions are to:

1. Hook the user by explaining why this is the site you want to explore for your real estate needs.
2. Introduce the type of material that is in the site.
3. Get the user to make contact.
4. Strengthen the legal protection for the company.

The first draft body text below satisfies many of our requirements for good web writing.

- Brief: the user can see the entire home page without scrolling.
- Strong lead sentence that summarizes content.
- Inverted pyramid style: put most important content first. The integrity of the Verani family is secondary to the size, experience, and capabilities of their company.
- Concrete words: uses nouns and verbs, avoiding adjectives and adverbs. There is little fluff here. The user is not told that Verani is the best company around. Instead, the company is described in very concrete terms: the number of agents, years of experience, sales figures, and affiliations. This information shows rather than tells the user that this is a hot company.
- The word "contact" in the last sentence is a link to a contact information page encouraging the user to get in touch.

```
FIRST DRAFT: More than 60 agents, 35 years of experience, and $100
million in sales make us the right choice to help you buy or sell
residential and commercial properties.
    The Verani family has lived in New Hampshire for three generations. As
your neighbor, we will treat you with the trust and integrity for which
the Verani family is known.
    Enjoy our site, then contact us for a personal consultation about your
real estate needs.
```

SECOND DRAFT: This version concentrated more on services offered and less on the family. Following legal advice, a link to terms and use was added in the body text. The Terms of Use is an important legal document that can help reduce the site owner's liability. Every commercial site should have one. But don't worry, this is not one more job for the writer. A lawyer usually writes the Terms of Use.

```
A leader in New Hampshire real estate for 35 years, we specialize in
southern NH real estate: homes, land, and commercial properties. Our
60+ agents and the global connections of the Prudential Real Estate
Network make us the right choice for residential and commercial real
estate.

Please review our Terms of Use, enjoy our site, then contact us for a
personal consultation about your real estate needs.
```

Complete First and Second Draft Home Page Text

After the previous discussion about writing the home page, review the first and second drafts of the home page text to get an overall understanding of the impact of the changes. Changes are in bold.

First Draft Home Page Text	Second Draft Home Page Text (Changes are in bold)
TITLE: Welcome to Verani Realty SECTION MENU: Residential New construction Commercial/industrial Relocation Services Mortgage and Title News and Special Events Search/sitemap About Us/Contact Resources LINKS TO EXCITING ELEMENTS: • Search for Properties • Calculate your mortgage • Get Email updates SLOGANS/HEADINGS: We're not just your real estate company ... we're your neighbor. BODY TEXT: More than 60 agents, 35 years of experience, $100 million in sales, and the global connections of the Prudential Real Estate Network make us the right choice to help you buy or sell residential and commercial properties. The Verani family has lived in New Hampshire for three generations. As your neighbor, we will treat you with the trust and integrity for which the Verani family is known. Enjoy our site, then contact us for a personal consultation about your real estate needs.	TITLE: **New Hampshire Real Estate: Specializing in Southern NH Real Estate, Homes, Land, and Commercial Properties** SECTION MENU: **Homes and Land** New construction Commercial/industrial Relocation Services Mortgage and Title News and Special Events Search/Sitemap About Us/Contact **Tools and Information:** **Calculators, Maps, and More** LINKS TO EXCITING ELEMENTS: • Search for Properties • Calculate your Mortgage • Get Email updates SLOGANS/HEADINGS: We're not just your real estate company ... we're your neighbor. BODY TEXT: **A leader in New Hampshire real estate for 35 years, we specialize in southern NH real estate: homes, land, and commercial properties. Our 60+ agents and the global connections of the Prudential Real Estate Network make us the right choice for residential and commercial real estate.** The Verani family has lived in New Hampshire for three generations. As your neighbor, we will treat you with the trust and integrity for which the Verani family is known. **Please review our Terms of Use,** enjoy our site, then contact us for a personal consultation about your real estate needs.

Main Section Introduction Pages

If you have a large site with sections of unique content, then you will need to write an introductory page for each section of the site. Of course, not all sites are broken down this way, so this page will not always be needed. But if it is needed, the primary function of a section introduction page is to:

1. Explain what is in the section.
2. Lure the user to click deeper into the site.
3. Provide local navigation to complement the global navigation for the entire site.

There are three main parts of a well-written section introduction page:

- The body text
- Local navigation
- Global navigation.

Homes and Land Section Introduction Page

Navigation

A surprisingly large number of websites make the error of using global navigation throughout the site to the exclusion of local navigation. This error loses an excellent opportunity to encourage a user to explore deeper into the site. In the Homes and Land example, global navigation allows the user to go to the home page and from there access the menu for the main sections of the site. Global navigation also allows the user to go to a search page that has a site-wide search and a sitemap. Local navigation introduces the elements of this section and hopefully lures the user deeper into the site. The writing challenge here is the same as it was writing the main menu on the home page. The menu items need to be succinct, descriptive, and engaging.

Body Text

The body text of the section introduction page introduces the key features in this section and provides easy access to get to these subsections. The introductory sentence explains in concrete terms why Verani can serve your Homes and Land needs, highlighting key terms.

Main Content Pages

If the writer and designers have correctly written the home page and the main section introduction page, then the user will be drawn to the primary content pages of the site. The content pages contain the major information that the site has to offer. For a commercial site, such as the example here, the primary function of these pages is to:

1. Present information.
2. Lure the user into other parts of the site.
3. Get the user to explore the client's products and/or contact the client.

The content pages have a local and global navigation system similar to that described for the section introduction pages, except the local navigation links on the content page are of course focused on that particular content.

Content Page Example

The main challenges to presenting complex content on a website are to write succinctly and to break the content down into bite-sized bits with meaningful headings. Nothing sends website visitors running more than a long uninterrupted wall of text. The following example is an explanation of mortgages, a topic that could easily fill a book. Notice how the material is broken down into short paragraphs with meaningful subheadings. There are also abundant links to some of the more interactive elements in the site. Last, there is a link to the agents' directory to encourage the user to get in touch.

This page does not directly connect to the client's product, in this case real estate, but the pages to which it links do. For example, after users use the mortgage calculator to determine how much property they can afford, there is a line of text on the calculator results page that asks them if they want to search for properties in that price range. This takes them to the search page and the client's product.

MORTGAGES 101

How Much House Can You Afford

Before starting serious house-hunting, it is a good idea to get an estimate of how much house you can afford. Review some of the basic concepts below, then try out our How Much House Can You Afford and our Renting vs. Buying Calculators.

The Down Payment Most mortgages require a minimum down payment of 5% of the house purchase price ($20,000 dollars on a $400,000 home). If you are a military veteran or a first-time buyer and qualify for a VA or FHA loan, it is possible to pay 3% or no down payment at all.

Debt to Salary Ratio Generally, your housing payment should not exceed 25% to 35% of your gross monthly income, and your total long-term debt should not exceed 38% of your gross monthly income. Long-term debt includes school loans, car loans, credit cards, etc.

Total Monthly Payment (PITI) It is important to keep in mind that your monthly housing payment includes more than the loan for the property. It includes principle, interest, taxes, and insurance. In New Hampshire, property taxes can be a large percentage of your costs. Use our **Mortgage Calculator** to determine your monthly payment.

Closing Costs In addition to the down payment, there are a number of other expenses when you finalize or close the purchase on your property. These other costs may include: points (fees paid to the lender for lower interest rates), taxes, title insurance, private mortgage insurance (PMI), property appraisal, credit report, homeowners insurance, and real estate taxes. Use our **_Closing Costs Calculator_** to get an estimate of your closing costs.

Types of Mortgage

There are various types of mortgages available:

* Fixed rate mortgages maintain the same interest rate over the life of the loan.
* Adjustable rate mortgages (ARM) adjust their rate according to fluctuations of interest rates in the market.
* FHA and VA mortgages are guaranteed or insured by the federal government. These mortgages often have lower down payments and lower interest rates than standard mortgages. VA loans require the borrower to be a military veteran.

Preapproved and Prequalified

Visiting your mortgage lender early in the house-hunting process is a good idea. After looking at your financial materials, the lender can prequalify you, which means give you an estimate of how much house you may be able to afford. Preapproval takes this one step forward by actually submitting your full loan application. Once this is accepted you know for sure how much you can spend on a house. Preapproval also speeds up the house-buying process when you finally make a decision.

See an Expert

The calculators on this site and the above material are meant to give you general information about mortgages, but you should see a qualified mortgage lender before making any final decisions. There is a **_list of mortgage lenders_** in the directory section of our site. Your **_Verani agent_** also has other resources for mortgage information, such as the free "Easy Moves" magazine.

When this page was being written, there was some discussion about breaking it into several shorter pages, but the final decision was that users would be interested in all the mortgage topics and made sense to keep them in one article.

Graphical Content

The writer should examine the content to be communicated and determine if there is a way to present it that would be more effective than straight text. Video, audio, or even a graphic chart might be an option.

The example that follows is a portion of a chart that explains all the steps that occur in the buying process. For reasons of space, only the last half of the chart is presented here. Because of the various directions the buying process can follow, this chart provides a more effective way of visualizing this information than would a list or an essay. The

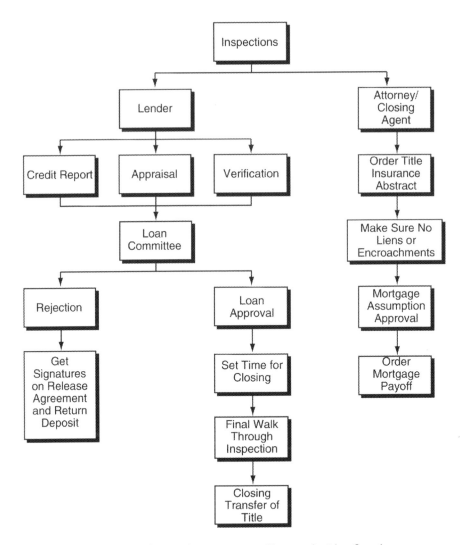

Figure 12–4 A portion of the real estate buying process illustrated with a flowchart

writing challenge here is to break the information into smaller units, chart the process, and write brief, clear symbol titles. Depending on the team, a visual designer might help create the chart.

Interactive, Personalized Content

Whenever an interactive media project can get the user to interact with the content beyond clicking and reading, and thereby customize the content for that particular user, the user is more likely to feel connected and dig further into the information.

The Verani site has a number of examples of interactive content. Calculators allow the user to compute how much house they can afford, renting vs. buying options, closing costs, and mortgages. The homes and land search can be customized to the user's needs through multiple criteria. Email updates allow the user to get email notification of houses that meet their criteria as soon as they come on the market. The interactive checklist creates a customized list of user preferences.

The execution of these tools owe their success to the developers. But the writer's skills are still required to explain how these tools work and to write the interactive content.

Interactive Content Writing Example 1: Checklists

The custom checklist allows the user to define their dream house by clicking a series of options. When they push "submit" a custom checklist with only their criteria is produced. They can then take this checklist with them as they visit properties for sale.

On the site, this custom checklist has the Verani name and contact information at the top to encourage the user to get in touch with them. This list also gives the user the option of emailing the completed checklist to Verani and/or getting email updates that match the criteria that they have defined in the checklist.

Writing something like this checklist makes the writer realize that one of the major jobs of the writer is selecting, sorting, and organizing information. Once that is done, then this information needs to be expressed as clearly as possible. This is only a section of the complete checklist.

CUSTOM CHECKLIST FOR YOUR NEW HOME	
DEFINE YOUR IDEAL HOME Create a custom checklist using the form below to: • Focus your priorities for your new home for you and your realtor • Evaluate and track the properties you visit	DIRECTIONS • Select your choices below • Push the "Create Custom Checklist" button at the bottom of the page • Print out one copy of the resulting Custom Checklist for each property you will visit
CRITERIA Type of home What type of home are you looking for?	CHOICE ° Single family ° Multifamily ° Condo/Condex ° Mobile Home
Price range What is your price range?	° Under $200,000 ° $200,000–$250,000 ° $250,000–$300,000 ° $300,000–$350,000 ° $350,000+
Neighborhood What type of neighborhood are you looking for?	° Urban ° Subdivision ° Rural

Conclusion

The goal of this chapter was to outline all the different types of writing that goes into the development of a basic content website from the first proposal to the final content. The example used here was for a smaller website, but the suggestions above hold true for other interactive media projects as well, with larger projects being much more complex.

Reference

Nielsen Norman Group. *How Users Read on the Web.* https://www.nngroup.com/articles/how-users-read-on-the-web

13 Educational Simulation
The Nauticus Shipbuilding Company

Summary

Name of Production: *The Nauticus Shipbuilding Company*
Writer: Steven Barney
Developers: Tarragon Interactive, Chedd-Angier Production Co.
Audience: General
Medium: Touch screen display in museum kiosk
Location: Nauticus: National Maritime Center, Norfolk, Virginia
Subject: Shipbuilding
Goals: Entertain, teach
Architecture: Simulation, hierarchical branching

The script samples and illustrations used in this chapter are courtesy of Chedd-Angier Production Company and the National Maritime Center. © Chedd-Angier Production Company, National Maritime Center.

Program Description and Background

Program Description

The Nauticus Shipbuilding Company is an educational simulation displayed in a museum kiosk at Nauticus: National Maritime Center in Norfolk, Virginia. This simulation allows museum visitors to experience the basic concepts of shipbuilding. Users engage with the simulation by touching images on the large touch screen in the museum display. Near the display is a wall of graphic and text information on shipbuilding that supports the simulation program. *The Nauticus Shipbuilding Company* is also being used in classrooms as part of the museum's curricular outreach.

Interactive Media in Museums

A single-user kiosk presentation, such as *The Nauticus Shipbuilding Company*, is a common way to present interactive media in a museum or other public site. Because of the need to accommodate large groups, interactive media in museums is also presented in a group

DOI: 10.4324/9781003430612-17

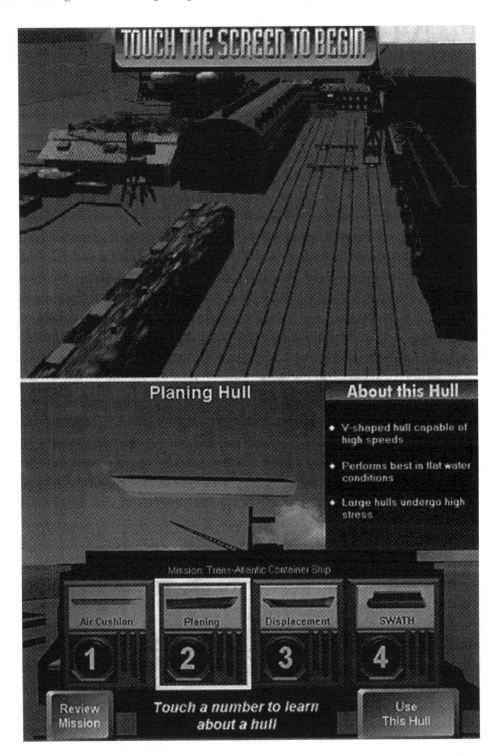

Figure 13.1 Top screen: From the attract program for *The Nauticus Shipbuilding Company*
Bottom screen: Where the user chooses hulls

format, where a number of people control the action on the screen. An example is the National Scouting Museum's *Boy Scout Patrol Theater*, which allows eight users to take on the roles of the individual Boy Scouts portrayed in the interactive media program. (See Boy Scout Patrol area of the *Writing for Interactive Media* website.) A growing trend in museums, conventions, and other public events is the immersive exhibit which often also includes live performance, audience participation, and displays of actual objects related to the presentation. See Chapter 19, "Using Narrative to Present Information: *The New England Economic Adventure*" for more on this type of program.

In addition to exhibits, many museums also have learning centers, which house a variety of interactive media "edutainment" programs for groups or individuals. Larger museums are active in educational outreach, providing curricular support for schools. The old fossils-on-wheels programs, which brought artifacts to schools, is now being supplemented by interactive media programs, such as *The Nauticus Shipbuilding Company*, and by online programs from museums, such as the Museum of Science in Boston, the Exploratorium in San Francisco, and the Franklin Institute Science Museum in Philadelphia.

Production Background

The Nauticus Shipbuilding Company was jointly developed by Chedd-Angier Production Company and Tarragon Interactive for Nauticus: National Maritime Center. The National Maritime Center, located on the Norfolk, Virginia waterfront, offers exhibits, films, and interactive media programs dealing with shipping, the Navy, and the sea.

The Chedd-Angier Production Company is a Boston-based media production company that Nauticus hired to develop several media programs for the museum. Chedd-Angier then recruited Tarragon Interactive to develop *The Nauticus Shipbuilding Company* project. At the time of production, Tarragon was a custom developer of interactive media titles for marketing and sales, training, and infotainment. Tarragon has since been sold and no longer exists as a separate entity. The writer of this program is Steven Barney, who was president of Tarragon Interactive. He is a designer-programmer with a background in instructional design.

Writing and Developing *The Nauticus Shipbuilding Company*

The Development Process

On this project, the writer's primary involvement occurs during the first two stages of development: project definition and design, but the writer is also often called in during production to make last-minute changes.

The project definition identifies:

- Design objective
- Target audience
- Delivery platform/location

Design documents include:

- Proposal. Outlining the program's approach.
- High-level design document. A text-based content treatment and a navigation flow diagram.
- Script. Program navigation flow plus narration, dialogue, screen text, and full description of visuals.

Development Challenges

Many of the challenges facing the developers of *The Nauticus Shipbuilding Company* are common to media development for museums and other public sites. These challenges are discussed below.

Design Objective

The design objective of *The Nauticus Shipbuilding Company* is to provide museum visitors with an interactive environment in which to explore how ships are built for specific missions. This program uses technical information that must be precisely accurate. The project was reviewed for accuracy by the faculty of MIT's Department of Naval Engineering and members of the National Board of the Society of Naval Architecture and Marine Engineering. The entertainment aspect of this piece was tested through focus groups and by placing a test exhibit at a museum and evaluating viewers' reactions.

Another objective of this program is replay. It should be designed so that users will go through the game and want to return to play it again. This means that diversity and depth must be designed into the experience.

Target Audience

Developing a program like this for the typical museum audience poses a number of challenges:

- Diversity. Museum audiences include people of all ages, backgrounds, education, and levels of interest in the subject. An exhibit has to have a little something for everyone.
- Short attention spans. Because there are so many exhibits competing for their attention, museum goers generally will not play a program for more than 2 minutes (60–90 seconds is the typical experience time). A program has about 5 seconds to capture a user, but even when captured, many leave after 30 seconds. A complex subject puts demands on the developer to present the material succinctly or to create a piece, such as *The Nauticus Shipbuilding Company*, that is so appealing it can lure users into longer than typical play times.

Delivery Platform and Locations

The nature of the delivery platform and location has a significant impact on what is creatively possible. A kiosk program running off a fast hard drive allows the use of video, 3-D graphics, and other features that would be difficult to deliver on media with slower access time.

Meeting the Challenges

The program's objectives and the challenges must be met by the writer-designer's proposals, high-level design documents, and scripts. There were many revisions of the written material. Here are a few of them.

The Proposal

The initial proposal is the earliest stage of a project. Compare the proposal with the treatment that follows it and consider what changes were made before reading the analysis.

INTERACTIVE MODULE—#5,7
SHIPBUILDING:

Objective

To simulate modular ship construction at work.

Treatment

Visitors will use a stylus to draw any kind of ship on a pressure-sensitive platen. Children might sketch out a simple shape. Others can create more sophisticated designs. When the drawing is complete, the user will push a button. The ship will disappear from the platen and will then be "built" on the video screen.

To do this, the program will divide the ship drawing into modular sections (based on the platen's grid and predetermined guidelines). These modules will then be "constructed" on screen, to the accompaniment of appropriate sound effects, such as hammering, riveting, and perhaps even the shouts of work crews. When all the modular sections are complete, they will be united, forming a replica of the visitor's original design.

The video game will be, in effect, a simulation of the CAD/CAM process, whereby ships are designed on screen and then built with the aid of computers—in separate modules.

If feasible, the computers can be linked to a printer, and visitors can take home sketches of their creations.

Technique/Method

Visitor-activated platen with video monitor.

High-Level Design Document

After the initial proposal was revised several times and the basic concept refined, the high-level design document, which includes a design objective, creative treatment, and a navigation flowchart, was prepared:

1.0 Design Objective

The objective of the program is to provide museum visitors with a fun, interactive environment to explore how ships are built to accomplish specific missions. Visitors will be able to experiment by building custom ships from a variety of components. Through this experience, visitors will learn to apply the principle of "form follows function" to the process of building ships. Visitors will learn about the major design components of a ship: hull, hold, engine, and special equipment. Visitors will learn how variations in these design components affect a ship's ability to carry out a specific mission.

2.0 Creative Treatment

ATTRACT ROUTINE: When no one is using the program, an attract routine will invite visitors to come explore the program. The attract routine will contain a brief glimpse of one of the mission introductions, picked randomly This will be followed by a series of snapshots of components being selected, and a ship being built by the program. Text overlays will repeat continuously. Sample text: "Build a Ship to Accomplish a Mission"; "Touch the Screen to Begin."

INTRODUCTION: Immediately upon touching the screen during the attract routine, the visitor is greeted with a brief sequence introducing the program with audio and text. Sample text: "Pick one of the five missions; then go to the shipyard to build your own custom-designed boat. When you are done, see if your boat succeeds in accomplishing the mission." "Let's go to the briefing room to choose a mission."

BRIEFING ROOM: The metaphor of a briefing room will be used to allow the visitor to select from a menu of missions, and then to review each mission. Upon selecting a mission from the menu, the visitor is briefed. Each briefing will consist of a full-screen graphic with text. A video clip with a talking head keyed over stock footage will introduce the mission. Design criteria for the mission will appear on a checklist. At the conclusion of the briefing, the visitor can either select this mission or return to the mission menu.

Mission 1. North Sea Fire Fighter The North Sea is full of gigantic oil-drilling platforms that use mile-long pipes to drain oil from under the sea floor, then store it in tanks until tankers come to take it to the mainland for processing and distribution to the general public.

    Sometimes these platforms catch on fire. Your job is to design a ship that will be able to put out these fires.

    The ship must be stable enough to remain near the platform until the fire is put out and must have pumps powerful enough to drive large amounts of water through its hoses. It must also be able to withstand the rough seas and weather of the North Sea.

Mission 2. Alligator Census Many years ago, the Everglades were viewed as a wasteland, home to millions of potentially disease-spreading mosquitoes. Because of such concerns, the Everglades were drained to create farmland. People now recognize that the Everglades is a beautiful, but fragile ecosystem that was greatly disrupted by the drainage and dredging projects. Many birds and other creatures died as a result. These species are believed to be making a comeback, but the only way to know for sure is to go into the Everglades by boat and count them. The ideal boat for this mission must be quiet so as not to disturb the wildlife, and it should be able to navigate shallow waters and swamp.

Mission 3. Coast Guard Drug Interdiction Undercover police and FBI investigators routinely attempt to infiltrate suspected drug rings and break up shipments of drugs from South America and other countries. They have just ordered a ship from your shipyard that will be able to intercept shipments of drugs coming into Miami, Florida. It must have a high top speed, be able to travel at or near that speed for long distances, and be outfitted with weapons sufficient to threaten and subdue vessels operated by suspected criminals. It should also have a low profile, making it difficult to spot from a distance.

Mission 4. Trans-Pacific Freighter Exports account for an increasingly large portion of our country's economy. Trade with the Far East is expected to double in the future. Efficient freighters are needed to transport the large flow of goods to and from this important economic region. The design should be cost-efficient, have enough range to travel to Korea, Japan, Singapore, China, and Taiwan, and be able to carry large quantities of cargo. Speed is a secondary design consideration.

Mission 5. Arctic Ice Breaker The "Land of the Midnight Sun" is an accurate name for the Arctic. Due to the Earth's orbit and tilt, the region experiences six straight months of darkness, followed by six straight months of light. This prolonged darkness contributes to temperatures as low as negative 70 degrees Fahrenheit, more than sufficient to freeze Hudson Bay and the rest of the Arctic Ocean. Ice breakers are needed to clear shipping channels otherwise blocked for months. You must design such an ice breaker to clear a path from Churchill, Canada, to Barrow, Alaska. It must be heavy, as indestructible as possible, and be able to remain at sea for months.

   After the user selects a mission, he or she is told: "You have selected a difficult mission. Now let's go to the shipyard where you can design and build your own custom boat to accomplish the mission."

The Shipyard

OPENING ANIMATION: A 3-D animation sequence will give an overview of the shipyard, then zoom in to the point of view of a shipbuilder entering the gates.

   After the opening animation, the visitor selects components from a series of menus. The design features for each component are summarized upon selection. After selecting each component, the partially completed boat moves along a track to the next component selection area.

Components

Hulls
Single V:
Efficient, stable, with a large amount of room for supplies, cargo, fuel, and passengers, they make an excellent choice for almost any ship. Single V-shaped hulls are by far the most common.

Double V:
Double V-shaped hulls are far less common than single V's, but they also make a good choice for ships where the main hull not being penetrated is of the utmost importance, such as oil tankers.

Single Flatbottom:
Single flatbottom hulls are used mainly for riverboats and other craft where a shallow draft is important. They are less efficient and stable than other designs but sometimes a shallow draft is the top consideration.

Hydrofoil:
Hydrofoils are radically different than the other three designs. The boat is fitted with several projections with angled metal plates on the bottom. They lift the boat out of the water when it runs at high speed. This design works only for smaller boats.

Hold

Cargo:
Cargo holds are used for holding large amounts of goods while on the ship. These range from weapons, to cars, to food, frequently packaged in cargo ship containers, which were transported to the harbor by rail or truck.

Passengers:
Passenger space usually consists of many small rooms, of which the interior varies according to type of ship. Cruise lines commonly have rooms to rival the best hotels, where military ships often have hammocks.

Ballast:
Ballast is used as a stabilizer for ships with little weight in their hulls. It is usually just a room that has sea water pumped into it.

None:
Small boats infrequently have ballast, as there is not a huge need for it.

Engine

Nuclear:
Nuclear power plants in ships work much like their electricity-generating counterparts on land. Steam is heated passing next to radioactive material. It is then used to push turbines connected

to the propellers, giving the ship its power. The shielding around nuclear plants is very heavy, making them efficient only for large ships.

Gas:
Gas power plants are much the same as jet engines, just on a larger scale. Their advantages are high speed and short start-up times, but they are noisy, inefficient for large ships, and require many people to run.

Diesel:
Diesel engines have many of the same characteristics as their counterparts in vans and trucks. They are efficient, low-maintenance engines with an ability to run at low revolutions per minute (RPMs). They are ideal for moving large ships at moderate to low speeds.

Steam:
Steam engines burn oil or gasoline to heat water until it is steam, and then use that to drive turbines.

Special Equipment

Weapons Mounts:
Turrets and mounts with machine guns and small cannon, from .50 caliber to 5 inches.

Cranes, Booms, and Winches:
Equipment for lifting cargo from the decks and holds of ships.

Pumps and Hoses:
Used for spraying water on burning vessels, docks, and other objects in or near the water. Water is drawn from the ocean or river that the boat is in.

Reinforced Hull:
An extra layer of reinforcements to increase hull integrity in certain areas. Useful for ships with a high potential of running into reefs and other obstacles.

Grappling Hooks:
Lines and hooks for latching on to other ships or objects while at sea.

CONCLUSION:
After the last component has been selected, a 3-D animation sequence depicts the launching of the vessel. If the design is suitable for the mission, the visitor will see a depiction of the design successfully carrying out the mission. If the design is fundamentally flawed, the vessel will be shown sinking. Some evaluation will be provided as to the ability of the visitor's design to carry out the selected mission. Finally, the visitor will be given the opportunity to print out the design and evaluation.

A design document would usually also have a project schedule and budget, but because this book's focus is writing and design, these sections are not included here.

Proposal and Design Document Compared

Comparing the design document's treatment to the proposal shows some striking changes in the evolution of this project. The proposal's initial idea, to have a computer "build" a ship based on a user's rough sketch, was replaced in the treatment by the more structured approach of having the viewer build a ship to achieve a specific mission based on defined ship components. Another key aspect of the treatment is that the user's design is evaluated at the end of the process, and the user is encouraged to play the game again to improve the design.

Although the initial proposal is fun, it illustrates the importance of balancing interactivity with control to teach a specific subject. The proposal provides a rough demonstration of CAD/CAM, but the more controlled approach in the treatment accomplishes much more. It allows users to utilize well-defined principles concerning hulls, engines, and other components to build a ship. The evaluation function suggested in the treatment allows users to learn from their efforts and build on them in repeat plays. With no evaluation function in the proposal, the user does not even know if his or her ship would float.

There are also some practical concerns here. It is important to give the general museum audience a positive experience. The treatment approach of assembling parts means that even a young child can piece together an impressive boat. This may not be true with the proposal approach. What will the CAD/CAM process be able to do with the rough squiggles of a seven year old? There could be a few default ships automatically rendered from unintelligible sketches, but this would not be the ship the user drew, and on repeated plays, he or she could be disappointed if the same ship was produced from different drawings.

Navigation Program/Flow

The creative treatment of the design document lays out the basic content of the production; the navigation/program flowchart defines how that content will be accessed interactively. Compare the flowcharts on the next pages, Figures 13–2 and 13–3, and consider the changes that were made before reading the analysis that follows.

Changes in Navigation/Program Flow

Different flowcharts serve different functions. Some, such as the one shown in Figure 13–2, lay out the possible navigation flow early in a project. Because this chart will be read by clients who may not be sophisticated in interactive media navigation, there is an advantage to keeping it as simple as possible. Detail is limited, particularly in the component section, where the multiple choices under each component are reduced to one broad category.

The second chart comes when the program is more defined. At this point, it is possible to chart all the paths in the project. A chart like this is useful to a sophisticated client and can also be the basis of a planning document for the production team.

Both of these charts are designed very simply, but there are a few conventions in the second chart worth noting. The diamond symbol suggests that this is a point where the

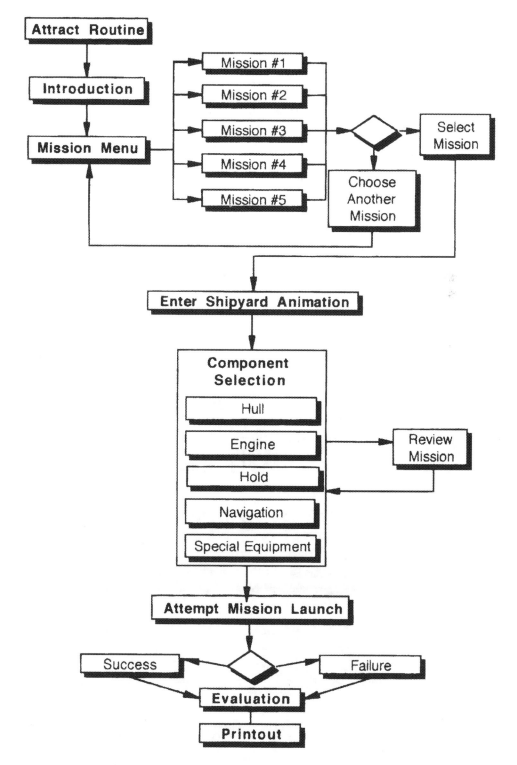

Figure 13.2 First draft navigation/program flow

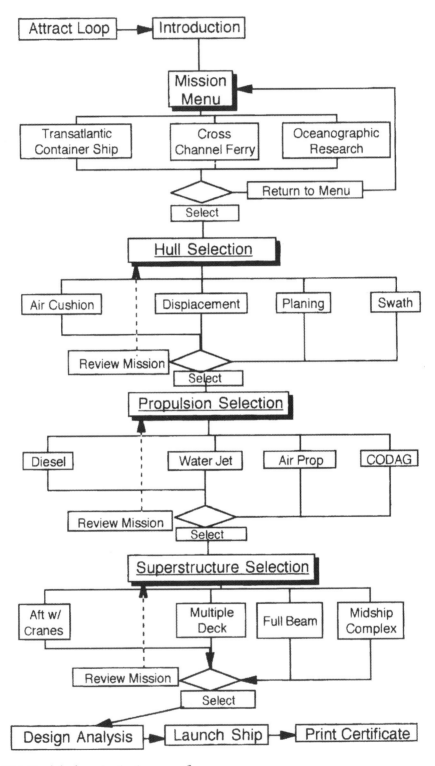

Figure 13.3 Final draft navigation/program flow

user can make a choice. The text in main categories is underlined. The first program flow uses arrows and lines to suggest directions. Some designers also use arrows to suggest a link where the viewer has no choice, such as the Attract Routine to the Introduction. No arrows indicate a place where the viewer has multiple choices, such as in the Missions.

The Final Script

The script is the complete and detailed description of the program on paper. A well-written script also communicates the look and feel of the project.

    After reading the script, consider what changes were made from the design document before reading the analysis.

SCENE	NARRATION
ATTRACT ROUTINE	(Note: The following text banners are repeated throughout the attract routine:)
When no one is using the program, an attract routine will invite visitors to come explore the program.	1. "The Nauticus Shipbuilding Company" 2. "Urgent: Naval Architect Needed" 3. "Touch the Screen to Begin"
Attract Routine steps 1. Flyover of shipyard in 3-D.	
2. Cut to rotation of planing hull.	"The Nauticus Shipbuilding Company— the most highly advanced shipbuilding facility in the world." "Touch the Screen to Begin"
3. Cut to assembly area with planing hull rolling in.	"Urgent: Naval Architect Needed." "Touch the Screen to Begin"
4. Cut to launch area, showing ship launch.	
INTRODUCTION	
Immediately upon touching the screen in the attract routine. Flyover of shipyard in 3-D.	Background sound of helicopter rotors.
Cut to helicopter descending and landing on heliport.	"Welcome to the Nauticus Shipbuilding Company. Thanks for being our visiting naval architect at such short notice. The Nauticus Shipbuilding Company is the most highly advanced shipbuilding facility in the world. We can custom-build many different types of ships. Each ship we build is unique and is designed to

efficiently meet our client's nautical mission requirements."

"Let's go to our Design Center to see what ships are on order."

Cut to POV [point-of-view] animation leaving the heliport, past office building to Design Center.

Loudspeaker VO: "Naval architect on premises. Ready production facilities."

DESIGN CENTER

Doors of Design Center open, wipe to view of the briefing room.

"We currently have a backlog of orders for 3 ships":
1. "a trans-Atlantic container ship which will sail out of Norfolk."
2. "a ferry that will transport passengers and cars between England and France."
3. "an oceanographic research vessel that will operate off the coast of New England."

"Touch an order to learn more about its mission and design requirements."

TRANS-ATLANTIC CONTAINER SHIP:

Map animating the route between Norfolk and several European ports.

"A large shipping company has asked us to design and build a ship which can safely and economically transport large amounts of cargo between their home port, right here in Norfolk, Virginia, and several European ports. The ship:
- must be able to withstand the rough seas of the Atlantic
- have a very large cargo hold with container-handling facilities
- be moderately fast
- have a long cruising range."

Dynamically build mission checklist.

Container Ship Checklist
1. Ability to withstand rough seas of Atlantic
2. Large cargo hold with container-handling facilities
3. Moderately fast
4. Long cruising range

Visitor is prompted to build the ship or review another mission.

"Press the flashing panel to build a ship for this mission or select another order."

PASSENGER AND CAR FERRY:

Map animating the route between Dover and Calais

"An English ferry operator has asked us to design and build a

ship which can quickly cross the English Channel between Dover, England, and Calais, France. The ideal design:
— will be very fast, have a cargo capacity for 200 passengers and 50 cars
— be easy to load
— be able to navigate shallow, crowded harbors."

Dynamically build mission checklist.

Ferry Requirements:
1. Very fast
2. Cargo capacity for 200 passengers and 50 cars
3. Easy to load
4. Able to navigate shallow, crowded harbors

Visitor is prompted to build the ship or review another mission.

"Press the flashing panel to build a ship for this mission or select another order."

OCEANOGRAPHIC RESEARCH VESSEL:

Show map animating area of research.

"A marine research instituterequires a new flagship for itsexploration of the ocean floor.The ship should:
— be a safe platform for working with complex equipment
— be able to withstand rough seas
— have good performance at all speeds
— have accommodations for extended research work at sea"

Dynamically build mission checklist.

Research Ship Requirements:
1. Safe platform for working with complex equipment
2. Able to withstand rough seas
3. Good performance at all speeds
4. Accommodations for extended research work at sea

Visitor is prompted to build the ship or review another mission.

"Press the flashing panel to build a ship for this mission, or select another order."

ORDER SELECTED

After selecting an order to build, scene cuts to POV animation leaving the Design Center, past building to hull subassembly area.

"You'll need to make 3 major design decisions to build the ship, allaffecting the ship's performance and ability to carry out its mission. You must choose:
— a hull shape
— a propulsion system, and
— a superstructure."

CHOOSE A HULL SHAPE

Hull subassembly area, 4 compartments are shown.

Loudspeaker VO: "Hull type being selected."

"Touch a number to learn about a hull."

After a compartment is selected, 3-D hull appears above the subassembly area and rotates around 360 degrees in y-axis, then 360 degrees in x-axis. As hull is rotated, text describing characteristics appears on data screen.

After learning about the characteristics for a particular hull, the visitor is prompted to use this hull or examine one of the others.

"Use this hull or press another number."

Images of the different types of Hulls are shown on screen to illustrate the text descriptions.

Air Cushion:
— flat hull rides on cushion of air
— capable of high speeds
— needs flat water conditions
— flat, rectangular deck easy to load

Planing Hull:
— V-shaped hull capable of high speeds
— performs best in flat water conditions
— high stress levels on hull

Displacement Hull:
— deep, rounded hull very stable in all conditions
— very large cargo capacity
—stable platform for large propulsion systems
— needs very large propulsion system

SWATH (Small Waterplane Area Twin Hull)
— 2 submerged hulls very stable
— flat deck provides good work area

After selecting a hull to use, cut to Design Assembly screen, animation of hull rollout.

Loudspeaker VO: "Planing hull being moved into position."

Cut to POV animation moving to propulsion subassembly area

Background sound of motors whirring and machinery clanging. "Next, you'll need to choose a propulsion system."

PICK A PROPULSION SYSTEM

Propulsion subassembly area, 4 compartments are shown.

Loudspeaker VO:
"Propulsion system being selected."
"Touch a number to learn about a propulsion system."

After a compartment is selected, 3-D propulsion system appears above the subassembly area and rotates around 360 degrees in y-axis. As propulsion system is rotated, text describing characteristics appears on data screen.

Diesel
— best performance at lower speeds
— fuel efficient
— infrequent maintenance

Images of the different types of Propulsion Systems are shown on screen to illustrate the text descriptions.

CODAG (Combination Diesel and Gas)
— good performance at all speeds
— improves maneuverability
— frequent maintenance

Water Jet
— low to moderate power
— high speed for right hull
— few underwater projections

Air Prop
— low to moderate power
— high speed for right hull
— no underwater projections
— affected by bad wind conditions

After learning about the characteristics for a particular propulsion system, the visitor is prompted to use this propulsion system or examine one of the others.

"Use this propulsion system or press another number."

After selecting a propulsion system to use, cut to Design Assembly screen, animation of propulsion system being dropped into selected hull.

Loudspeaker VO: "Air Prop propulsion system being moved into position."

Cut to POV animation moving to superstructure subassembly area.

Background sound of motors whirring and machinery clanging.
"Next, you'll need to choose a superstructure."

CHOOSE A SUPERSTRUCTURE

Superstructure subassembly area, 4 compartments are shown.

Loudspeaker VO:
"Superstructure being selected."
"Touch a number to learn about a superstructure."

After a compartment is selected, a 3-D superstructure appears above the subassembly area and rotates around 360 degrees in y-axis. As superstructure is rotated, text describing characteristics appears on data screen.

After learning about the characteristics for a particular superstructure, the visitor is prompted to use this superstructure or examine one of the others.

"Use this superstructure or press another number."

After selecting a superstructure to use, cut to Design Assembly screen, animation of superstructure being lowered onto selected hull.

Loudspeaker VO: "Multiple Deck superstructure being moved into position."

Images of the different types of Superstructures are shown on screen to illustrate the text descriptions.

Bridge with Cranes
— shipboard crane system for container handling
— high bridge provides good visibility

Multiple Deck
— forward bridge provides excellent visibility
— sleek structure reduces wind drag

Full-Beam Bridge
— very high bridge house provides excellent visibility
— work spaces and accommodations close together

Complex Amidships
— compact and integrated work area
— good deck space fore and aft

DESIGN ANALYSIS

Animation of completed designs rotating 360 degrees in y-axis.

"Completed design ready for inspection and evaluation."
1 of 3 possible completed design outcomes:
"Very good! You have chosen an optimal design!"
"You have chosen a functional design."
"You have chosen a nonfunctional design."

Animation of hull choice rotation 360 degrees in y-axis	1 of 3 possible hull outcomes: "Hull Choice: Optimal" "Hull Choice: Functional" "Hull Choice: Nonfunctional" Followed by mission-specific feedback for chosen component (see Feedback below).
Animation of propulsion system choice rotation 360 degrees in y-axis.	1 of 3 possible propulsion system outcomes: "Propulsion System Choice: Optimal" "Propulsion System Choice: Functional" "Propulsion System Choice: Nonfunctional" This is followed by mission-specific feedback for chosen component (see Feedback below).
Animation of superstructure choice rotating 360 degrees in y-axis	1 of 3 possible superstructure outcomes: "Superstructure Choice: Optimal" "Superstructure Choice: Functional" "Superstructure Choice: Nonfunctional" Followed by mission-specific feedback for chosen component (see Feedback below).
User is prompted to touch graphic of champagne bottle. After button press or 5 seconds, animation of completed ship design being launched.	"Press the champagne bottle to launch your ship." "Ship being launched."
If design was optimal, user is prompted to touch graphic of certificate to receive his/her printout of Optimal Design Certificate	"Press the button to print your Optimal Design Certificate!"

DESIGN ANALYSIS FEEDBACK

Selected Mission:
Trans-Atlantic Container Ship
Hulls:

Air Cushion	"Hull Choice: Nonfunctional — Can't withstand rough seas of Atlantic — Can't support heavy bridge and crane system — Cargo capacity too small"

Planing	"Hull Choice: Nonfunctional — Can't support heavy bridge and crane system — Cargo capacity too small"
Displacement	"Hull Choice: Optimal — Very stable in rough seas — Very large cargo capacity"
SWATH	"Hull Choice: Nonfunctional — Cargo capacity too small"

Propulsion System:

Diesel	"Propulsion System Choice: Optimal — Fuel efficient — Performs well at low to moderate speeds"
Air Prop	"Propulsion System Choice: Nonfunctional — Not powerful enough — Needs flat water conditions"
Water Jet	"Propulsion System Choice: Nonfunctional — Not powerful enough — Needs flat water conditions"
CODAG	"Propulsion System Choice: Functional — Performs well at high speeds — High maintenance — Gas turbine features not necessary"

Superstructure:

Bridge with Cranes	"Superstructure Choice: Optimal — Cranes allow easy handling of containers — High bridge provides excellent visibility"
Multiple Deck	"Superstructure Choice: Nonfunctional — No way to handle containers"
Full-Beam Bridge	"Superstructure Choice: Nonfunctional — No way to handle containers"
Complex Amidships	"Superstructure Choice: Nonfunctional — No way to handle containers"

Selected Mission

Cross-Channel Ferry

Hulls:

Air Cushion	"Hull Choice: Optimal

	— Capable of high speeds
	— Shallow draft allows easy access to harbors
	— Rectangular deck perfect for loading cars"
SWATH	"Hull Choice: Nonfunctional
	— Requires large propulsion system for speed
	— Deck shape makes car loading difficult"
Displacement	"Hull Choice: Nonfunctional
	— Requires very large propulsion system for speed
	— Deep draft limits access to harbors"
Planing	"Hull Choice: Nonfunctional
	— Requires large propulsion system for speed"

Propulsion System:

Diesel	"Propulsion System Choice: Nonfunctional
	— Performs best at lower speeds
	— Hull projections increase draft"
Air Prop	"Propulsion System Choice: Functional
	— Needs large power plant
	— Affected by bad wind conditions"
Water Jet	"Propulsion System Choice: Optimal
	— Good for high speeds
	— No hull projections keep draft shallow"
CODAG	"Propulsion System Choice: Nonfunctional
	— Hull projections increase draft
	— Diesel features not necessary"

Superstructure:

Bridge with Cranes	"Superstructure Choice: Nonfunctional
	— Cranes not necessary for cars and passengers
	— Reduces desk space for cars"
Multiple Deck	"Superstructure Choice: Optimal
	— Multiple levels perfect for cars and passengers
	— Forward bridge good for high speeds"

Full-Beam Bridge

"Superstructure Choice:
Nonfunctional
— Can't handle lots of passengers
  comfortably"

Complex Amidships

"Superstructure Choice:
Nonfunctional
— Can't handle lots of passengers
— Reduces deck space for cars"

Selected Mission:
Oceanographic Research Vessel

Hulls:

Air Cushion

"Hull Choice: Nonfunctional
— Can't withstand rough seas"

Planing

"Hull Choice: Functional
— Capable of high speeds
— Not very stable in rough seas
— Limited work and living space"

Displacement

"Hull Choice: Functional
— Stable in rough seas
— Plenty of work and living space
— Deep draft limits access to
  shore areas"

SWATH

"Hull Choice: Optimal
— Very stable in rough seas
— Plenty of protected work and
  living space
— Shallower draft provides access
  to shore areas"

Propulsion System:

Diesel

"Propulsion System Choice:
Functional
— Fuel efficient
— Infrequent maintenance
— Performs best at low speeds"

Air Prop

"Propulsion System Choice:
Nonfunctional
— Not powerful enough
— Needs flat water conditions
— Affected by bad wind conditions"

Water Jet

"Propulsion System Choice:
Nonfunctional
— Not powerful enough
— Needs flat water conditions"

CODAG

"Propulsion System Choice: Optimal
— Good performance at all speeds
— Makes hull more maneuverable"

Superstructure:

Bridge with Cranes

"Superstructure Choice:
Nonfunctional

	— Container handling system not necessary"
Multiple Deck	"Superstructure Choice: Nonfunctional — No work space on deck"
Full-Beam Bridge	"Superstructure Choice: Nonfunctional — Too big for appropriate hull — Too far aft"
Complex Amidships	"Superstructure Choice: Optimal — Good work space on deck — Well-integrated space for labs"

Script Sample Courtesy Chedd-Angier Production Company © Chedd-Angier Production Company.

Script and Design Document Treatment Compared

There were a number of substantial elements changed from the design document's creative treatment to the final script. These changes illustrate solid interactive writing principles.

Attract Routine: attract routines play when no one is using the kiosk. Clearly, they are very important as bait to lure or attract the players. Without a strong attract routine, a kiosk program is ineffective because no one will play it.

Treatment: the attract routine in the treatment suggests showing one of the program's ships being built and the text: "Build a Ship to Accomplish a Mission."

Script: the script starts with a 3-D animation flyover of the shipyard and the text: "The Nauticus Shipbuilding Company—the most highly advanced shipbuilding facility in the world. Urgent: Naval Architect Needed."

The script changes give a much better introduction to the program by using the shipyard flyover, a standard cinematic establishing shot of the location. The location is extensive and impressive. The script's text also helps build the simulation and the excitement of the program. We are now dealing with the most advanced shipbuilding company in the world. Players are also asked to assume the role of architect and become a part of *The Nauticus Shipbuilding Company*—and they are needed urgently!

BRIEFING ROOM

Treatment: the treatment includes a video clip of a talking head of the shipyard president keyed over stock footage to explain the mission.

Script: the script eliminates the video talking head and the stock footage, replacing this material with more graphic elements, such as maps showing where the ship would travel.

There are several good reasons for this change. One is that the video talking head and documentary footage in a world of 3-D animation creates a conflict in style, one of the effects of which is to point out the artificiality of the animation. By eliminating this conflict, the program has stylistic consistency, and it is raised up one level of abstraction. The user can now more easily enter this fantasy world where he or she is the only real person.

The graphic elements, such as the maps, also ground the user visually in the mission, as opposed to being told about it by the talking head. Finally, the talking head video expanded the number of elements on screen, creating clutter and confusion for the viewer.

MISSIONS

Treatment: the treatment has five missions, ranging from North Sea Fire Fighter to Arctic Ice Breaker.

Script: the script has three missions: Transatlantic Container Ship, Cross-Channel Ferry, and Oceanographic Research Vessel.

The script reduces the number and changes the types of missions. Three factors motivated these changes:

1. The budget and running time of the program.
2. The particular missions that best presented a wide view of naval architecture.
3. The missions that best suited the game design. The ideal missions had to present shipbuilding problems where the answers weren't obvious but not impossible. The information had to allow clues that could be subtle.

COMPONENTS

Treatment: the treatment's ship components include hulls, hold, engine, and special equipment.

Script: the script's ship components include hulls, propulsion, and superstructure.

The special equipment was combined into the superstructure, and the hold was eliminated to reduce one variable in building the ship. It is important that the overall experience be as short as possible and still be effective. This has an impact on production cost and the time that the user would have to interact with the program.

EVALUATION OF DESIGN

The script increased the amount of evaluation of the ship design at the end of the program. The goal here was to encourage the user to go back and try the process again. This is ultimately a more successful learning approach than a one-shot deal where the user gets it right or wrong. The chance to try, fail, and redo something without penalty is an important learning feature of interactive media.

Conclusion: Response to the Project

The response to *The Nauticus Shipbuilding Company* has been positive in both the museum and in classroom use. It makes strong use of the simulation model and hierarchical structure to accomplish its goals of teaching a subject to a general audience in an entertaining fashion.

14 E-Learning

Interactive Math and Statistics Lessons

Summary

Name of production: Interactive Math and Statistics Lessons
Writer: Shawn Hackshaw
Developers: Houghton Mifflin Harcourt; Dolphin MultiMedia, Inc; Larson Texts, Inc; InterWrite
Audience: College Students
Medium: Online (web, network)
Presentation location: College labs, student computers
Subject: Math and statistics
Goal: Teach
Structures: Linear with scene branching

Materials used with special permission of Houghton Mifflin Harcourt. All Rights Reserved. © Houghton Mifflin Harcourt

NOTE: Since the original writing of this case study, Houghton Mifflin has merged and operates under a new name Houghton Mifflin Harcourt.

Program Description and Background

Program Description

In the United States alone, billions of dollars are spent annually on course materials for schools and colleges. Billions more are spent for government and corporate training. Because of cost and ease of access, there is a particular demand for digital course material. This material includes digital textbooks, online courses, and supplementary or ancillary material that supports print textbooks. The supplementary materials include background material, drill and skill exercises, interactive lessons explaining key concepts, and more. Publisher Houghton Mifflin Harcourt's *Interactive Math and Statistics Lessons* are an example of supplementary material that explains key concepts.

The *Interactive Math and Statistics Lessons* were developed to teach math and statistics to a college audience. Each lesson takes a key math or statistic concept and uses audio, animation, video, text, and graphics to present this concept in an engaging way. The goal in these lessons is to reduce each concept to a format easily understood by students who may

DOI: 10.4324/9781003430612-18

not have had great success in math. Most lessons can be completed in less than ten minutes. The lessons are primarily used to support and extend math textbooks.

Each lesson has up to eight modules or sections:

- Prepare for the Tutorial (includes Prep Tests)
- Study the Concept
- Try an Example
- Explore the Concept
- View a Video Example
- Practice Exercises
- Apply the Concepts to Real Life
- Mastery Test

The lesson structure listed above follows a traditional but effective instructional design: introduction, pre-tests, concept explanation, example, apply/explore concept, and posttest to verify mastery. A closer look at each of the lesson modules explains their function.

Prepare for the Tutorial

A brief summary of the lesson in a bulleted list, a photograph describing a real-life application of the concept, a summary of the basic pre skills needed to do the lesson, and links to pretests (Prep Tests) on these skills.

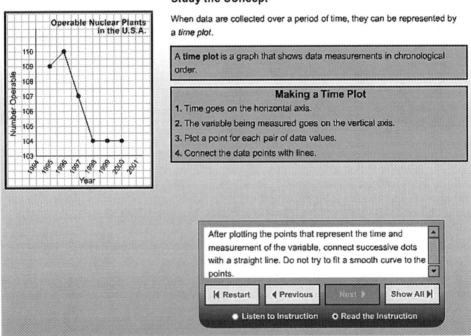

Figure 14–1 Study the Concept screen

Study the Concept

A detailed explanation of the concept including animation, static images, text, and audio narration. The student has the option of listening to audio narration, reading text, or both. The text appears section by section with corresponding images and narration. For example, in Figure 14–1, the animated time plot appears step by step as it is explained in the text. The student can move the lesson back, forward, or replay the entire lesson if they wish.

Try an Example

The Try an Example screen uses animation, static images, text, and audio narration to present an example of the concept explained in the previous screen. Usually at least two examples are presented. One without user input, and the other requiring students to input data to complete the example as pictured in Figure 14–2.

View a Video Example

This screen includes a short video of a classroom lecture explaining the concept.

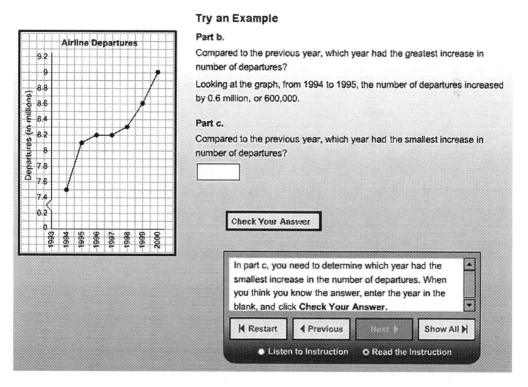

Figure 14–2 Try an Example screen

Practice Exercises

These exercises provide a chance for the student to work with the concepts they have just learned in previous screens.

Apply the Concepts to Real Life

In an attempt to make the concept more meaningful to students, this module gives them a chance to solve a real-life problem using the concept. Elements included on this screen are animation, static images, text, and audio narration.

Explore the Concept

This is a highly interactive exploration of the concept. This is custom made for the concept and the most challenging module for the writer to create.

Mastery Tests

These are the posttests that demonstrate the student has learned the material.

Hundreds of these lessons have been produced. They support many of Houghton Mifflin Harcourt's *Math and Statistics* college textbooks. Material that can support more than one textbook is an important criterion when designing ancillary material. It is too expensive to create unique ancillary material for a single book unless the textbook is very popular. Instead, the approach is either to create generic material on the subject, such as these math lessons, or to create a software shell/engine that can be customized for each book with additional unique content. A software shell/engine is a piece of software that has certain capabilities, such as presenting various types of exercises, video, audio, etc. Different information can be added to the shell without rebuilding it.

Production Background

The math editors of the Houghton Mifflin College Division (prior to Harcourt merger) conceived the idea for the *Interactive Math and Statistics Lessons*. The idea was refined and the Interactive Lessons software engine created by Dolphin MultiMedia, Inc. Initially, math content development and lesson production was by Larson Texts, Inc. Later, InterWrite was also brought into the project to help develop and create additional math and statistics content.

Headquartered in Boston, Massachusetts, Houghton Mifflin Harcourt is one of the top educational publishers in the United States. It publishes textbooks, instructional technology, assessments, and other educational materials for teachers and students of every age. The company also publishes reference works, fiction, and nonfiction for adults and young readers.

Dolphin MultiMedia provides strategic consulting to help their clients communicate their messages to their audiences. They create interactive material, video, web, and computer-based demos or presentations for sales, marketing, education, and executive briefings. The media may include graphics, interactivity, web links, and video or animation. Dolphin created the software engine and integrated the produced lesson components for the Interactive Math Lessons.

Larson Texts, Inc. has several divisions. Larson Texts produces math textbooks for sixth grade through calculus. Larson Learning, Inc. offers interactive educational math software, print materials, and staff development workshops. TDLC.COM, publishes on-line math course materials. For the Interactive Math Lessons, Larson developed math content and created lesson elements, including creating animations, graphics, and audio narration.

InterWrite was an interactive media consulting and development company located north of Boston. They created teaching, training, and customer information projects for interactive media. InterWrite performed a similar function as Larson Texts on the Interactive Math Lessons project, developing math and statistics content and creating the lesson elements.

There were numerous math writers on this project working for both InterWrite and Larson Texts. Some of the writers are math teachers by trade. Others are professional math content developers. The writer interviewed for this case study was Shawn Hackshaw who worked for InterWrite. Shawn teaches high school and college math. He has a master's degree in math education at the secondary level and is a certified math teacher in the State of New Hampshire. Shawn wrote 15 Interactive Math lessons and provided storyboards for the graphics and animations.

Goals and Challenges Writing the *Interactive Math and Statistics Lessons*

Goals

One of the authors on the project, Shawn Hackshaw, outlined his primary goals in creating the lessons in the quote below. Note that the lessons need to support a variety of textbooks. The authors of the lessons draw their basic content from these texts.

> My goals with each lesson were to summarize and simplify materials in a given text or series of texts without compromising the integrity of the material. The multimedia presentation had to be accurate and brief. . . .
>
> I needed to be able to describe and illustrate a process in clear and precise steps that any user could follow, regardless of their mathematical background. Each individual lesson had goals that were outlined in the texts that the lessons were being created to support, and I needed to be cognizant of the [book] authors' intentions as well as understanding of the attention span and learning needs of the average student user.
>
> (Hackshaw)

Challenges

The challenges to these straightforward goals were numerous. Some challenges relate to the content. Others to the production process itself.

Production Challenges

- To master software and technical skills to write the lessons.
- To come up with a script format that will satisfy the needs of the client's non-technical math content reviewers, the production team's programmers and animators, and the narrator who will read the audio narration.

Content Challenges

- Understand the specific restriction, format, and style of the Interactive Lessons.
- Ensure that the concepts could support a variety of textbooks.
- Reduce large amounts of content in the books to smaller amounts that could be effectively presented in an interactive, online format, keeping in mind the needs of the audience, particularly their short attention span with math subject matter.
- Find ways to explain, visualize, and make interactive the complex math and statistics concepts.

Writing the *Interactive Math and Statistics Lessons:* Meeting the Production Challenges

Software and Technical Skills

Writing for most technical subjects, such as math and science, requires more software and technical skills than writing non-technical material, such as English and history. For example, chemistry writers often know modeling and visualization tools for creating images of molecules and other scientific elements. The writer is not responsible for creating the final production graphics, but the clearer he/she can be in sketching out the illustrations, the easier it is for the project's graphic designers and programmers to create accurate models and interactions. When a writer can create very clear preliminary models, it also saves the production team time and money. So, it is definitely a plus for the writer to have some graphic and technical skills related to his/her subject matter.

On the math and statistics interactive lessons, writer Hackshaw used several tools to write math symbols and present illustrations. MathType is a professional equation editor that makes it much easier to write out complex mathematical symbols and formulas. A limited version of MathType is included with Microsoft Office, AppleWorks, and other products, but the professional version is much more powerful. MathType easily integrates with most word processing software and has handy features, such as an ability to export equations from MathType to MathML, an XML-based language used to present math in interactive media, such as websites. MathML was the standard for this project, so this export feature saved considerable time for the XML programmers.

For the Interactive Lessons, it was also useful for the author to have some basic graphic skills. There were many images and animations that had to be created to explain math and statistics concepts. Because the author could provide clear preliminary illustrations, it was a great help to the designers and programmers. The software that Hackshaw used on this project for charts, graphs, and illustrations includes: GraphSight, Excel, and TI Connect (to capture screen shots directly from the TI graphing calculator). In general, if you are interested in writing for the STEM educational market, you may not only need writing skills and a knowledge of the subject matter, but you may also need some basic technical and graphic skills, such as those described above.

Developing a Script Format

Designing the right script format for a project is essential. The script format helps the writer present on paper a complex interactive media program. Developing a script format for a project is not usually the exclusive responsibility of the writer, although sometimes it is. Often the production team and/or the client will have an approach that they prefer, particularly if the content is being developed for an existing software engine. In this project, the production team, InterWrite, revised the client's suggested format with significant input from the writer Shawn Hackshaw.

The challenges of designing a script format for this project are shared with many technical, interactive media projects. The script format has to present the content for a variety of audiences that have different needs:

- Client: needs to have a clear, uncluttered visual representation of how the screens will look so that they can evaluate and comment.
- Production Team: animators, programmers, and other team members need very specific technical details so they can execute the author's vision. Hackshaw said that explaining his vision clearly for the development team was one of his biggest challenges on the project.
- Narrator: copy that can be easily read out loud.

After some experimentation, a multi-part script format was used by InterWrite for this project. A detailed explanation of the script format follows.

The Storyboard

As mentioned earlier, each lesson is divided into several modules, including: Prepare for the Tutorial, Study the Concept, Try an Example, Explore the Concept, Apply the Concepts to Real Life, etc. Except for the tests and the video screen, all of the screens are represented visually by a storyboard. A storyboard attempts to represent how the screen layout will actually look by showing placement of illustrations and screen text. A storyboard is a commonly used tool in developing content for both interactive media and linear media such as film and TV. Some storyboards, particularly in the advertising industry, can be very detailed and well-crafted productions. For this project, however, a much simpler storyboard was adequate. The storyboard was created using MS Word tables. A graphic designer created the art based on the rough illustrations of the writer.

The storyboard below is the storyboard from which the final lesson pictured in Figure 14–1 was created. This was a storyboard for a simple module. Others were more complex. Note the following in the storyboard below:

- Title bar clearly indicates the concept title and the unique concept tag: m02c01. It is important in a complex project for each element to have a unique tag. This is essential in production, but also helps the development team and client refer to a specific module without confusion. In this case, "m02" means the second concept within this lesson, and c01 lets us know it is the Study the Concept module within this second concept. You can create whatever tagging system makes sense to you and your team, but the important thing is to use it consistently throughout the script.
- In the produced lesson, the screen text and animation appear gradually. But on the storyboards, all the text is presented at once along with the final frame of the animation. This is because the storyboard is supported with a more detailed script (discussed later

in this chapter). If the storyboard were the only production document, there would need to be multiple storyboards, showing exactly how the text and animation elements appear.

- The grayed-in boxes indicate that these are process boxes or definition boxes and should also be grayed boxes in the final lesson. Process boxes list the steps of a procedure. Definition boxes define a term. See Figure 14–1 to see how these boxes look on the final screen.

Study the Concept *(Storyboard)*

Concept: Creating Time Plots	m02c01
	Creating Time Plots When data are collected over a period of time, they can be represented by a *time plot*.
	A **time plot** is a graph that shows data measurements in chronological order.
Operable Nuclear Plants in the U.S.A. 111 110 109 108 107 106 105 104 103 1994 1996 1998 2000 2002 Year	**Making a Time Plot** 1. Time goes on the horizontal axis. 2. The variable being measured goes on the vertical axis. 3. Plot a point for each pair of data values. 4. Connect the data points with lines.

Script Animation Page

In the storyboard shown previously, the animation is shown as a static image in order to illustrate the approximate layout of the page, but it was also necessary for both content review and production development to have a precise idea of how the animation would unfold. This is handled on a separate animation page, which follows the storyboard. The animation page has the file name of the animation frame on the left, an image of the frame in the middle, and the corresponding text that triggers that frame appearing on the right.

Study the Concept *(Animation Page)*

Concept: Creating Time Plots		m02c01
	Animation Frame Image	Corresponding Text
File # il0262m02c01anim01.swf **Frame #**		
il0262m02c01anim01F1_IW.ai		To make a time plot, use the fol-lowing procedure.
il0262m02c01anim01F2_IW.ai		After you draw your horizontal and vertical axes, time should be placed on the horizontal axis.
il0262m02c01anim01F3_IW.ai		The variable being meas-ured goes on the vertical axis.
il0262m02c01anim01F4_IW.ai		Plot a point for each pair of data values.

i10262m02c01anim01F5_IW.ai	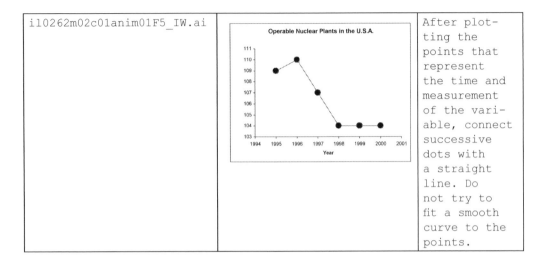	After plotting the points that represent the time and measurement of the variable, connect successive dots with a straight line. Do not try to fit a smooth curve to the points.

Programming, Text, and Narration Script

The final written script section for each module is the Programming, Text, and Narration Script. This script has all the details necessary for the production team, including the narrator, to create the actual lesson.

The script on a complex project becomes the bible for the development team. All elements must be spelled out clearly. In the sample script that follows, all the file names for this module are listed at the top of the page. This allows the graphic designer to give a name to files and the programmer and animators to create links to those file names correctly. The file names follow a standard project naming convention. Writers should be aware of that convention if they are going to be listing file names, such as in this script.

Below the file names are multiple rows and four columns. All the content in a row appears on the screen at one time, followed by the next row, etc. The four columns each describe different content:

- Images, Text, Programming: this column lists the file names of the images, on-screen text, and any programming, such as indicating a Definition Box.
- Narration (Text Transcript): the next column over is the text transcript, which appears in the box at the bottom of the screen for the student to read. See Figure 14–1. This is an accurate text rendition of the audio narration.
- Narration (Audio Transcript): the audio transcript is what the narrator will say. Even though the Text Transcript and Audio Transcript are identical in content, they are written somewhat differently to make it easier for the listener and reader. In the sample below, there are no differences, but examples of what appears in other scripts are numbers written out in narration but appearing as numerals in text and difficult words written out phonetically in the narration.
- Project Note: this is used by the production team for a variety of purposes, including timing narration for developing the lesson and tracking bug fixes. (Bugs are errors discovered during review.)

The real script is created in landscape format to allow the columns to be wider. It is restructured here in portrait format for easier display in the book.

Concept: Creating Time Plots

Study the Concept (*Programming and Text Script*)

File Names This Module (Study the Concept)

Animation:

ID: m02c01
Audio: il0262m02c01.mp3

il0262m02c01anim01.swf
il0262m02c01anim01F1_IW.ai
il0262m02c01anim01F2_IW.ai
il0262m02c01anim01F3_IW.ai
il0262m02c01anim01F4_IW.ai
il0262m02c01anim01F5_IW.ai

Images, Text, Programming	Narration (Text Transcript)	Narration (Audio Transcript)	Project Note
1) (Title) Creating Time Plots			
2) (Main Screen Text) When data are collected over a period of time, they can be represented by a **time plot.**	When data are collected over a period of time, they can be represented by a **time plot.**	When data are collected over a period of time, they can be represented by a **time plot.**	
3) (Definition Box) A time plot is a graph showing data measurements in chronological order.	A time plot is a graph that shows data measurements in chronological order. It is important to note that the interval of time between measurements should be the same. So, if you take a measurement once a week, it should be on the same day every week. Or, if you take a measurement every day, the same time period, such as one-half hour, should be used.	A time plot is a graph that shows data measurements in chronological order. It is important to note that the interval of time between measurements should be the same. So, if you take a measurement once a week, it should be on the same day every week. Or, if you take a measurement every day, the same time period, such as one-half hour, should be used.	

Images, Text, Programming	Narration (Text Transcript)	Narration (Audio Transcript)	Project Note
4a)(Procedure Box) Making a Time Plot [il0262m02c01anim01F1_IW.ai]	To make a time plot, use the following procedure.	To make a time plot, use the following procedure.	
4b)(Procedure Box) • Time goes on the horizontal axis. [il0262m02c01anim01F2_IW.ai]	After you draw your horizontal and vertical axes, time should be placed on the horizontal axis.	After you draw your horizontal and vertical axes, time should be placed on the horizontal axis.	
4c)(Procedure Box) • The variable being measured goes on the vertical axis. [il0262m02c01anim01F3_IW.ai]	The variable being measured is placed on the vertical axis.	The variable being measured is placed on the vertical axis.	
4d)(Procedure Box) • Plot a point for each pair of data values. [il0262m02c01anim01F4_IW.ai]	Plot a point for each pair of data values.	Plot a point for each pair of data values.	
4d)(Procedure Box) • Connect the data points with lines. [il0262m02c01anim01F5_IW.ai]	After plotting the points that represent the time and measurement of the variable, connect successive dots with a straight line. Do not try to fit a smooth curve to the points.	After plotting the points that represent the time and measurement of the variable, connect successive dots with a straight line. Do not try to fit a smooth curve to the points.	

With the production challenges solved, the writer next must face the content challenges.

Writing the *Interactive Math and Statistics Lessons*: Meeting the Content Challenges

Understanding the Requirements for this Project

Any complex interactive media project will have a series of rules that will affect the writer. If you are writing for a unique product that will be built from the ground up according to your script, you will have fewer restrictions. But if you are writing for an existing software engine, which is often the case, you must know what the engine can or cannot do. As mentioned previously, the interactive math lessons were written for an existing software engine. Be sure to ask for the project guidelines before you start a project. They are usually included in a document called a "Style Guide" or "Project Specifications." Sometimes no Style Guide exists, and it is part of the writer's job to create a style guide to ensure consistency in content development. Some of the things you need to know before writing a complex project include the following.

Screen Layout

You need to know what kinds of media or text can go where in the interface. Can the screen scroll? Is the amount of text limited in certain areas? Figure 14–3 is part of the Interactive Lessons style guide that tried to answer some of these questions.

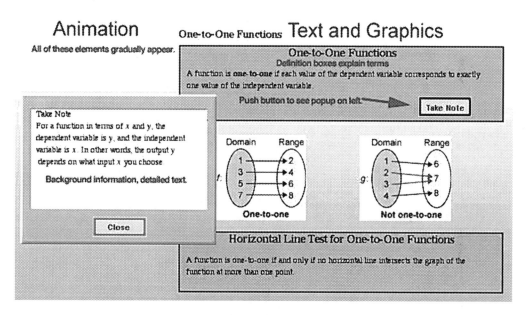

Figure 14–3 Illustration from style guide explaining layout for writers

Engine Capability

You also need to know what this software engine can do. What kind of media can it present, such as video and animation? What kind of exercises is it capable of, such as multiple choice, true and false, etc.? Does it have any other tools or functions, such as note taking tools or tracking student progress.

Unique Project Elements

If there are unique elements in the project that require special terms and layout, you need to be sure you understand them. These unique elements are often related to production issues.

Dividing Content into Various Display Areas

Once the writer understands the screen layout and engine capability, then he/she is better able to make effective use of all the display elements in a project and not just put all the content in one location. For example, in the Interactive Lessons, it is usually best to limit the amount of text on the screen because reading lots of text on screen is tiresome for most users. On-screen text should just cover key points. Concepts should be visualized as much as possible in diagrams and animations. If details need to be discussed, leave them off the main screen text, and cover them instead in the audio and other special elements, such as Definition Boxes and Hints. This allows a more sophisticated user to move through the main screen text and visuals to finish the lesson quickly, while allowing an average student to get additional help by referring to other lesson elements.

Writing Style Guide

Important information for the writer is the writing style guide. This guide lays out exactly how elements should be handled in text. This will include how to write certain types of technical material, such as math formulas; style of items such as bulleted lists; and consistent use of certain words that may be handled in a variety of ways. For example, "doughnut" and "donut" are both correct, but within a project, a specific word should only be spelled one way.

Writing style guides are used even in print projects, but the added complication for an interactive media project is that depending on where the text appears in the program, it might be handled differently. For example, in this project, there were different style rules for the narration and the text script. The goal was to make one easier to be read by the student and another easier to read out loud by the narrator. A sample from the style guide follows.

```
1.Math Symbols are spelled out and numbers are represented
  in Arabic.
```

Audio Transcript (A)	Text Transcript (T)
negative nine over six	negative 9 over 6

```
2.Superscripts and subscripts are written as symbols. Subscripts
  are always written "variable" "sub" "number".
```

Audio Transcript (A)	Text Transcript (T)
x squared	x^2
x sub one	x_1

Reducing and Structuring Content for Interactive Media

Once all the project rules as discussed above are understood, the author can finally begin the actual writing. The first challenge for most interactive writers is to chunk the content. This means taking the large amount of continuous content that can be covered in a book or even a chapter of a book and break that content into smaller units that can be portrayed interactively. In the case of this project, math and statistics concepts needed to be broken down to fit into the module structures of the Interactive Lessons. Also, keeping in mind the needs and attention span of the student audience, the amount of content covered by a particular concept must be reduced as much as possible to make it bite sized, and easily digestible by the audience.

The writer also had to keep in mind that the one concept that he/she was working on, was part of a much larger body of concepts that explained other issues. This meant that the author did not have to include background material on his concept because that background material would be covered in a completely different lesson. It is important for an interactive writer to understand the big picture of a project and how all the elements fit together. This helps avoid repeating material that is presented elsewhere in the project.

The Outline

The client's math editors help with this process of chunking by presenting the writer an outline of the concepts for a particular math or statistics concept, such as this outline for the time plots (second concept below) presented earlier in this chapter in script samples and screen shots. In general, an outline can be a good starting point to chunk content.

```
Prepare for the Tutorial
View a Video Example
Explore the Concept
Concept: Creating Bar Graphs and Circle Graphs

   • Study the Concept
   • Try an Example
   • Practice Exercises

Study the Concept Try an Example Practice Exercises
Concept: Creating Time Plots

   • Study the Concept
   • Try an Example
   • Practice Exercises

Concept: Creating Histograms and Relative-Frequency Histograms

   • Study the Concept
   • Try an Example
   • Practice Exercises

Concept: Creating Stem-and-Leaf Displays

   • Study the Concept
   • Try an Example
   • Practice Exercises

Mastery Test
```

The first job of the writer is to analyze this outline and determine if the concept is too large to be handled in one lesson or should be broken down into multiple lessons. In the outline above, the elements in each module are pretty straightforward with each of them including: Study the Concept, Try an Example, and a Practice Exercise. The writer could suggest adding more elements to better explain the concept. For example, he/she may think that a certain concept needs multiple examples, a video, or a real-life application.

Continued Refinement: The Writing and Review Process

To effectively present the information, the writer should be involved in as much of the content development process as possible. The outline discussed above is the beginning, but once the outline was refined, the author next had to study the various textbooks that these lessons needed to support. For this project, there were multiple textbooks written by many authors. Writer Hacksaw's process was to sit at a large table with all the textbooks open in front of him. Each textbook would be turned to the section covering the concept being written. Hackshaw then marked up the textbooks with numbers, underlines, etc. to highlight the points he wanted to cover. Then he began writing his first draft storyboard and script.

The finished first draft would be reviewed by InterWrite and then more extensively by the Houghton Mifflin math editors. They would return suggested changes to the author. The author had the option of arguing for his approach instead of the client's suggestions. It is not a good idea to rubber stamp a client's changes if you strongly oppose them. If later they prove to be bad choices, it is the writer who will often carry the blame for the client's suggestions, because the writer is responsible for the script. Of course, when arguing any point with the client, the client will have the final word, and the writer should learn how to give in gracefully if he/she has not been able to persuade the client to adopt the writer's point of view.

With the Interactive Lessons, once the client approved the script, then the developer produced it. In the case of the time plots lesson described earlier, the developer was InterWrite. Because the writer on a project, such as this, is also the subject matter expert, he was also responsible for reviewing the first draft of the produced lesson. If a writer can be involved in this way, it is often helpful. Sometimes ideas that looked great on the script do not come off as well in the final production. Sometimes explanations are not clear and need additional text or illustrations. Last, the author must make sure that no errors were introduced in production. A single deleted math symbol can make an entire calculation incorrect. Unless there is some issue that needs to be resolved later in the production, usually this ends the writer's involvement with a particular concept. Being involved from outline to production is important to guarantee accuracy and a consistent presentation of the content.

Explain and Visualize Concepts in an Engaging Way

One of the biggest challenges for the writer was to find ways to clearly explain the concept and engage the student interactively. Hackshaw found a few techniques that were particularly helpful.

Step-by-Step Instruction and Reinforcement

Hackshaw said that one of the most important techniques in explaining technical subjects is careful step-by-step instruction. For example, when graphing a line, such as the lesson pictured in Figure 14–1:

> students need to understand how points on that line are found. If you don't take the time to show how to find the points, and just plot them on the graph, students won't make

the connection. That line just showed up without an explanation . . . Students need to be constantly reminded in systematic step-by-step process of how the concept works. (Hackshaw)

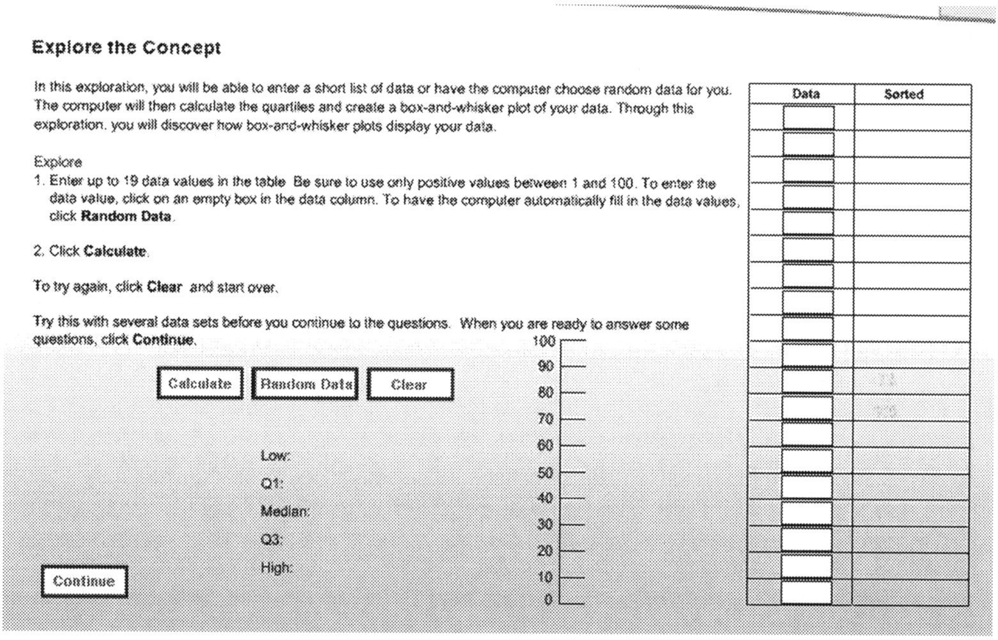
Explore the Concept
In this exploration, you will be able to enter a short list of data or have the computer choose random data for you. The computer will then calculate the quartiles and create a box-and-whisker plot of your data. Through this exploration, you will discover how box-and-whisker plots display your data.
Explore
1. Enter up to 19 data values in the table. Be sure to use only positive values between 1 and 100. To enter the data value, click on an empty box in the data column. To have the computer automatically fill in the data values, click Random Data.
2. Click Calculate.
To try again, click Clear and start over.
Try this with several data sets before you continue to the questions. When you are ready to answer some questions, click Continue.
Calculate
Random Data
Clear
Low:
Q1:
Median:
Q3:
High:
Continue
Data
Sorted
100
90
80
70
60
50
40
30
20
10
0

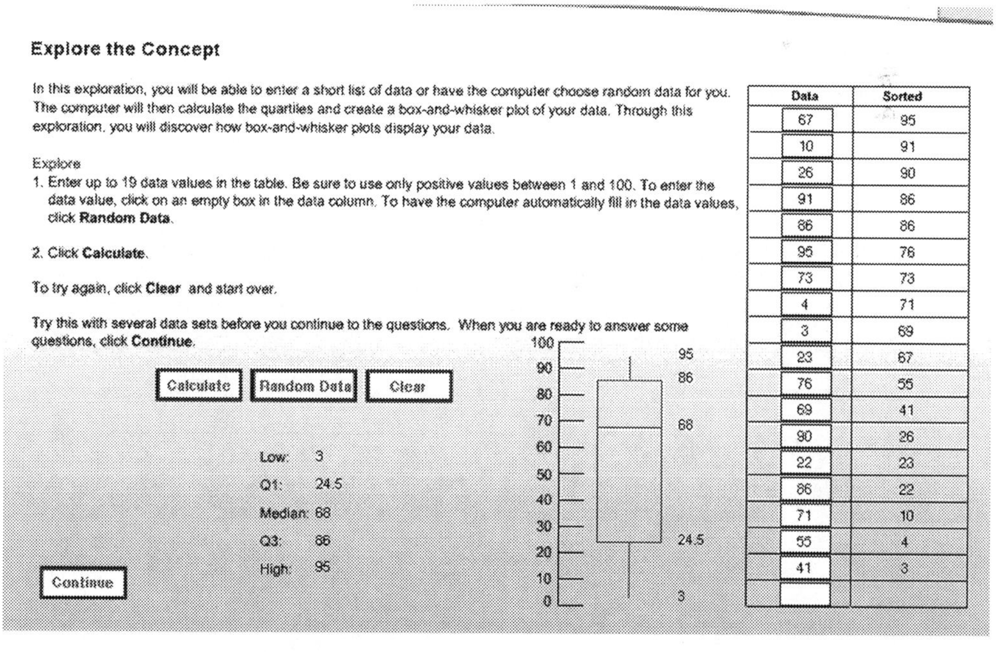
Explore the Concept
In this exploration, you will be able to enter a short list of data or have the computer choose random data for you. The computer will then calculate the quartiles and create a box-and-whisker plot of your data. Through this exploration, you will discover how box-and-whisker plots display your data.
Explore
1. Enter up to 19 data values in the table. Be sure to use only positive values between 1 and 100. To enter the data value, click on an empty box in the data column. To have the computer automatically fill in the data values, click Random Data.
2. Click Calculate.
To try again, click Clear and start over.
Try this with several data sets before you continue to the questions. When you are ready to answer some questions, click Continue.
Calculate
Random Data
Clear
Low: 3
Q1: 24.5
Median: 68
Q3: 86
High: 95
Continue
95
86
68
24.5
3
Data
Sorted

Data	Sorted
67	95
10	91
26	90
91	86
86	86
95	76
73	73
4	71
3	69
23	67
76	55
69	41
90	26
22	23
86	22
71	10
55	4
41	3

Figure 14–4 Box and Whisker Plot, showing empty screen on top and after data has been inputted at bottom

The structure of the Interactive Lessons encourages this step-by-step process and reinforcements with multiple media. Hackshaw said:

> when you teach a concept, first explain what is it, then visually represent it in numerals or a formula, then present it in audio, then develop picture or animation that illustrates it.
>
> (Hackshaw)

Allow Multiple Ways to Interact with a Concept

Allowing multiple ways to interact with content is an effective use of interactive media as a teaching tool. The writer tried to foster this type of interaction within the lessons he wrote.

In Figure 14–4 that follows, the top image has no data entered. The student has the option of entering his or her own number or clicking the Random Data button. Clicking the Random Data button enters numbers in the left column of the table located on the right of the screen. Then by clicking the Calculate button, the numbers are sorted in the column on far right, a whisker plot is created in the middle, and a range is shown under the buttons. (See the bottom image.) This setup allows students to see all the elements of a concept on one screen and to view them interactively. Students can change a number or two and click "Calculate" to see the changes in the three main screen elements (sort, plot, and range). The Random Data button is also a recommended feature for an exercise like this. It allows

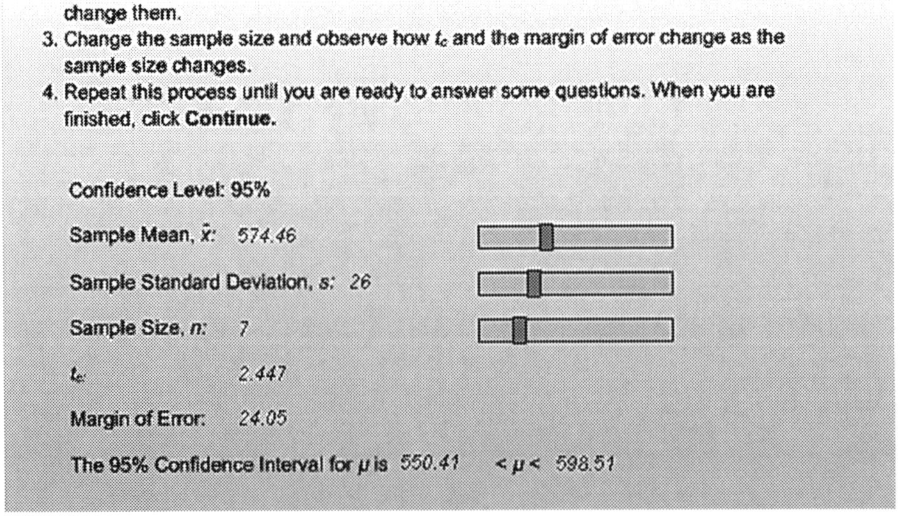

Explore the Concept

Explore
1. Using the sliders, select a value for the sample mean, the sample standard deviation, and the sample size.
2. Once you have set the values for the sample mean and the sample deviation, do not change them.
3. Change the sample size and observe how t_c and the margin of error change as the sample size changes.
4. Repeat this process until you are ready to answer some questions. When you are finished, click **Continue**.

Confidence Level: 95%

Sample Mean, $\bar{x}$: 574.46

Sample Standard Deviation, s: 26

Sample Size, n: 7

t_c: 2.447

Margin of Error: 24.05

The 95% Confidence Interval for μ is 550.41 $< \mu <$ 598.51

Figure 14–5 Confidence intervals lesson using sliders for data input

students to experience the exercise without having to spend several minutes inputting data. Once they understand how the exercise works, they are then often tempted to enter their own data for further exploration of a concept.

Another example occurs in a lesson dealing with confidence intervals. See Figure 14–5. In this exercise, instead of being asked to input numbers, students are given sliders to input a wide range of numbers. As they slide the dark bars, the numbers next to the bar change. When they slide the bottom bar, the bottom four numbers change. Students can experiment with sliding this bar to see how an entire range of numbers changes the calculation. This is far more flexible and interactive than having students simply input single numbers.

Figure 14–6 shows another effective way to manipulate data. In this module, pushing one of the arrows moves the parabola on the graph and changes the corresponding formula over the arrows. This allows students to avoid entering lots of data, and it gives users a different way to experience the information, thus engaging them in the learning process.

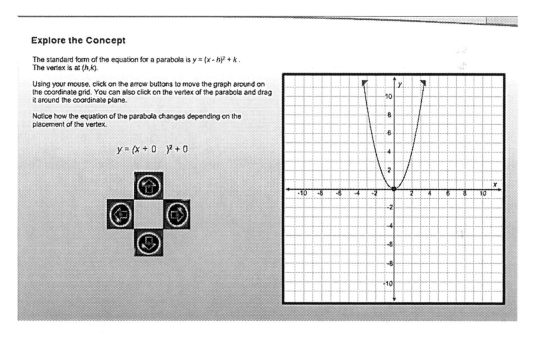

Figure 14–6 Graphing parabolas using arrows to shift graph

Conclusion: Response to the Project

Several hundred interactive math and statistics lessons were produced. They had a positive response with both students and teachers who found the approach to be a major help in understanding math concepts.

Reference

Hackshaw, Shawn. Phone interview and emails with the author

15 Key Points from Part III: Writing and Structuring Long Form Interactive Information—Websites, E-Learning, Simulations

Gathering Information

As in any other information-based project, the first thing to do when writing an informational interactive media program or website is to gather as much information as possible on the subject and the audience. Study that information, and let your approach emerge from the material. If you are writing for a client, you also need to learn as much as you can about their expectations of the project and the business goals.

Defining the Goal: Business Context, Data, and Users (Chapter 10)

Before you can start building an informational interactive media program, you need to clearly define your user and your goal for the project. Because users are so well defined for most informational programs, it is essential to understand the user before coming up with a program's goal. One of the ways that interactive programs try to understand their users is in the writing of personas and use cases. A persona is a description of the key characteristics and information needs of a typical user. A use case is a way to capture the step-by-step information or interaction needs of a specific user of your interactive media project.

Defining the user is actually just one of the three main components of defining the project's goals. These elements are listed in the table below.

Components of Project Goal Definition

Business Context	Data	Users
• Corporate Goals • Resources • Brand	• Document types • Formats	• Information needs • Research modes • Expertise • Technology • Culture & Language
	Business Context + Data + Users = Project Goals	

Techniques to Achieve Common Informational Goals (Chapter 10)

Informational interactive media programs cover a wide range of information including general reference, infotainment, education, interactive news, marketing, training, public relations, customer support and much more. The good news for the writer trying to grasp the

DOI: 10.4324/9781003430612-19

techniques used to create this wide array of informational programming is that most of these productions have one or more of the following general goals, each of which have their own techniques for execution:

1. To persuade
2. To entertain
3. To enable transactions
4. To create a sense of community
5. To inform
6. To teach

Discovering an Approach (Chapter 11)

If it suits your goals and your type of information, attempt to find an approach that goes beyond click-and-read to utilize the full power of interactive media to engage the audience.

Simulation (Chapter 13)

If your information is focused on a process, consider a simulation, such as *The Nauticus Shipbuilding Company*. In a simulation, you first assign a role and a task to the user, such as a naval architect building a ship. You then define all the elements of the task and describe the attributes and behaviors of each element. For example, the elements of the shipbuilding process include choosing hulls, propulsion systems, and superstructures. An attribute of an air cushion hull is that it has a shallow draft; a behavior is that it will sink in rough seas. Once the attributes and behaviors are defined, the user can perform the simulated task and receive realistic feedback.

Organizing Loosely Related Content (Chapter 10)

If your information is on a broad, loosely related subject, such as the Harlem Renaissance, the key concern is organizing information into discreet units or categories and making this information accessible to the user. One way to do this is to organize the information around a concept map, such as the journey through the streets of 1920s Harlem. Another way is to use a guide or agent to lead the user through the material. It also helps the user's comprehension to present information with a variety of media (video, text, graphics, audio) and in a variety of ways, such as games, quizzes, and explorable spaces.

Training

If the information is narrowly focused and is on a subject the audience needs to learn precisely, consider a training model. A classic approach to training is to present the material in a variety of ways, starting at the simple and moving to the complex. This is the structure of *Vital Signs*, a program training nurses to take vital signs.

Its sequences are: (1) Registration, (2) Pretest, (3) Humorous Introduction, (4) Overview, (5) Basic Terms, (6) Detailed Instruction, (7) Practice, (8) Case Study Experience, and (9) Posttest. By presenting information in a variety of ways you are accommodating each user's learning pattern.

It might serve students well to make the interactive media education process resemble the interpersonal education process by giving your program characteristics, such as immediacy of response, nonsequential access of information, adaptability, feedback, options, and interruptibility (Chapter 10).

E-Learning (Chapter 14)

If your subject can be broken into repeatable modules and potential users are spread over a wide area, you might consider creating an online tutorial, such as the *Interactive Math and Statistics Lessons*, in Chapter 14. You might consider a module structure similar to the one used for this program:

- Prepare for the Tutorial
- Study the Concept
- Try an Example
- Explore the Concept
- View a Video Example
- Practice Exercises
- Apply the Concepts to Real Life
- Mastery Test

Structure (Chapter 11)

Once your basic approach is determined, then you need to decide what type of structure and navigation will work best for your material. Several different types of structure and navigation are often combined in one piece. Some possible structures and navigation include linear, linear with scene branching, hierarchical branching, multi-path navigation, single-level linking, worlds structure, and simulation.

Writing Formats (Chapters 10 and 12)

The writing formats for information programs vary, but a fairly standard approach for simulations and other types of highly interactive programs is demonstrated in *The Nauticus Shipbuilding Company* (Chapter 13). After an initial proposal is approved, writers produce a design document. This document often includes the design objective, creative treatment, project schedule, and a navigation/program flowchart. The final stage is usually a complete script, which includes all the dialogue, narration, and descriptions of the images and actions. There are a number of script format options (Chapter 3), depending on the type of project and degree of interactivity.

Writing a website can require many different types of writing, such as writing proposals, outlines, flowcharts, on-screen text, and site maintenance manuals. (See Chapter 12.)

Mechanics of Writing (Part I)

There are many organizational devices that help in the planning of informational presentation, such as flowcharting and databases (Chapter 3). You also have to keep in mind the basic techniques of the print, radio, and script writer, such as keeping sentences short, using the active voice, and writing visually (Chapter 2).

Figure IV–1 The psychedelic introduction for the Magic Circles Challenge in the computer game *Amped III*

© Indie Built, Inc.

Part IV

Writing and Designing Interactive Narrative—Games, Immersive Experiences

Part IV Overview

Part III discussed interactive informational writing.

Part IV examines writing for interactive narrative—telling a story with interactive media. Interactive narrative appears most often in games and e-learning programs, but can also be integrated into an immersive experience to present information. as will be discussed in Chapter 19 on "The New England Economic Adventure."

This part includes an introduction to this type of writing and three case studies:

Ch. 18 Adapting a classic book to a computer game for the female audience case study: Nancy Drew: *Secret of the Old Clock*
Ch. 19 Using narrative to present information: *The New England Economic Adventure*
Ch. 20 Adding story to a simulation *Amped III*

DOI: 10.4324/9781003430612-20

16 Interactive Multimedia Narrative vs. Linear Narrative

Portions of this chapter originally appeared in the *Journal of Film and Video*.

Chapter Overview

A narrative is what we commonly refer to as a story. An interactive narrative allows the user to explore several variations of a story or stories. Interactive narratives are produced primarily for video game and e-learning programs. Interactive narratives share many elements with linear film and video narrative. Because of this, this chapter analyzes the basic elements of linear narrative before exploring the intricacies of interactive narrative in later chapters.

Narrative and Interactive Narrative Defined

A narrative is what we commonly refer to as a story. A "story" is one of those terms that we intuitively understand but are hard pressed to define. Critics have written many books defining narrative, but for our purposes we will define a narrative as a series of events that are linked together in a number of ways, including cause and effect, time, and place. Something that happens in the first event causes the action in the second event, and so on, usually moving forward in time.

Narrative interactive media involves telling a story using all the interactive media elements we've discussed in previous chapters, including the use of many media and interactivity. In narrative interactive media, the player explores or discovers a story in the same way the user explored information in the programs discussed in the previous part of the book. Often the player is one of the characters in the story and sees action from that character's point of view. But even if he or she is not a character, the player still has some control over what the characters will do and how the story will turn out. Interactive narratives can be used for pure entertainment or to present information in an experiential way.

Interactive Narratives vs. Simulations, and Worlds

A narrative or story is an ancient form of communication, but interactive media programs can also utilize newer forms that are sometimes confused with narrative. These new forms are simulations and worlds structures.

In a virtual world program, the player explores an environment. Examples include the classic *Myst* (updated *RealMyst*) and the long running online role-playing game *World of Warcraft*. The designers of a virtual world create a physical space, such as a mysterious island or an entire war-ravaged mythical world, where the player has the freedom to move about and interact with various elements, such as opening doors, examining objects, talking

DOI: 10.4324/9781003430612-21

to other characters, and even completing noble quests against mighty enemies and monsters. Worlds programs are not narratives even though some of the characters and locations may have background information presented about them.

In a simulation, such as *The Nauticus Shipbuilding Company* (Chapter 13) or *Amped III* (Chapter 20) a player explores all the different possibilities in an activity, such as building a ship or going snowboarding. Simulations are not narratives. Even if they have a script attached to them, if the elements in the program come up in a random pattern, they do not comprise a narrative.

In an interactive narrative, a player explores a story. Interactive narratives have beginnings, middles, and ends, even though each user may experience these elements differently. There is nothing unplanned in an interactive narrative. Someone who plays the program long enough will eventually see all the material the writer created. An interactive narrative essentially allows each player to discover the story in a different way. The Nancy Drew mystery games (Chapter 18) are excellent examples of interactive narratives.

Simulations, worlds, and narratives can, of course, be combined and that is the most common way they are currently presented. *Dust: A Tale of the Wired West* integrates a narrative into the virtual world of a desert town in the old West. The *Just Cause* series takes the same worlds approach by making the player an agent who follows various stories on the island of San Esperito. The island is a fully developed world that the player can explore and interact with. *Amped III* takes a different approach and combines simulations and narrative by adding story segments to the snowboarding simulation. Although, the original *Sims* game was closer to a pure simulation of building a house and creating a family, the later releases in this series create a more elaborate world for the characters to inhabit and becomes a combination of a simulation and a worlds structure. Even most shooter games will also add a little story to help set up the action. For example, in the beginning of this game, you are told that the only way you can save your true love is to hunt down and destroy a horde of deadly enemies. Once the setup is in place, the vast majority of the rest of the game is shooting the enemies. All these combinations are valid entertainment, but in this book our focus will be on games where the narrative is the primary or at least a major component.

Interactive Multimedia Narratives

Interactive Multimedia Narrative Genres

Although, there have been some interesting interactive narrative experiments with interactive TV, the most sophisticated, commercial, interactive multimedia narratives are primarily found in video games.

The major types of video games that include story elements are action games, role-playing games, and adventure games, with adventure games being the only genre primarily devoted to storytelling. The main focus of action games is speed and action that usually takes the form of shooting other characters or blowing things up. Role Playing Games (RPGs) involve a character taking on a role and exploring a world usually as part of a mini quests with limited story interaction and development of other characters. A sub-genre of this game is the Massively Multiplayer Online Role-Playing Game (MMORPG) that can involve hundreds of thousands of people at one time.

As Aaron Conners, the writer of the games *Amped III* and *The Pandora Directive* explains, in an adventure game, telling the story is the primary focus. There are strong characters and sophisticated story development. Characters overcome obstacles to achieve a final quest. Puzzles are also an important element. *Nancy Drew: Secret of the Old Clock*

(Chapter 18) is an adventure game in the mystery sub-genre. The appeal of the mystery and adventure story is clearly that they are strongly goal oriented. The player has something to aim for, obstacles are easy to establish, and jeopardy is built into the genre.

The State of Interactive Narrative and Video Games

After a golden age of story-based adventure games in the mid-1990s, adventure games fell on hard times. Some interactive narrative adventures were poorly done and perhaps deserved to fail. But a number of adventure games with sophisticated stories, such as *Grim Fandango*, were released to rave review and critical acclaim and still did very little business. Because of this, many game publishers turned their backs on interactive narrative to focus on action games. Fortunately for lovers of interactive narrative, interest in interactive narrative eventually revived, primarily through the success of the hybrid genre: action-adventure—a game that has extensive action elements and a story. Most action-adventure games of this period, such as *Half-Life*, did not have the sophisticated stories of the classic adventure games of the mid-1990s, but they at least pointed the direction for the creation of commercially successful interactive narratives.

The major elements of this new direction for interactive narrative were the combining of different game genres and including more mature content and story elements. But other factors in the industry have also helped strengthen the resurgence of interactive narrative. A key factor is the introduction of more sophisticated game consoles that are capable of presenting content in a more cinematic and realistic fashion. This new capability has helped improve the success of Hollywood and game tie-ins and increased the convergence of narrative film/TV and the game industry. Another factor in more successful interactive narratives, particularly those tied to specific movie properties has been the involvement in games of major film narrative talents.

All of these factors have produced more recent successful video games with strong stories. Matthew Costello, the author of *The 7th Guest*, one of the most successful story based games ever, agrees that there has been a renewed interest in adding story to games. According to Costello, game companies have realized that story, characters, and dialogue are important components. They are hiring more writers with a grasp of narrative and they are starting early with the story script instead of just adding story elements to a game after the fact.

With the global video game market measured in the hundreds of billions of dollars, the outlook for the production of more games with story elements and complete interactive narratives looks strong.

Larger game budgets; more powerful consoles capable of a realistic, cinematic presentation; Hollywood convergence and story talent; blended game genres; a willingness to experiment with narrative in games; and broadband speeds on mobile devices and the web, allowing presentation of sophisticated video and animation, all point to a promising future for the interactive narrative.

Classical Linear Narrative Elements Defined

Although there are many different types of narrative, successful interactive narratives have largely focused on classical narrative, the same type of narrative that dominates linear film and video. Because of this, interactive narrative shares many of the elements of narrative film and video. Because these are forms that most readers are already familiar with, I will first review the basics of classical linear narrative in film and TV before diving into the intricacies of interactive narrative

Character

Classical linear narrative film and video are character driven. It is the character who grabs our attention and whose situation we are drawn into. Most successful film and video today clearly define their characters early in the piece. Who are the characters? Where are they from? What do they want or need, and why do they want it? What the character wants usually provides the action story of the film or video; why they want it provides the motivation for the actions and the underlying emotional story.

As an example, the classic film trilogy *The Lord of the Rings* establishes the lead character Frodo as a sincere, loyal, innocent, and cheerful nephew of his more adventurous uncle Bilbo. We learn all this information about Frodo through the simple clothes he wears, his interaction with friends, his own actions and statements, and the setting. The first time we see him, he is reading a book under a tree in a peaceful orchard. When he first hears of the power of the One Ring, he immediately wants to give it away to Gandalf. A little later he tells his adventurous uncle, "I'm not like you." But when it seems that no one else is suited to be ring bearer, Frodo does reluctantly take on the role. What Frodo wants in the film (his action need) is to destroy the One Ring, forged by the Dark Lord. Why Frodo wants to do this is to save the Shire but also to prove to himself that he has the internal courage to accomplish the task. If we are going to care about the story, it is important that we identify with this character and his needs. Identification can be achieved in a number of ways, including casting an appealing actor, creating sympathy for an underdog, and having the character do positive things. The best way to achieve identification, however, is to develop the character so that the audience clearly understands the character's needs. *The Lord of the Rings* does all of these things to get us on board with Frodo.

Structure

Once the character's needs are established, then the writer can begin to structure the script. The key elements of classical narrative structure are exposition, conflict, climax, and resolution. Figure 16–1 lays out the basic structure of the vast majority of film and TV shows produced today.

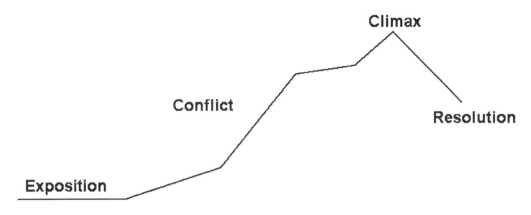

Figure 16–1 Classical linear structure

Exposition or Setup

The beginning of the story must set up the lead character, the setting, and what the character wants—the goal to be achieved or the problem to be solved. Current films and videos tend to limit pure expositional sequences at the beginning and jump right into the story, integrating the story with the exposition. Some pieces open with an action scene and then slow down the pace in the next scene for exposition. However it is done, near the beginning of a script, the audience must learn who the character is, where he or she is, and what he or she wants.

Conflict

Once the writer knows the lead character and his or her goal, then he or she can start the character on the way to achieving that goal. Of course, if the character achieves the goal in the first scene, it will be a very short story. To avoid this happening, the writer introduces conflicts or obstacles. There are three basic types of conflict:

1. Person vs. person.
2. Person vs. the environment.
3. Person vs. self.

In *The Lord of the Rings* example, there are many "persons" who oppose Frodo, particularly Gollum, the orcs, Ring Wraiths, Lord Sauron, and all their minions. The environmental obstacles include mysterious forests, snowy mountains, labyrinthine mines, and much more. The last type of conflict, person versus self, is a way of adding considerable depth to a piece. In the case of Frodo, he has serious self-doubts about his ability to carry the task to completion. These doubts are exacerbated by the evil power of the ring itself.

A number of writing critics, particularly Syd Field in Screenplay, point to a key plot point or event in the exposition that shoves the character out of the exposition and into the conflict. In Frodo's case, it occurs at the secret council in the elf land of Rivendell when he takes on the task of carrying the ring to Mordor to destroy it. Once the conflicts begin, then each conflict or obstacle should be more challenging than the last obstacle so that the story rises in intensity.

Climax

Finally, the story nears the peak of intensity, and a final event jack it up to the climax, which is where the character either achieves the goal or not. In Frodo's case, the final event is at the fires of Mordor when Frodo finally reaches his destination. However, because of the power of the Ring, Frodo has been corrupted and is unable to throw the ring into the fire. It is only by chance that another character, Gollum, tries to seize the ring for himself and ends up accidentally plummeting into the fire with the ring. With a little help from Gollum, Frodo has accomplished his physical goal of destroying the ring, but ultimately failed to accomplish his emotional goal of proving he has the strength to withstand the seductive power of the ring. This conflicted climax is one of the elements that adds power to this story. Typically, in a Hollywood film, the hero accomplishes both his physical and emotional goal.

Resolution

The resolution wraps up the story after the climax. The resolution of *The Lord of the Rings* involves the return to the Shire and ultimately Frodo's departure with the Elves to a land of peace.

In most stories, the character changes or travels a character arc, a character may start cowardly and by the end prove he or she is brave, or start the story unsure and by the end be full of confidence. Because Frodo never achieves his emotional goals and because he is so wounded by the evil power of the Ring, he also follows an arc. He travels from a point of carefree, innocence at the beginning to a point of being somber and restrained. Some critics see the journey of Frodo as one from innocence to experience or from childhood to adulthood.

Scenes and Sequences

A narrative is comprised of individual scenes and sequences. A scene is an action that takes place in one location. A sequence is a series of scenes built around one concept or event. In a tightly structured script, each scene has a mini-goal or plot point that sets up and leads us into the next scene, eventually building the sequence. Some scenes and most sequences have a beginning, middle, and end, much like the overall story.

Jeopardy

The characters' success or failure in achieving their goals has to have serious consequences for them. It is easy for the writer to set up jeopardy if it is a life-and-death situation, such as being butchered by orcs in *The Lord of the Rings*. It is harder to create this sense of importance with more mundane events. This is accomplished through properly developing the character. In a well written script, if something is important to the character, it will be important to the audience even if it is not a life and death situation.

Point of View

Point of view defines from whose perspective the story is told. The most common point of view or POV is third person or omniscient (all knowing). In this case the audience is a fly on the wall and can flit from one location to another, seeing events from many characters' points of view or from the point of view of the writer of the script. This is the point of view of *The Lord of the Rings*.

The other major type of point of view is first person or subjective point of view. In this case, the entire story is told from one character's perspective. The audience sees everything through his or her eyes. The audience can experience only what the character experiences. Used exclusively, this type of point of view has numerous practical problems. The primary one is that we never get to see the lead character's expressions except in the mirror. Because of this, stories that are told in subjective point-of-view narrative are sometimes told in third-person point of view in terms of the camera. This allows us to see the lead character. Voice-over narration is often used with subjective point of view.

Pace

Pace is the audience's experience of how quickly the events of the narrative unfold. Many short sequences, scenes, and bits of dialogue tend to make the pace move quickly; longer elements slow it down. Numerous fast-moving events in a scene also quicken pace. Writers tend to accelerate pace near a climax and slow it down for expositional and romantic scenes. A built-in time limit accelerates pace and increases jeopardy by requiring the protagonist to accomplish his or her task in a certain time frame. In *The Lord of the Rings* Frodo has to destroy the Ring before Lord Sauron and his armies amass the power to destroy all the good folks of Middle Earth.

Conclusion

The above has only scratched the surface of the complex topic of linear narrative, but it should be an adequate foundation for the interactive narrative discussion that follows. Our primary focus will be how the writing of interactive narrative differs from writing linear narrative.

17 The Elements of Interactive Narrative

Portions of this chapter originally appeared in the *Journal of Film and Video*.

Chapter Overview

The major elements of interactive narrative that must be understood by the writer include:

- The role of the player
- Character development
- Structure
- Exposition
- Plot points
- Scenes
- Pace and time
- Dialogue and other sounds

Linear vs. Interactive Narrative

Writer Matthew Costello, who has written successful films, novels, and computer games, points out a key difference between linear and interactive narrative. A film starts from characters. A novel can start with an idea and have characters gather around it. A game starts from the genre and expectations. The story world comes first. A designer comes up with a game story world for a project. Then the writer has to ask what is the world going to have in it: possible interactions, environments? What type of story does this suggest?

According to Costello, the story worlds of games are gravitating towards genre. Genres are categories of stories, such as horror, mystery, fantasy, science fiction, and crime genres. Using a genre story world makes it easier to develop a narrative because the user already understands the basic conventions of character and plot lines. The writer does not have to establish everything from scratch as in a non-genre story.

The key difference between linear narrative and interactive narrative is interactivity. With an interactive narrative, the writer gives up some control of the narrative to the game player. Finding the right balance between giving the player some control over the narrative, while allowing the writer to perform the necessary functions of the storyteller, including establishing characters and an engaging story structure—is a key challenge for the writer of interactive narrative.

DOI: 10.4324/9781003430612-22

Character and the Role of the Player

Characterization in an interactive narrative is vastly more complex than in a linear narrative because of the role of the player. In most interactive narratives, the player expects to be one of the characters in the story or at least to have significant control over the characters. The writer has to determine what this player/character gets to do and how his/her actions advance the narrative.

Player Control

The degree of the player's control over the characters is one of the first decisions in writing a program. If you are writing for an existing story engine, these choices may be already determined. So be sure to learn the capabilities of the program you are working with. The basic types of control the player is allowed are choice of scenes, the character's actions, or all the character's behavior.

Scenes

In this approach, the player can decide which path of the story the characters will choose, but once launched on that path, the characters function independently until the next branching point. *Boy Scout Patrol Theater*, an interactive narrative at the National Boy Scout museum, is a good example. The Boy Scouts in the story must decide whether to search the farm, the neighborhood, or the school. Once the player makes the choice to search the school, the characters function on their own without player interaction until the next interactive point. The characters are usually seen in third person. (See the *Boy Scout Patrol Theater* area in the "Chapters" section of this book's CD-ROM.) Many games that allow significant interactivity in most of the game will have sections where players can only choose complete scenes. These are often in the form of cut scenes—linear movie-like scenes in the middle of a game.

Actions

In some programs, the player will see the main character on the screen and can control the actions of the character, but not the dialogue. *Grand Theft Auto* works this way. We can see the lead character on screen, and we can direct him to steal cars or create other mayhem. This is a third person POV as described in the previous chapter. We do not directly control what the character says or what other characters say to them. The primary place CJ talks is in the cinematic cut scenes where we have no control. Often in games with this type of control, the scene tends to be seen in long or medium shots so that the player can direct the action.

All Behavior

This is the highest degree of interactivity. In this mode, the player chooses what the character does and what they say. In the Nancy Drew mystery games (Chapter 21), the player takes on the role of Nancy Drew in the first person POV. We do not see the character of Nancy Drew, but instead see everything through the character's eyes. This approach allows the player to essentially become the character. In the screenshot from *Nancy Drew: Curse of Blackmoor Manor*, shown in Figure 17–1, the player/Nancy Drew is talking to the rather scary aunt who is in charge of the manor. The aunt's dialogue is spoken and also appears in text in the darker color at the top of the window. In this screenshot, the player is clicking the question, "Is anyone else staying here?" which the aunt will reply to in audio and on-screen text.

Many games with interactive dialogue only show the player's choices in text and not the dialogue of the other characters as in the example above. In other games the player does not click the actual line of dialogue but instead clicks an attitude, which indicates the type of dialogue the on-screen character will speak. This way the actual dialogue becomes a surprise. Interactive dialogue works great for certain types of games, such as mysteries, but some designers feel that it overly slows the pace of genres such as action games where the lead characters sometimes never speak at all.

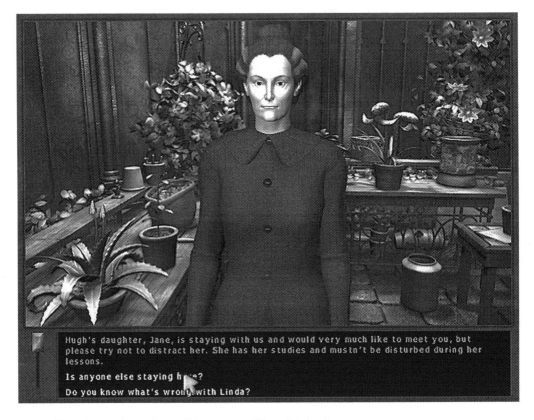

Figure 17–1 Interactive dialogue. Player controlling all behavior
© HeR Interactive Inc.

Player Control Combinations

Few programs function purely in just one of the approaches above. Many programs, such as *Amped III* (Chapter 20), combines different amounts of player control. During most of the snowboarding game play, you have complete control over the player's actions, but you can choose to take a break from snowboarding and view one of the story challenges. The story scenes are basically linear and there is no interactivity until the scene has finished.

Other games, such as *The Chronicles of Narnia: The Lion, The Witch and The Wardrobe*, allow you to change player perspective. In this case, you can choose which of the four main characters to play.

Variable Control

In some programs, players can decide on how much control they want. In *Voyeur* the player watches the events in the mansion across the street, sees the news on television, and receives telephone calls. If the player just sits and watches, the corrupt politician is the protagonist of the story. If the player decides to try to stop the corrupt politician, the player can have a major effect on the plot.

Impact of Player Options

The degree of player control, player point of view, and the type of character played in a first-person point-of-view story all have significant impact on the story.

Player as Protagonist

To maximize player interactivity and immersion in the story, one of the best options is to allow the player to become the protagonist of the story by controlling all the character's behavior and seeing the action in first-person point of view. There are, however, drawbacks to this approach. One is that it is difficult to portray certain types of action in first-person point of view. For example, how do you show someone kissing the protagonist? The player also never gets to see the protagonist's expressions and actions, which are the main ways that character is revealed. Because of this, first-person point-of-view interactive stories often rely on dialogue. Gender issues are also raised with first-person point-of-view interactive. Is the character male or female? If the character is assigned one gender, as in the Nancy Drew mysteries, are there character identification problems for the player? If no gender is assigned, how do the other characters address the player/protagonist?

If the player is the protagonist, it is also difficult for the writer to develop him or her as a complex character. If the writer does develop the protagonist in detail, you/the player are left with a fictional version of yourself who may say and do things that you would never do. The writer will also have to hope that the goal of the protagonist is something the player can identify with.

The alternative approach for the protagonist, as practiced in *Dust*, is to have a very general character, in this case, the Stranger. The player knows nothing about him, and so can perhaps more comfortably become him. But will the player be able to understand and empathize with the action and emotional needs of this sketchily drawn character?

Player Determining the Character

A way around the quandary of either defining a character that the player cannot fit into or leaving the character vague is to give the player a role in determining the character. In *Amped III*, at the beginning of the program, the player can choose the character's outfits, gender, voices (male or female), and attitude (cheeky or chill). *Grand Theft Auto* takes player definition of character one step further by having the lead character change depending on what type of activities he does. Lots of exercise, he is buff. Lots of food and riding around in cars, he gets fat. He can also shop for clothes at any number of stores. The non-playing characters in the game will also respond to the character differently based on his appearance. Having a customizable main character can change the experience of the storyline.

Player as Minor Character

A more unusual role for the player is that instead of being a major character, the player can be a minor character. The player may not seem so central to the action, but the advantage is that the portrayal of the minor character is not as crucial. If the minor character is only sketchily drawn, it will not have as much of an impact on the story as a poorly developed main character. It is also much easier to show the main action of the story in third person. For certain types of training and education programs, this type of third-person portrayal is essential. *A la rencontre de Philippe* is an interactive language program in which the player takes on the role of helping Parisian friends find an apartment. This allows the player to watch the native speakers interact in French, which was one of the goals of the program and which would have been more difficult if the player was a first-person protagonist.

Character Setup and Relationships

The player is only one of the characters in a program. Many others must be set up, but the demands of the interactive narrative do not make it easy to bring them to life. Space is always at a premium, scenes tend to be short, and character setup tends not to be interactive and thus is kept to a minimum.

An interactive writer needs to be able to introduce the characters quickly and simply. And once the characters are established, the writer also has to keep track of the different relationships of all the characters in all the possible versions of the story, using often complex character charts.

Structure and Navigation

Just as in a linear piece, in an interactive narrative, once the character and his or her goal are established, then the basic structure of the story needs to be developed. In interactive writing, however, this is far more complex than the simple linear structure illustrated in Figure 16–1 in the previous chapter. Because, in an interactive narrative, the writer must also consider navigation between all the elements of the narrative structure.

Will Wright, the designer of the popular *Sims* series of games, explains the difference between linear and interactive narrative well:

> When I watch Indiana Jones escaping from the Temple of Doom (in the movie of the same name), it's not what happens to him that I find interesting; it's what might have happened had he slipped in front of the boulder. Dozens of potential failure states are compressed into a few seconds of action and transmitted to my brain with amazing efficiency.
>
> Game players are given the ability to explore a space of possibilities—the phase space—and this is the real strength of the medium. It's sort of like the difference between a roller coaster and a car. The coaster is on a fixed track. It's a very exciting track, but it's always the same. I can add branches to the track, but it can still be viewed as a finite amount of track. If I put someone in a car, however, they can go almost anywhere. Since

I can't simulate the whole world in my games, I have to put up barriers and limit where they can go in the car.

(Bunn and Herz)

The road with barriers he describes are essentially the structure of interactive narrative. How the user can move between roads is the navigation. The most common interactive narrative structures are described below.

Linear Structure

Defined

Strictly speaking, this is not an interactive structure but it is often used in interactive projects. Linear structure has no branching choices for the user.

Use

Linear structure is frequently used in interactive narrative to set up the story. All of the narratives profiled in this book open with linear sequences before user interaction is possible. Linear video is also sometimes played within an interactive piece for additional background and to tie interactive segments together. The *New England Economic Adventure* (Chapter 19) uses linear video to present information that the audience will later use interactively in exercises and games.

Linear Structure with Scene Branching

Defined

This structure allows the user to choose alternative scenes, but after these alternative scenes are played out, the user is always routed back to the same main story line.

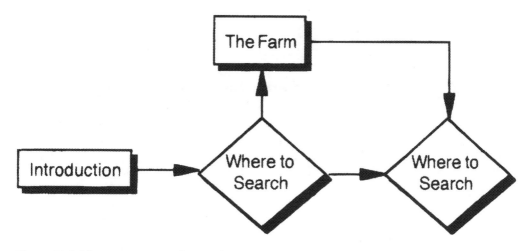

Figure 17–2 Linear structure with scene branching

Use

This is a common structure in training and educational narratives. In *Boy Scout Patrol Theater* the basic structure is a linear story about trying to find a lost girl. At various decision points, however, the players get to make a choice, such as choosing to search the farm, the school, or the neighborhood. If they choose the farm, then they detour momentarily from the main story and search the farm, but eventually return to the main story (see Figure 17–2). A similar structure is used in narrative, corporate training programs where the user takes on a role and tries to accomplish a task. Players can choose alternate scenes for helping to accomplish the task, but are always routed back to the main task scenario.

A variation on this approach is the structure has only one critical story path through the game. The user can explore different scenes off the critical path, but they usually cannot get very far on any alternate path. This structure is basically a linear story that sometimes appears to present alternate scenes. But if the players venture down one of those alternate scenes and stay too long, they can expect to fail the task or get into serious trouble, even death.

Hierarchical Branching

Defined

This structure involves taking the story in a completely different direction based on the viewer's choice at a preset decision point. This is a common informational architecture but presents problems in interactive narrative.

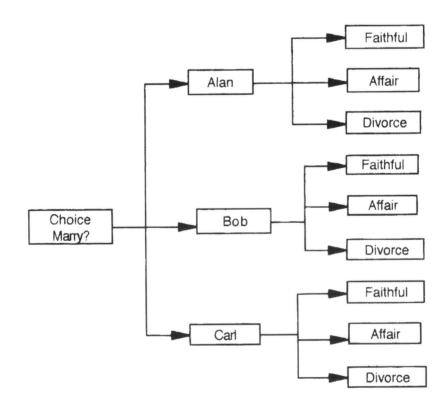

Figure 17.3 Hierarchical branching explosion

Used in a Complete Story

Using hierarchical branching to take the complete story into different directions has limited options. For example, as illustrated in Figure 17–3, the character comes to a point where she can choose one of three options: marry Alan, marry Bob, or marry Carl. After that choice is played out, then the character can choose to be faithful, have an affair, or get divorced. The problem here is obvious: the number of choices increases exponentially. Adding one more set of choices to this chart would mean an additional 27 scenes, the next level would be 81 additional scenes, and the level after that 243 scenes! This is called combinatorial explosion. This is clearly too much material for a writer to present or a viewer to access.

Used with Endings

Although it is rare for an entire story to be completed with hierarchical branching, it is commonly used for the ending of programs. This device gives the viewer a feeling of greater control over the narrative, and branching explosion is obviously limited because the story ends. The end of *The 11th Hour*, where the viewer must choose to save one of three women, is a good example. Each woman equals a different ending to the story. The wrong choice is oblivion; the right choice is bliss.

Used with Dialogue

This type of branching is also used in interactive dialogue where the user makes a dialogue choice that leads to several new choices. This has less chance of the interactions going out of control, as in a full story, because each dialogue scene is limited.

Parallel Path Stories

Defined

With parallel structure, several versions of the same story play parallel to each other. Depending on choices that the player makes in the story, he or she can move from one path to another. This is a way to give the player an option of multiple paths in a story without the branching explosion of hierarchical branching.

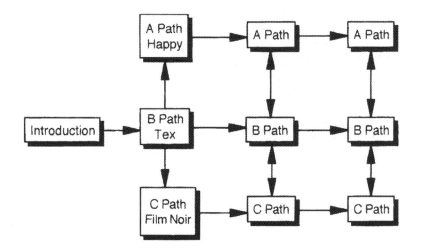

Figure 17.4 Parallel path stories lead to one of several possible endings

Use

The Pandora Directive (Figure 17–4) uses parallel path stories. After a linear introduction, the player enters an interactive scene. Depending on the choices that he or she makes, the player can move up to: the A path, which is a Hollywood-type version of the story where the hero wins true love; the C path, a bleak, film noir experience of the story where everything goes wrong; or the B path, which is a middle ground. Each new interactive scene gives the player options to move back and forth between paths depending on the choices they make. Depending on the choices they have made earlier in the game, they arrive at one of several possible endings. Although this can be an effective structure, it is challenging to use in complete games because of the difficulty of tracking and creating multiple story paths and the changing relationships of the characters.

It is a little easier to use parallel path structure as part of a more linear game instead of the overall structure. In this case, the character has several different paths to choose in a particular scene that will ultimately affect the ending of the story.

Linked Worlds—String of Pearls Architecture

Defined

This approach moves away from simple branching. A string of pearls architecture is a linked series of worlds structures connected by plot points or tasks that the player must accomplish to move forward in the narrative. As defined at the beginning of Chapter 16, the worlds approach lets the user explore a location. By itself, a worlds structure cannot form a coherent narrative, but combined with other forms it can.

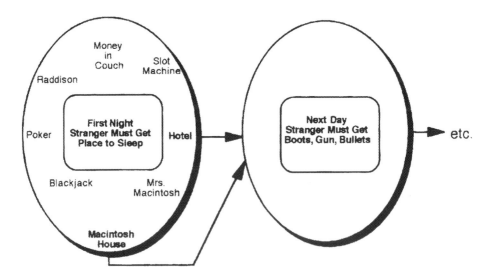

Figure 17–5 String of pearls structure

Use

Dust: A Tale of the Wired West uses the string of pearls approach. When the player/Stranger first comes to town in the middle of the night, he is free to roam the town of Diamondback for as long as he wants. There are poker games to be played, hookers to talk to, and mysterious buildings to explore. This is a clear worlds structure—interesting, but by itself there is no story.

To move to the next day and advance the narrative, the player/Stranger must find a place to sleep. He can either stay at the hotel or get one of the town's citizens to take him in. There are a number of ways to accomplish this goal. To stay at the hotel, he needs money. He can get cash at the saloon if he is lucky at blackjack, poker, or the slot machine. If he is nosy, he might also find the four bucks that somebody lost in the hotel couch. But when he does get the money, the hotel owner says there are no vacancies. To get a room, it helps to meet Raddison, another character who lives there and who will introduce the Stranger (the player) to the owner. An alternative to the hotel is to get a citizen to take the player/Stranger home. To accomplish this, the player needs to sweet-talk the abrasive Mrs. Macintosh.

The player can perform all of these actions in any order desired, but eventually he or she has to find the right combination of actions to get a place to sleep and thus exit from the first night of the story and begin the next day or pearl on the string. In the second pearl, the next day's action, the player must get boots, guns, and bullets before moving on to the third pearl (see Figure 17–5). All of the player's accomplishments move the story forward to the final shootout and to solving the mystery in one of six possible endings.

In addition to being used in the classic *Dust*, this worlds structure linked by a narrative thread has become a popular architecture in many other games. For example, *Grand Theft Auto* uses this structure. A series of tasks to accomplish form the critical path of the game. These missions must eventually be taken on to move to all the locations (worlds) of the game, but you can decide when you want to take on the mission. You are free to explore GTA's huge virtual world as long as you want. *Amped III* (Chapter 20) is a game that is mostly a snowboard simulation but also provides the opportunity to explore the locations of top boarding resorts. Similar to the other string of pearls examples mentioned, *Amped III* has a series of story challenges that link together the simulation sections and form the core narrative of the story.

In some ways, the ideal story for a string of pearls structure is a mystery story. This is the structure used in the Nancy Drew mysteries (Chapter 21). Nancy Drew and any detective's goal in a mystery story is to discover what happened—the narrative of the crime. Initially the detective is in the top or outer world of the crime, but as she gets clues and solves puzzles, she gradually gains access to the inner worlds of the narrative, finally concluding with the mystery's solution. See Figure 21–1 near the beginning of Chapter 21 for a diagram of the mystery version of the string of pearls structure as used in the Nancy Drew games.

Variable State Environment and Types of Links

Defined

The most sophisticated interactive narratives, many of which have been discussed previously in this chapter, have moved beyond direct links and simple branching to a variable state environment. With the help of software and sophisticated design that responds in a sensitive way to the player's actions, there are multiple outcomes to scenes, depending on where the player has been and to whom he or she has talked. In short, the environment responds to the player, much as it does in real life.

A variable state environment can take into account hundreds of actions as opposed to just the A or B choices in branching. And as each interaction is played differently, it will yield different responses. Different combinations of different interactions will also yield different responses.

Use

In a detective story, what the murderer cleans up after the murder and how he/she escapes, affect what clues can be used against him and the testimony of witnesses. In *The Pandora Directive*, if you as the player are tactless with your girlfriend, you will get into a fight. This causes you to get drunk, and because you are drunk, you are unable to save a nightclub singer's life. These types of convoluted reactions to the player's actions are far more like real life than the direct reaction to a player's choices in some video games.

Exposition or Setup

Exposition is another issue that presents special challenges for the interactive writer. Exposition involves introducing characters, setting, and story situation to the player. Exposition is particularly important in games because the player will need that information to make choices and take actions later in the game. Some designers feel that the key is to make the exposition entertaining and brief. Get the story setup and get on with the game. *Nancy Drew: Secret of the Old Clock* presents the exposition efficiently and entertainingly. The game opens with Nancy driving her roadster to the Lilac Inn, the location of the mystery. As she is driving, we hear in voice-over what sounds like a 1930s radio show (the era of the game). The radio show/voice-over gives us the key background in audio illustrated with cuts to game scenes illustrating the narrator's description. When Nancy's car pulls into the driveway of the Inn, the radio show/exposition is complete.

See this Nancy Drew video on the book's website.

Amped III also chooses a brief introductory scene to introduce the characters and setting. In this case, the characters are riding up the chairlift at a ski resort and the lead character/player is wearing a head-to-toe pink bunny suit. He is meeting a dare, which is to ski the mountain in the funny suit. Through the banter about the dare and the suit, we get to know the characters and the basic situation.

Other designers, such as David Riordan, try to avoid introductory scenes. He said that if you spend time introducing the characters, the viewer is not being asked to do anything, which is a problem in interactive media. Instead, he said that you need to discover the backstory as you go through the story.

One way to accomplish this is through the use of sets and props to give exposition. They can provide background information subtly, such as a gun in a suitcase, or more overtly, such as a letter the player is allowed to read, or even active props, such as a television set that gives background information on the characters. The use of props in interactive media differs from their use in linear video because in interactive narrative, the player gets to choose which props to examine, has far more props to choose from, and can do things that would be impossible in linear, such as move closer to a letter to read it or choose to turn on the television.

Another key way for a player to learn exposition is through what other characters say to the player as scenes unfold. For example, a friend in the game can give the player key background. A variation on this approach is to introduce a stranger to the story. Someone in the story now has to explain the story background and characters to the stranger and in the process to the player/us.

Designing a game around an established story genre helps with exposition. For example, if a game is in the spy genre, we already know a lot about the story conventions for this genre from secret agent movies and books, such as the James Bond series. Because of the shared genre narrative conventions, many of the story elements do not have to be explained again in the game. We know that the secret agent character will have access to extraordinary gadgets, will be sexy, and must operate primarily on his own or with the help of a beautiful lady.

Guaranteeing that Essential Exposition Is Seen

Because this is interactive media, depending on the game, the player may have a choice to not view certain scenes, including exposition. One solution is to require viewing of the exciting linear exposition scenes, such as those discussed earlier. As soon as the game starts, the exposition plays. Most games will allow the introduction to be skipped on later plays of the game. A somewhat dated approach is to include the back-story in a separate document or book that goes along with the game. A better solution is to design the game to lure the player into choosing the essential exposition, often with engaging interactive devices, such as televisions that can be viewed, mini-games of missions that reveal background, and interesting game characters who want to tell us everything we need to know.

Demonstrating How the Program Works

A type of exposition unique to games is that players need an explanation of how the game works. What can the player do? How do they move? Can they pick things up? How does the interactive dialogue work? The best programs integrate this information into the exposition and do not make the users read vast amounts of instructions before they can play.

One way to do this is to set up a simple situation at the beginning of the program that shows how the game works. For example, the player is confronted with a nasty dog. To get by this dog, the player must pick up objects, talk to characters, access help, and move about. A less integrated approach is to have a tutorial that plays a scene for the user and shows what to do.

Plot Points

Plot points or beats are story information that moves the plot forward. For example, in *Lord of the Rings*, it is a major plot point when Gandalf tells Frodo that he must destroy the one ring. The point moves the story forward in a major way. In an interactive story, making essential plot points is as difficult as presenting exposition. Because the user can choose which scenes to view, there is no guarantee that the user will choose a specific scene and learn a specific plot point.

One solution is to place essential plot points in a required sequence. With this option, the player cannot learn later plot points and progress in the game until they have seen earlier ones. In the example from *GTA* in the previous paragraph, the player must choose the first cut scene/mission before they can progress in the story to additional major missions and complete the game's story. The first cut scene is not actually forced on the player. They have the option of not choosing it, but if they do not choose it, they are limited to the initial location and basic crime activities of stealing cars and having fights.

Another solution to the problem of guaranteeing key plot points are seen is to put several plot points in a scene. This way if the user selects a scene, multiple plot points will be established. Another approach is to have the same information appear in a number of different scenes. The difficulty here is that the information can't be presented in exactly the same way or players will get bored if they select several of these scenes. The solution is to feed the essential information into multiple scenes but to do it differently each time.

In a narrative that includes multiple story variations, establishing plot points is even more complex than setting up exposition. Often much of the exposition will be the same for all possible stories. For example, in *Voyeur*, the back-story on the corrupt politician and his desire to be president does not change from story to story. Plot points are, however, usually different in each story variation. This means that essential plot points have to be established for each story. It also means that scenes that are common to all variations cannot include plot points that contradict the plot in a specific story variation. Some writers use charts of plot points to keep all of these elements clear.

Scenes

As the examples above suggest, strong scene writing is important to the interactive writer. Writer Maria O'Meara believes that crafting a scene well is the most valuable technique of the interactive writer. Every experience in an interactive ought to be a tiny story or scene. Even if it's short, it still needs to have a beginning, middle, and end. Because in many cases, the player can choose which scenes to access, an idea cannot be split across multiple scenes in case the player does not select all the scenes presenting the idea. Instead, each scene must be complete.

Scenes also tend to be smaller in interactive. When writing about a character in a location, you need to consider all the scenes that might happen in that location based on character choices.

The interactive writer, in other words, must write vertically as well as horizontally. He or she cannot be concerned only with what scene follows another. The writer also has to be aware of what other scenes in other possible stories might be connected to this one. Some interactive writers script ten or fifteen related scenes at the same time in order to keep tabs on all the connections. And rewriting can be ghastly. Change one element in one of fifteen connected scenes, and all the other scenes need to be rewritten.

Pace and Time

An interactive narrative has no set running time. It depends on how the player plays the game. The challenge here for the writer is to create a consistent sense of time in the piece when a player might spend 20 minutes in a scene or might skip it altogether. Because time is also an important factor in pace, how does the writer deal with the way this variability of time affects pacing?

Player Creates the Pace

In a linear narrative, such as a movie, the writer can carefully create and sequence a number of scenes to create a faster or slower pace. In interactive narrative, the player creates the pace. For example, a player goes into a haunted house and has to find a way out. The writer's job is to make sure that the scenes are dramatic in themselves and that the player is surprised when things happen. How the player interacts with this environment creates the pace of the sequence, but that interaction is affected by the kinds of elements the writer-designer gives the player to interact with. Another way to heighten the feeling of pace is to create a sense of urgency. Set up the story so that if players dawdle too long in any one location, they have a good chance of being killed. If the player has to keep moving, it keeps the pace of the narrative moving.

Interactive Media Pace = Series Pace

The combined running times of multiple plays of an interactive movie is much longer than the running time of a two-hour feature film. An interactive movie can be thought of more like a TV series. For example, the writer can deal with much of the exposition the first time the game is played, which allows the pace to be increased in later plays.

Manipulating Time to Affect Pace

Other writers and designers have actively manipulated time to affect the pace of the story. For example, the player has to achieve his goals in a set period of time. This type of game often has a clock in the game that tracks time and adds urgency. In the real time of playing the game, going to a library and talking to someone may only take 30 seconds, but in game time the player may be deducted an hour. And while he or she is at one location, other scenes happen whether the player sees them or not, just as they would in real life. If the player is knocked out, he or she will miss several scenes and be docked 80 minutes on the clock. This time manipulation can add a sense of urgency to the game. The story material stays the same; it is how it is played that affects the overall pacing.

Nancy Drew: Secret of the Old Clock uses a similar device but it evolves more from the characters. The owner of the Inn is a young girl who is getting progressively more upset by all the weird events. Nancy has to solve the crime before the girl gives up and sells the Inn—the goal of the crooks.

An interesting use of time is if the time spent in one scene affects what happens in later scenes. For example, in one scene the heroes have to battle a group of villains to find the heroine who is held captive. If the heroes take a long time to defeat the first set of villains, the villains holding the heroine have more time to hide her, increasing the difficulty of the final rescue. This use of time is an important step in making games reflect how time is experienced in real life. It can also give the designer more control over pacing. For example, if the player spends a long time on one scene, the next scene could automatically be altered to increase the pace of the sequence.

Dialogue and Other Sound

One of the difficulties of characterization in interactive media is the limited dialogue that is allowed because many scenes are very short, and it usually takes longer to develop a strong dialogue scene. The interactive writer has to learn how to weave together these short dialogue scenes into effective sequences.

The potential use of other sounds, particularly nonsynchronous sounds, is also important. *Under a Killing Moon* uses the tradition of the ironic voice-over in the detective story and includes over five hours of voice-over that gives the player information about characters, objects, and situations. Other games use phone calls to establish plot points and back-story. Ambient sounds are also essential for setting mood. Harsh industrial sounds can create an uneasy feel, sounds of nature create a feeling of peace and calm.

Conclusion

This chapter provides an overview of some of the common elements and structures of interactive narrative. The next chapters will examine specific interactive narrative programs to explore how these structure and elements were utilized in specific situations. Every project is different, sometimes storytelling is fairly linear and structured. Other times there is great randomness and more freedom in how the player participates in the story. There is no one right way to create interactive narrative as the case studies in the following chapters will demonstrate.

18 Adapting a Classic Book to a Computer Game for the Female Audience

Nancy Drew: Secret of the Old Clock

Summary

Name of production: *Nancy Drew: Secret of the Old Clock*
Writer: Anne Collins-Ludwick; Lead Designer: Mari Tokuda
Developer: HeR Interactive, Inc.
Audience: 10 and up, rated E for "Everyone" by the ESRB
Presentation location: Home, where entertainment games are played
Subject: Nancy Drew Mystery Adventure
Goal: Entertain
Architecture: Parallel Paths, linear, dialogue branching

The script samples and images used in this chapter are reproduced by permission of HeR Interactive Inc. © HeR Interactive Inc.
Nancy Drew is a registered trademark of Simon & Schuster, Inc. and is used under license. Copyright in the Nancy Drew books and characters is owned by Simon & Schuster, Inc.

Program Description and Background

Program Description

Nancy Drew: Secret of the Old Clock is the 12th in the series of Nancy Drew mystery computer games produced by HeR Interactive. In these games, the player takes on the role of Nancy Drew and sees and hears the events of the game from her perspective. This is a first-person game; we never actually see Nancy Drew. The *Nancy Drew: Secret of the Old Clock* game was inspired by the first Nancy Drew mystery book ever published. The game is set in 1930, the same year as the original book's publication.

In this game, Nancy drives her blue roadster to the Lilac Inn to help seventeen-year-old Emily Crandall, who has just inherited the Inn from her mother. At the Inn, an anxious Emily explains to Nancy that she was surprised when her rich uncle left most of his wealth to Richard Topham, an expert on paranormal activities. Emily believes there is a second will that leaves her uncle's money to her.

This sets Nancy off on her investigation. Nancy talks to the paranormal expert Richard Topham, the town banker Jim Archer, and Emily's flakey new guardian Marian Aborn.

DOI: 10.4324/9781003430612-23

Nancy soon learns that Emily's uncle was a paranoid eccentric who devised elaborate puzzles and games to protect his privacy and wealth. In order to find out more about the uncle and his will, Nancy has to solve these puzzles and games. The solutions to puzzles gradually point the way to secret tunnels, hidden rooms full of gadgets, and finally the solution to the mystery. The game has two levels of game play: Junior and Senior Detective

Production Background

Nancy Drew: Secret of the Old Clock was developed and produced by HeR Interactive Inc. of Bellevue Washington. HeR Interactive was founded in 1995 to create interactive games for the female audience. This is an audience that was, and is today, largely underserved in the gaming industry, which tends to focus on action and sports games aimed towards young males.

To ensure success, HeR Interactive licensed the game rights to an established name with female audiences—Nancy Drew mystery books. The Nancy Drew mysteries have been a success with girls of all ages since the first book was published in 1930. There are currently more than two hundred million Nancy Drew books in print worldwide.

HeR Interactive also knew it was important to produce a high-quality product at a reasonable price. To do this, they set a firm six-month production schedule for each Nancy Drew game, producing two games a year. Each game uses the same basic game engine, but each new game has different characters, locations, puzzles, and game engine innovations. For example, in *Secret of the Old Clock*, players can drive around in Nancy's car for the first time and they can spend and earn money.

The HeR Interactive formula for success could be summarized as:

- Find an underserved segment of the audience.
- License a known brand.
- Produce a good-quality product at a reasonable price through careful production scheduling and quality control.

An aspiring game writer or designer might consider this formula and think of other underserved audiences to write for instead of attempting to duplicate current hits.

Anne Collins-Ludwick was the writer and producer of *Secret of the Old Clock*. Before being involved in writing for games, Collins-Ludwick wrote for television. She was the Story Editor on *Vegas* and *Fantasy Island*, wrote scripts for *The New Twilight Zone*, and wrote and edited scripts for the entire eight year run of the detective show, *Matlock*.

When *Matlock* ended, Anne worked in web development and online games before joining HeR Interactive. She has an M.A. in Radio/Television/Film Production from the University of Texas at Austin.

Comparing TV and game writing, Collins-Ludwick says:

Computer games, especially the Nancy Drew games, are a lot like TV shows, in that you have a main character who meets and talks to other characters in the course of solving some big problem. Although technically the two media are quite different, the principles that guide the writing and production of their content are amazingly similar.

(Collins-Ludwick)

Collins-Ludwick stresses that writing the Nancy Drew games is very collaborative. She is part of a team with the designers and other creative team members who all contribute to the final game story and design.

The lead designer on *Secret of the Old Clock* was Mari Tokuda, who worked closely with executive producer Robert Riedl. Tokuda holds degrees in Zoology and Creative Writing from the University of Washington.

Goals and Challenges Writing *Nancy Drew: Secret of the Old Clock*

Goals

Many of the goals in creating *Secret of the Old Clock* are shared with other games in the Nancy Drew series. The writer and designers wanted to create a game that would appeal to their target female audience in a broad age range from ten to adult. They wanted the game to be an effective mystery, while still allowing significant interactivity, puzzles, and game play. Last, they wanted to add some new elements to this version of the game engine to make the game play fresh for repeat players of the Nancy Drew series.

Challenges

There were several challenges to achieving the above goals:

- Adapting a 1930s book to a 21st century computer game.
- Developing a single game that would be challenging and interesting both to a preteen and a late teens female, plus still have some nostalgia interest for older women.
- Accomplishing all of the above, particularly the period elements within budget and schedule.

Meeting the Challenge of Adapting a 1930s Book to a 21st Century Computer Game: The Process of Writing *Secret of the Old Clock*

Criteria for Choosing a Book for a Nancy Drew Game

Adapting a book to a computer game has many of the same issues as adapting a book to film or television. A book's action must be visualized. Viewers and players do not want to listen to lengthy narration, dialogue, and particularly internal dialogue, which can be an important part of a book. Dialogue in games (and film/TV) needs to be shorter than what is often in a book, more conversational in tone because it is actually being spoken, with more interaction between two or more characters instead of long speeches or musings.

In addition to the issues above that are shared with film and TV, there are issues unique to writing for a game. A major issue is that, as in the case of the Nancy Drew games, the book may have to be adapted to an existing game engine, which has specific requirements. The Nancy Drew engine is based on the user finding clues and solving mysteries, because of this, the story on which a Nancy Drew game is based needs:

- intriguing locations for the user to explore to find clues, but the number of locations must be limited because of cost and user orientation
- interesting characters for the player (Nancy Drew) to talk to

- potential for puzzles and activities to be integrated into the story
- objects as clues in the story that can be created in a game and viewed or manipulated by a player.

Besides the needs of the game engine, the HeR Interactive team added another restriction on themselves as explained by Anne Collins-Ludwick, the writer of *Secret of the Old Clock*:

> To never to show Nancy, her family or her friends in our games is a stipulation that we imposed on ourselves. This was not because of game engine limitations, but because we'd rather leave what Nancy and associates look like up to the imagination of our Players, which affords them the pleasure of believing that Nancy looks just like they do, that Bess and George look just like their best friends, that Carson looks just like their dad, etc.
>
> (Collins-Ludwick)

Choosing the Book and Product Concept

With the above criteria in mind and no book yet chosen, the task to develop the concept fell to the creative director at that time, Max Holechek, and later to lead designer Mari Tokuda. The first task was to choose the Nancy Drew book(s) the game would be based on. This choice is explained in the Initial Design Outline. This document is the first stage of story development and includes the product concept, characters, and narratives.

Initial Design Outline (Product Concept Section)

Product concept:
As Creative Director, acting as Lead Designer for ND12, I requested permission to use Nancy's first adventure, *Secret of the Old Clock*, as the basis for the game. In order to differentiate the game's visual style from the Nancy Drew games that preceded it as well as showcase the specific elements that have contributed to Nancy Drew's unending popularity, I also requested that *Secret of the Old Clock* game storyline take place in 1930, the year in which the first four Nancy Drew Mysteries were published. These requests were approved by the HeR Interactive President, the V.P of Marketing and Sales, and by Simon and Schuster.

Concept challenges:
Secret of the Old Clock was a difficult book to adapt to the HeR Interactive Nancy Drew game format. The main challenges were that Nancy, her family, and her recurring friends can never be viewed in the HI games, yet most of the action of the book takes place in or around River Heights and greatly involves Nancy's home and family. Second, *Secret of the Old Clock* is much less of a mystery story as it is an adventure tale. Because of this, the crime or mystery aspects of the book are, at best, flimsy.

Challenge solutions:
I studied the first four Nancy Drew books as they were originally written in 1930. (*Secret of the Old Clock*, *The Hidden Staircase*, *The Bungalow Mystery*, and *The Mystery at Lilac Inn*.) Though I found the storylines of all the books too weak to base a game upon

```
individually, I took some of the strongest and most identifiable
aspects of each book and wove them together to create a new, cohesive
story. The new story not only stands solidly on its own, but it
equally represents the spirit and basic conflict of all four books. In
the end, the Secret of the Old Clock game will be a tribute to all of
Nancy's original 1930 adventures.
```

Note that his description of the book's story's as flimsy means in terms of what would work in the Nancy Drew mystery game engine. As books, the stories hold up just fine.

Defining Characters and Narrative: Initial Design Outline

Once the books are chosen and the basic concept is approved, the next step in the development of a Nancy Drew game is describing the key characters and the basic story narrative. The Nancy Drew engine allows four main characters or suspects besides Nancy Drew. The narrative at this point does not include interactivity, but just lays out the main beats of a story, similar to a film treatment. The narrative and characters are also included in the Initial Design Outline referenced above. Below are samples from this same document describing characters and narrative.

Initial Design Outline (Character and Narrative Section Excerpts)

The Secret of the Old Clock –
Game Characters:

```
Emily Crandall
A 17 year old, casual school chum of Nancy's. Up until recently, Emily
and her mother ran a popular roadside restaurant, the Lilac Inn, but
the untimely death of the mother has closed the restaurant for a few
weeks until matters are settled. It's Emily wish to continue the
family business, and is looking forward to officially owning the
property when she turns 19.

Marian Aborn
37-year-old Marian is an old, close friend of Emily's mother. It was
their agreement that Marian would become Emily's legal guardian should
anything happen and Marian has come to care for Emily and assist in
running the Inn for a year or more. Marian has a reputation for being
a skilled aviator and amateur archeologist.
```

(Book Author's Note: The rest of the characters are described in a similar manner in the full Initial Design Outline.)

Game narrative:
```
The story opens with Nancy arriving at the Lilac Inn in her blue
roadster. Nancy wishes to check-in on and support Emily, as Nancy can
relate to her recent tragedy. The Inn has been closed for a time, but
is rescheduled to reopen within the week.
    After meeting Emily and having a brief introduction to Emily's new
guardian, the friendly and outgoing Marian, the Inn shakes with a
stove explosion in the kitchen. Amid shouts, the women take action to
put out the fire and keep it from spreading.
```

After the fire has successfully been extinguished and the fire marshal has assessed the damage, Marian tells Nancy that the kitchen was mostly spared, but the large stove is too badly damaged to use. Money is very tight and Marian is not sure how it will be replaced. The Inn may have to be sold. Marian says that she is concerned about Emily and how she'll react to this additional tragedy in her life. She says that Emily has been behaving in an increasingly curious manner and Marian fears for the poor girl's nerves.

Emily has indeed taken the news very badly and she confides her woes to Nancy. Emily loves the Inn and feels akin to its many regulars. She knows that her mother would have wanted her do whatever she could to save the Inn and Emily says that she's ready to do so ... even though the prospects seem grim.

Emily also relates the story of her Uncle Josiah Crowley who died just before her mother did. Emily and her mother had been assisted financially from time to time by her eccentric, gregarious uncle and he promised that they would be taken care of upon his death. However, to their surprise, Crowley's will only left them worthless stocks (that had been worth several thousands of dollars before the Wall Street crash) and his remaining assets were bequeathed to Richard Topham's Physic Science Organization, of which Crowley had been a sponsor.

Emily feels that there has been an error and that Josiah must have left a second will somewhere. If it could be found, the inn would be saved! Nancy promises to take the case.

Josiah Crowley used to live roughly a quarter mile away from the Inn and Nancy figures that his house would be a good place to start the search. When she gets to the house, it is revealed that Richard Topham, the new property owner, is now living there. After allowing Nancy a brief tour and an explanation of his work, Topham cuts the visit short when he realizes that Nancy is looking for a second will. Nancy gets all but the bum's rush out the door.

The quest also takes Nancy to the local bank, where she meets Jim Archer. Nancy is curious if Crowley has left any unclaimed assets at the bank (safety deposit boxes, etc.) and Jim seems very eager to help her. So eager, in fact, that Nancy senses that he's quite taken with her. Unfortunately, nothing is found at the bank. Jim promises to visit Nancy and Emily at the Inn soon.

Nancy's investigation reveals that Josiah was a kooky guy and was rather obsessed with the safety of his valuables. Finding records of his assets proves difficult, as he has hidden them behind layers of codes, riddles and puzzles. Her first lead is a journal she finds in an old clock that he left with Emily's mother.

Though Carson Drew and Nancy's old chum, Helen Corning, are quite busy (Carson with a big case, Helen a counselor at a Girl's Summer Camp), they assist Nancy with the case via phone calls and written letters when they can.

In the full Initial Design Outline the complete concept, all the characters and the full narrative are described. The above is just a sample for purposes of illustration.

Collins-Ludwick, the *Old Clock* game writer, said that the designer works closely with the writer. The designer primarily does the puzzles, broad story line, and interactions. The writer is in charge of writing all dialogue, voice-overs and getting them recorded. The process is very collaborative between designer and writer.

Structuring the Interactivity: The Project Flowchart

After the narrative and characters are laid out in the Initial Design Outline, the next step is designing the interactivity. This is done primarily by the designer in the project flowchart but with the writer's collaboration.

The actual chart is very complex. Before viewing a sample of the actual chart, it will be helpful to understand the basic game structure. Please refer to Figure 19–1. This flowchart is simplified for the sake of illustration. In the actual game, there are many more locations, puzzles, activities, etc. The structure of the Nancy Drew games is a string of pearls structure as discussed in Chapter 17. The game presents a series of locations or worlds that Nancy can search. As she uncovers more clues, additional worlds are available to her, and she moves forward in the narrative.

Looking at the chart in Figure 18–1, notice that after the introduction, the player can:

- choose to go to several locations
- move from location to location without completing all game elements in one location, but eventually must complete all major elements to solve the game
- move back and sideways on paths to various locations and even redo some of the puzzles, but to move forward new puzzles have to be solved
- use material from one location to solve puzzles in another location.

All major elements eventually lead to the final puzzle, which must be solved by the player to unravel the mystery.

One of the challenges of this type of structure is to integrate puzzles and activities so they do not slow the story pace but do help move the mystery forward. The puzzles and activities in this game were integrated primarily by establishing the character of Josiah Crowley as an eccentric who created all sorts of puzzles and games to provide security for his possessions and ideas. Once this basic premise is accepted, then the existence of many of the puzzles make sense. Puzzles and activities not directly related to Josiah Crowley were sometimes harder to justify.

The other major challenge with the structure as illustrated in Figure 18–1 is to give players the impression of significant interactivity, while still maintaining control of the unfolding of the basically linear mystery. The player is allowed interactivity through dialogue choices, activities, puzzles, and freedom to move from location to location by walking or driving. But the game's writer and designer are constantly nudging the player into the right direction to solve the mystery. Nudging techniques include:

- comments in the conversations, such as Emily's guardian telling Nancy Drew that she has to talk to Emily
- voice-overs by others and Nancy Drew herself that indicate the importance of an item or a possible follow-up activity
- written assets, such as books, newspapers, etc. that Nancy can read
- hints delivered via the telephone from Nancy's dad or friends
- Nancy's Journal and Task List, which are combined in her notebook. These are available at any time from buttons on the main interface (see Figure 18–2). The journal recaps key information discovered so far. The Task List for Junior Detectives lists the things Nancy has to do to solve the mystery. The game writer has to write both the Journal and Task List.

All of these tools work together to help the player get to the successful conclusion of the game while still maintaining the impression of interactivity.

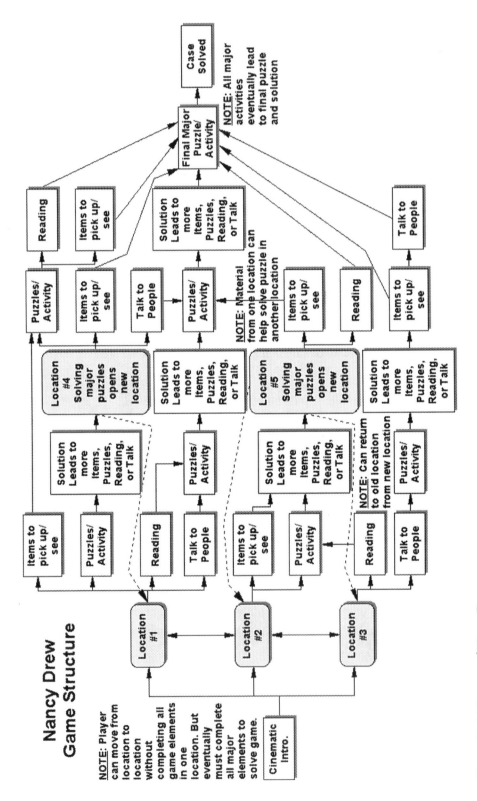

Figure 18–1 Diagram of Nancy Drew game structure

Figure 18–2 Main interface showing buttons for Tools, Journal, and Money

Keeping the structure in Figure 18–1 in mind, now look at Figure 18–3, which is a section of the actual flowchart used to structure *Secret of the Old Clock*. Note that this chart follows the same structure as the simple chart shown earlier, but is more complex and each symbol has specific labels. This is only a small section of the complete game chart, but it does illustrate many of the actual chart conventions. These include: coding of symbols to indicate type of game element, indicating where money is spent, and use of dashed lines to indicate non-essential action. A player can perform a non-essential action, but it is not absolutely necessary in order to win the game.

The production flowchart is a key tool in planning the interactivity of the Nancy Drew games. The first iteration (version) of the flowchart is basically the story line as described in the initial outline. As the design and writing process progresses, puzzles, games, conversations. and other interactions are added to move the story forward and develop the mystery.

The game is usually designed so that all options are not open to the user at the beginning. Otherwise, it would be overwhelming to have too many initial choices. Instead, several locations are available to explore and a few individuals are willing to talk. As the player solves puzzles, finds items, and completes activities, more options open up to the user. These additional options can be new locations or additional people to talk to.

For example, when the player/Nancy Drew first tries to talk to Richard Topham, the paranormal expert, Topham will not talk with the player until they first solve a logic puzzle

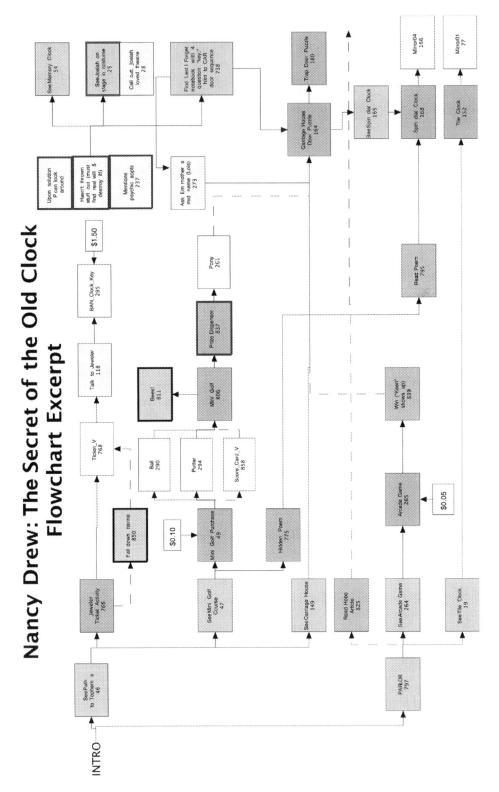

Figure 18–3 Section of *Secret of the Old Clock* production flowchart

and prove their intelligence. Topham does not want to waste time with a dullard. Another example is that the door to the carriage house behind Josiah Crowley's old house has an elaborate word combination that must be solved before getting access to the building.

In addition to helping plan the story and basic interactions, the flowchart is a valuable tool for planning the production and avoiding design pitfalls in the game. Key to this use of the chart is the flowchart symbol legend as shown in Figure 18–4.

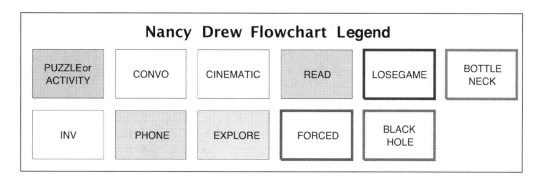

Figure 18–4 Symbol legend for *Secret of the Old Clock* production flowchart

Every type of element that is added to the flowchart has a specific symbol and color so that the designers, writer, and other team members can easily see how the structure and interactions are developing. Following are descriptions of what the various symbols stand for. This description also gives a better understanding of the various elements in this game and in this type of game in general.

- PUZZLE OR ACTIVITY (tan): a puzzle the player solves or something they can do such as playing a record on a phonograph.
- CONVO (light green): a conversation. The player can talk to another character at this point.
- CINEMATIC (light blue): a linear movie scene, such as the opening with Nancy driving to the Inn. There are no options for interactivity in a movie scene.
- READ (purple): a book, notebook, newspaper, etc. that the player can read and get clues.
- INV (yellow): an item that can be picked up by the player and added to their toolbox (inventory) as if the player physically had the item. The item can later be used to solve puzzles and get information.
- PHONE (gray): an opportunity for the player to make or receive phone calls.
- EXPLORE (dark green): an option to move around or look into a location, such as a room, a drawer, or a tunnel.
- FORCED (green border around one of the other boxes described above): a game element with no interactivity. Once started, the element must be completed. The cinematic introduction of the game is an example. Once you launch the game, the cinematic introduction plays and you cannot stop it until it finishes. An example on the chart in Figure 18–3 is Prize Dispenser in the middle of the chart. Once you make Par on the golf game, you automatically are taken to the prize dispenser where a prize pony toy is given. This toy is important later in the game.

- BLACK HOLE (red border around one of the other boxes): Collins-Ludwick explained this item in an email, "A black hole is an event which, although it may enhance a Player's enjoyment of the game, goes nowhere in terms of the central plot. Conversations which don't impart critical information – a name, a code, directions, etc. – could all be correctly termed black holes, which is why usually only plot critical convos are indicated on the flowchart. We mark them on the flowchart to remind ourselves that those elements are "unnecessary" in terms of the critical path." (Collins-Ludwick)
- LOSE GAME (blue border around one of the other boxes): some action that causes you to lose the game. There are two examples on the Figure 18–3 chart sample near the top of the chart: Bees! and Fall Down Ravine. If you do lose a game, you do have the option of clicking the Second Chance button and restarting from right before you lost.
- BOTTLE NECK (magenta border around one of the other boxes): Collins-Ludwick explained this item in an email (see below):

A bottleneck is a place where "sub-paths" converge, and which therefore has the potential to produce some awkward game play. For instance, if the design of a particular game dictates that a new environment will not open until the Player has gotten two different pieces of information from the same phone character, it's possible – maybe not likely but still possible – that the Player, because of previous choices he/she has made during the game, will have to get those two pieces of info with two phone calls that follow one right after another. We mark bottlenecks to remind ourselves that they are places where the Player could get confused and/or frustrated because they cannot advance until they do one certain thing, or until something happens over which they seemingly have no control (they must enter a certain environment to trigger the needed phone call). When we can't avoid bottlenecks in design, we at least make sure that the Player, at that point in the game, has some indication of what needs to be done, through hints, the journal or the task list.

(Collins-Ludwick)

Once the interactivity is sufficiently laid out in the flowchart, then the next stage is writing the dialogue.

Writing the Dialogue: Animated Characters and Off-Camera Scripts

As details are filled in on the flowchart, the writer can start writing the script. The flowchart summarizes roughly what Nancy says and what other characters say to her; the script has the actual dialogue. The script starts off as two scripts. One is for animated characters who we see talking on screen to Nancy, and the other is for off-camera characters who we don't see. These off-camera characters can be on the phone, actually off-camera, or Nancy musing to herself. See Figures 18–5 and 18–6 for examples of the two types of conversations. When both scripts are done, they are combined into one huge script.

Anne Collins-Ludwick, the writer of the *Secret of the Old Clock* game, said that the major difference in writing the dialogue for a game as opposed to film or TV is having to write multiple dialogue responses for interactivity. There are dialogue choices for the player to make for many of the conversations. These are indicated by the lines of light blue text on the bottom of the interface. Unlike some other games, the dialogue choices made by the player don't change the direction of the story. As explained earlier in this chapter, in the section on structure, this game is structured along multiple location paths that all eventually lead to the same linear story no matter what choices you make in the dialogue or what information

Figure 18–5 On-camera conversations with animated character

Figure 18–6 Off-camera conversations

you discover. However, asking the right questions in the dialogue does make you get to the end of the story and solve the mystery sooner. Also, in some cases, by asking the wrong questions, you may miss information and lose the game.

There is extensive use of voice-over dialogue in this game. When you are traveling around the town and "park" at one of the buildings, you are greeted by a picture of the building in a photo or on the drive "map," and you hear the building's resident(s) in voice-over but do not see him or her. There are also voice-overs of Nancy musing to herself as she explores. This functions as hints, making sure the players understand what they are seeing and possibly nudging them in a new direction. The games formal Help or Hint system is also delivered in voice-over on the pay phone just outside the Inn. Nancy can call her father or friends and get advice on how to solve specific aspects of the mystery.

Both on-camera and off-camera dialogue is also listed in text at the bottom of the screen so that the game can be played without sound or by the hearing impaired.

Script Sample #1: Jane's Introduction

All on-camera dialogue (conversation) is written in a Word document script that follows a proprietary format required by the game engine. All journal and check list entries (see Figure 18–2), as well as the text for most of the voice-overs, in the game are contained in a customized Excel spreadsheet. The writer found it initially hard to work with these specialized formats but over time has gotten used to it. The conversation script has to not only indicate what the dialogue will be but also branching dialogue possibilities based on previous things the player has heard and seen. The conversation script was more than three hundred pages long, so the samples below are just a fraction of the complete script.

The first sample below is a fairly simple interaction that takes place near the beginning of the game. Because the player has not experienced much else in the game, the branching possibilities are fairly straightforward. The conversation in straight brackets, [ ], indicates the speech by the animated character Jane. In Figure 18–5, this appears at the top of the dialogue block in the darker blue. The dialogue in arrow brackets, < >, indicates the dialogue choices for the player/Nancy Drew. The words "Go to" followed by a number, indicates which scene a dialogue choice will lead to. Note that often the dialogue choices do not actually make a difference in the evolution of the story or in the responses the player gets, but they do give the player a feeling of additional interactivity. Follow further down the script to see each dialogue choice. Note that each piece of dialogue has its own unique code for tracking purposes, such as [JWP82].

```
Scene 1082
[Emily didn't say anything about you coming until just this morning.]
[JWP82]

<{uncertainly}Is it okay that I'm here?><NJP82b> Go to 1004

<She didn't?><NJP82a> Go to 1004

Flag Set: None
Info Check: No
Bye: No

===========
```

Scene 1003 Moved

===========

Scene 1004
[Don't get me wrong. She can invite anybody here she wants. It's just that she's gotten so darn forgetful lately.][JWP04]

<Is she all right?><NJP03a> **Go to 1005**

<Maybe she's just ... you know, still thinking about her mom.><NJP03b>
Go to 1006

Flag Set: None
Info Check: No
Bye: No

===========

Scene 1005
[{with a sigh} Well, now, that's hard to say.][JWP05]

Go to 1006
Flag Set: None
Info Check: No
Bye: No

===========

Scene 1006
[She misses her mom, that's for sure. So do I. Gloria and me, we were best friends, ya know. The two of us ran this swell little dress shop over in Capital City.][JWP06]

Go to 1007
Flag Set: None
Info Check: No
Bye: No

===========

Scene 1007
[But then, she got hitched, and I didn't, and the next thing I know, she's writing me saying it would sure take a load off her mind if I could take care of her little girl should something ever happen to her.][JWP07]

<Emily's father ...?><NJP07a> **Go to 1008**

<It was nice of you to say yes.><NJP07b> **Go to 1009**

Flag Set: None
Info Check: No
Bye: No

===========

Scene 1008
[Died in the War. Cantigny, I think. Anyway ...][JWP08]

```
Go to 1009
Flag Set: EV_JW_Said_Cantigny = True
Info Check: No
Bye: No
```

==========

Scene 1009
[I couldn't say no. I mean, what're best friends for? {troubled}I just wish I knew how to help Emily.][JWP09]

<You make it sound like she's in some kind of trouble.><NJP09a> **Go to 1010**

<Help her do what?><NJP09b> **Go to 1010**

```
Flag Set: None
Info Check: No
Bye: No
```

==========

Scene 1010
[She's been acting so ... {then} Look, go talk to her. She probably just needs to spend some time with a bearcat like you instead of some dumb Dora like me.][JWP10]

Script Sample #2: Nudging the Player to Talk to Emily

Another function of the interactive dialogue is to nudge the player in the right direction so they can proceed forward and solve the mystery. If at the end of the previous discussion, the player clicks on Jane again, they are told to talk to Emily in Scene 1012 below. If player clicks on Jane a third time without talking to Emily, they are told even more tersely what to do in Scene 1013 below.

Scene 1012
[Go on up. She's in her room. Just make like a Boy Scout and be prepared.][JWP12]

Go to Node
```
Flag Set: None
Info Check: No
Bye: No
```

==========

Scene 1013
[Talk to Emily, then talk to me.][JWP00c]

Go to Node
```
Flag Set: None
Info Check: No
Bye: No
```

==========

Script Sample #3: More Complex Conditions

In order to solve the carriage house door puzzle, the player needs to discover Emily's mother's middle name. But the player will only know that they need to ask this if they have seen several other clues previously in the game. These conditions are laid out in the first line of the script sample below in the "If . . . then" string of conditions. In the example below, the player asks Jane, Emily's guardian, who comes up blank. The writer Collins-Ludwick, explains the "If . . . then" logic in the script below.

As the writer, I'm responsible for the logic – that is, for indicating what conditions have to be true (or false) in order for something to happen, or for certain dialog to be available (and oh, can the logic get complicated!). Every time something significant happens in the game – the Player sees or hears something important, gets a piece of info from someone, encounters something new, etc. – we set a flag (i.e., EV_Saw_Questions = True), which the engine keeps track of.

When you played the game, you probably noticed that when you clicked on a character, he/she would look up at you and greet you. That greeting will vary depending on what flags have been set at that point in the game. Likewise, in the course of your conversation with a character, there will usually be a point at which you can either ask the character a question (usually there will be several to choose from) or say goodbye. We refer to those questions as "Information Checks." It's a structure, which tells the engine that when certain conditions are met (certain flags have been set), make this question available to the Player. Once the Player asks that question, we (usually) set a flag, which will prevent Player from being able to ask that question again.

It's important to note, too, that while convo.doc (the script) is one of two documents that provide the engine with the text that will be displayed onscreen during the game, the script also serves as a roadmap for the person who is building the scenes that comprise the convo sequences. So, in the example you cited, "If EV_Saw_Questions = True and EV_EC_Said_Lois = False and EV_JW_Said_Mid_Name = False" means when those three flags have been set as indicated, then Player will be able to click on (ask) the question that follows the conditions (it will be tagged with < >), and the character will respond with the line that's in square brackets ([ ]).

The three lines, "Flag Set: None, Info Check: No, Bye: No", just tell the scene-builder whether a flag should be set when that particular info check plays, whether the scene should go to another info check, and whether Player can say goodbye at that point. Sometimes an info check scene will be hard-coded to go directly to another scene (Info Check: No); sometimes an info check will go to another info check, which the engine will make available (Info Check: Yes). If all info checks have been exhausted at that point, Player can click on the goodbye response.

(Collins-Ludwick)

The sample she explains follows.

Scene 1047 Information Check
```
If EV_Saw_Questions = True and EV_EC_Said_Lois = False and EV_JW_Said_
Mid_Name = False

<What was Emily's mom's middle name, do you remember?><NJP47>
```

['Course I do. It was ... {frustrated}Oh, piffle! It's right on the tip of my tongue. It was ... it was ...][JWP47]

Go to 1048
Flag Set: EV_JW_Said_Mid_Name= True
Info Check: No
Bye: No

===========

Scene 1048
[{with an exasperated sigh} It'll pop into this feeble brain of mine one of these days. Why don't you just go ask Emily.][JWP48]

Flag Set: None
Info Check: Yes
Bye: Yes

===========

Script Sample #4: Voice-Over Telegram Delivery

Delivering telegrams is the main way that Nancy Drew can make money in the game. Nancy picks up telegrams from the telegraph office then drives to the delivery. Nancy gets a different response each time she delivers the telegram. Below is just a small fraction of the telegram deliveries to Lowood Academy. Note the event conditions at the beginning of each scene beginning with "If."

Scene 5026 Lowood Academy
If EV_Tel_Temple_Academy = True and EV_Said_Tel_Temple_Academy = False and EV_First_Time = False

[<c0>Hello. I've got a telegram for Miss Temple?<c1>{NTA26a}

I am she.][TET26aX]

Go to 5140
Flag Set: EV_Delivered = True and EV_Said_Tel_Temple_Academy = True
Info Check: No
Bye: No

If EV_Tel_Temple_Academy = True and EV_Said_Tel_Temple_Academy = False and EV_First_Time = True

[<c0>Hello, Miss Temple. I've got another telegram for you.<c1>{NTA26bx}

Thank you.][TET26bX]

Go to 5141
Flag Set: EV_Delivered = True and EV_Said_Tel_Temple_Academy = True
Info Check: No
Bye: No

```
If EV_Tel_Brock_Academy = True and EV_Said_Tel_Brock_Academy = False
and EV_First_Time = False

[<c0>Hello, Miss Temple. I've got a telegram for Mr.
Brockelhurst?<c1>{NTA26c}

He's in class. I'll give it to him.][TET26cX]
```

Go to 5142
```
Flag Set: EV_Delivered = True and EV_Said_Tel_Brock_Academy = True
Info Check: No
Bye: No
```

```
If EV_Tel_Brock_Academy = True and EV_Said_Tel_Brock_Academy = False
and EV_First_Time = True

[<c0>Hello, Miss Temple. May I leave this telegram for
Mr. Brockelhurst with you?<c1>{NTA26d}

You may indeed.][TET26dX]
```

Script Sample #5: Hints

The Hints in this game are delivered by the pay phone just outside the Lilac Inn, usually by Nancy's father Carson. See the first two scenes below (5117 and 5119) to get an idea of the kinds of information Nancy can get through the hints. Notice the fairly long "If . . . then" conditions in the first line. This allows the programmers to deliver the correct hint based on the player's previous action in the game. Sometimes, there are no hints available and the player has to solve the puzzles on their own. Look at Scene 1901 below. If the long list of conditions at the beginning of the dialogue is met, there is no more help for Nancy, and she is told the line is busy.

Scene 5117 Information Check
```
If EV_Carson_Said_Hints = True and EV_Solved_Mirrors = True and EV_
Solved_Trap_Door = True and EV_Tried_Attic_Lock = True and EV_Solved_
Attic_Lock = False and EV_Attic_Lock_Hint = False

<I got the window in the carriage house open, but I'm not sure what to
do next. Any hints?><NCD117>

[Try moving the mirrors and see what happens to that beam of light
from the window. I suspect that having everything properly aligned
will put a brand new spin on things.][CDP117]

Flag Set: EV_Attic_Lock_Hint = True
Info Check: Yes
Bye: Yes
```

==================

Scene 5119 Information Check
```
If EV_Carson_Said_Hints = True and EV_Saw_Crystal_Note = True and EV_
RT_Said_Zener_First = False and EV_Quartz_Hint = False
```

```
<I have a feeling that getting Josiah's ham radio to work could be
pretty important. But it's missing piece of quartz. Any hint as to
where I might find it?><NCD119>
```

```
[Richard Topham may've taken delivery of it after Josiah passed away.
Why don't you check with him?][CDP119]
```

```
Flag Set: EV_Quartz_Hint = True
Info Check: Yes
Bye: Yes
```

Scene 1901
```
If EV_Carson_Said_Stole = True and EV_Carson_Said_Telegrams = True and
EV_JA_Said_Real_Will = True and EV_Carson_Said_JA = True and EV_Carson_
Said_Car = True and EV_JA_Said_Apologize = True and EV_Carson_Said_
Guardian = True and EV_Said_Behind_Wall = True and EV_Heard_Topham1 =
True and EV_Carson_Said_Topham = True and EV_Solved_Zener = True and
EV_Solved_Bertha_Lock = True and EV_Logic_Test_Hint = True and EV_
Memory_Clock_Hint = True and EV_Carriage_Lock_Hint = True and EV_Par_
Golf_Hint = True and EV_Poem_Puzzle_Hint = True and EV_Tile_Clock_Hint
= True and EV_Spin_Dial_Clock_Hint = True and EV_Gear_Clock_Hint = True
and EV_Bounce_Hint = True and EV_Mirror_Hint = True and EV_Trap_Door_
Hint = True and EV_Attic_Lock_Hint = True and EV_Quartz_Hint = True
and EV_Zener_Hint = True and EV_Pie_Hint = True and EV_Dress_Hint =
True and EV_Fish_Hint = True and EV_Journal_Hint = True and EV_Bertha_
Hint = True and EV_Bottom_Hint = True and EV_Mother_Hint = True and
EV_Special_Golf_Hint = True and EV_Trivet_Hint = True and EV_Secret_
Passage_Hint = True and EV_Snoop_Hint = True
```

```
[Hang on a minute.][OPP01]
```

Add appropriate SFX, then
Go to 1762

Scene 1762
```
[Sorry. The line's busy. Here's your nickel back.
<c0>Thank you. <c1>{NOP06}][OPP06X]
```

Script Sample #6: Voice-Over Gas Station

In addition to the telegrams and the phones, another kind of voice-over occurs when Nancy parks at various building in town. Below is what happens at the gas station. This scene is pictured in Figure 18–6. We never see the attendant, just a photograph of a 1930s gas station.

Gas Station Owner

```
===========
```

Scene 5000 Greetings
```
If EV_Tel_Zippy = True and EV_Said_Tel_Zippy = False and EV_First_Time
= False
```

```
[Welcome to Zippy's, where zipless service is zippily zapped and zippy
service is the zippiest.
<c0>{a beat}No offense, but that's kind of a silly slogan.<c1>{NZP00b}
{dejected}I know. My mother made it up. {then}Want some gas?][ZIP00bX]
```

```
Go to 5001
Flag Set: EV_Delivered = True and EV_Said_Tel_Zippy = True
Info Check: No
Bye: No
```

The Critical Path: Step-by-Step Outline

When design and dialogue are nailed down, then a document is prepared called The Critical Path. This is a step-by-step outline describing the ideal, fastest path to get to the end of the game and solve the mystery. This describes the most efficient way to play the game by asking all the right questions and solving the puzzles in the proper order. The Critical Path also provides the puzzle solutions. The Critical Path is usually written by the game writer, but sometimes the lead designer will write The Critical Path first as an aid to designing the game. It's largely a guide to understanding game flow, and in its final form is used mainly by the game testers, as well as reviewers. It allows reviewers to quickly play the game to the end. A sample of the critical path follows.

CLK Critical Path
Italics refer to optional steps

1. OPENING NARRATIVE/CINEMATIC. Radio announcer establishes that it's 1930 and sets the stage. ND has been invited to Lilac Inn by Emily Crandall (EC), a casual friend who lost her mom (Gloria Crandall) the previous month to illness. CROSSFADE TO ND turns onto drive to Inn in roadster, passes car parked at side of drive, pulls up in front of Inn.

2. P sees coin phone on porch and calls father, who asks her to pick something up for him from the telegraph office when she has a chance.

3. P talks to Jane Willoughby (JW) at desk area just outside kitchen/dining area. JW is EC's legal guardian according to the wishes of EC's mom, one of Jane's oldest and dearest friends. JW is worried about EC's mental condition.

4. P meets EC in her room. She seems nervous, distracted, a bit paranoid. She and mom ran the Inn; now it's just EC and Jane (who, compared to her mom, knows very little), and it's been hard. Without going into detail as to why, she retrieves the jewels she inherited from her mother and presents them to P, saying she wants ND to take them home and put them in Carson's safe.

5. Suddenly there's an explosion. From the other room we hear footsteps, and JW yelling "Fire!" EC reacts and we CROSSFADE TO:

6. Aftermath of explosion. P talks to JW; we learn that fire department just left. Stove exploded. Looks like someone (EC maybe) left the gas on. Much damage to kitchen. Line to phone on desk was destroyed. EC is in room, understandably upset. JW goes to answer the pay phone which is ringing. P hears an O.S. scream from EC and we cut to EC's room.

7. P reacts as EC says her jewels are gone! Someone must've stolen them in all the excitement. Now EC and the Inn are <u>really</u> in trouble. P asks whether jewels were insured; EC says their banker, Jim Archer (JA) would know for sure. If only Josiah

Crowley, an eccentric old man who died six months ago, had left money for EC and her mom like he always said he would ("Time will tell," he'd always say). Instead, he left them nothing. Everything went to Richard Topham (RT) instead.

8. *P may play Emily's phonograph on the phonograph player in her room.*

9. P walks over to see RT, who lives in the nearby house that used to be Josiah's and runs a school for the development of paranormal powers.

10. On the way to RT's P catches the receipt for the appraisal of a key that someone has dropped on the path back to the Inn (don't catch it when on the bridge).

11. At RT's house, his cat won't stop meowing until P finds the cat's favorite toy and gives it to him (it's under the table to the left of the front door when facing the fireplace).

12. Topham refuses to waste his time talking further to P unless she can "prove" herself worthy.

13. P solves the logic test he gives her and returns it to Topham. Answers: 1.) All Wet 2.) Doll Up 3.) Double Cross 4.) Dry Up 5.) Big Cheese

14. P is given permission to poke around Josiah's stuff. RT hasn't thrown anything out so the small rooms are very cluttered with mementos (i.e., interesting junk).

15. P will need to ask RT's permission to look around whenever she enters his house

16. *P sees a picture of Josiah in costume on stage; call out reveals that Josiah loved theatre.*

17. P finds old clock, learns that it belonged to Josiah.

18. P solves clock puzzle (matching tiles) and finds a mirror inside it, which she takes.

19. P finds Josiah's "Lest I forget ..." pad (in the elephant compartment on the secretary next to the robot) which includes four questions in with verbal reference to carriage house (What are you when you win Bard Bounce? What poet is the cat's meow? What will par on my miniature golf course get you? What's Gloria's middle name?) It also refers to the "tick tock on top," with four names Flute, Thisby, Pyramus, and Bottom. Stuffed into the "Lest I Forget ..." is a carbon copy of a letter with the name smudged out.

20. P exits and locates the carriage house out back and sees that it is locked with four four-letter word spin locks (hence the four questions) (to the right before the bridge when exiting RT's house).

21. P discovers Josiah's private mini-golf course on path back to Inn (on the left just after the bridge when exiting RT's house).

22. P rents a golf ball, putter, and score card.

23. P plays golf and pars all six holes (tricks for the golf holes – 3rd hole "Hole Lot of Lava" – to the right is a small hole in the volcano that is a shortcut for the ball – 4th hole "Sky Rail Inc." – get it into the middle hole for a shortcut –).

24. P is rewarded with a small, cheaply made toy pony, dispensed by a crudely made machine.

25. P notices a mini-game/puzzle next to the golf course (in a giant golf ball).
26. P solves the puzzle (The answer is random and the different colors can only be used once) and a poem is revealed.
27. P goes back to the Inn, discovers a "Bard Bounce" machine in parlor.
28. P solves Bard Bounce; a sign reveals the word "keen."

Junior
Move yellow left
Move green left
Move green down
Move blue left
Move blue down
Move blue right
Move red down
Move red right
Move red up
Move yellow down

Senior
Move blue left
Move yellow left
Move yellow up
Move yellow right
Move blue up
Move green up
Move green left
Move green down
Move blue down
Move yellow left
Move blue up
Move blue right
Move yellow right
Move red up
Move red right
Move green right
Move red down
Move red left
Move green left

Adapting a 1930s Novel to a Computer Game Conclusion

The process HeR Interactive followed adapting the first Nancy Drew novels to a computer game serves as a good example of this type of adaptation. As discussed above, their process included the following steps:

- Careful selection of original source material with a clear focus on the elements needed to make a strong game of this type—intriguing environments, interesting characters, and a complex mystery with potential for integrating puzzles and activities.
- Clear initial definition of characters and basic narrative in a written document.

- Systematic mapping out of the interactive options using a flowchart.
- Writing strong dialogue with multiple options for the users and in a format that can easily be integrated into the game engine.
- Create a step-by-step critical path walkthrough for a clear view of the game particularly for testing and reviewers.

By following these steps, HeR Interactive created an effective, modern computer game from a seventy-five-year-old book.

Meeting the Challenge of Developing a Computer Game for a Broad Female Audience

HeR Interactive's mission is: "To transport girls and women into the fun, interactive world of classic adventure games." The company writes that their games are "ideal for players ages 10 to adult" (HeR Interactive Corporate Backgrounder). There are a number of techniques and content considerations used by HeR Interactive to reach their target audience.

Considerations for a Female Audience

A key and somewhat obvious consideration is to avoid elements that are repellent to most females. This includes limiting violence and gender stereotypes. There are no bloodbaths in the HeR Interactive games, and you will never see Nancy or any female character act or look like the dumb bimbos popular in many of the hit games today. Even violent scenes, such as the car crash at the end of the *Old Clock* and the kitchen blowing up at the beginning are portrayed with great discretion. The kitchen explosion is just an off-camera noise and a cross fade to a boarded up charred door.

Besides avoiding elements negative to women, these games also, of course, include material women like. The game's writer points out that most women enjoy social interactions. So, the game's designer and writer make sure that the player has lots of opportunities to talk to people, just like in real life even if they are not telling you something important about solving the mysteries. There are a lot of phone conversations between Nancy and her friends that serve no purpose other than fun, like any teenager chatting on the phone with her girlfriends.

Collins-Ludwick writes that most of the time, the designers and writers do not have to consciously worry about creating games that appeal to a female audience because much of that appeal is built into the Nancy Drew source material.

> When we design a game, we frankly don't worry much about our audience. We simply try to create the most interesting, exciting game we can using the character of Nancy Drew to drive the story. If we make sure the story line showcases her defining qualities – her curiosity, determination, courage, compassion, sense of humor and sense of justice – our games will naturally appeal to females, just as Nancy has appealed to females for seventy-five years. True, we're well aware that most females seem to enjoy social interaction more than most men, and so we make sure there're lots of opportunities in our games for the Player to talk to people, but questioning suspects and pumping witnesses for information is totally in keeping with the Nancy Drew character. Snooping and talking and breaking codes were everyday activities for Nancy, and happily they lend themselves very well to the engine we've developed for our games. The fact that there is no mayhem, sadism, gore

or profanity in our games has more to do with the fact that these elements are absent from the books than with the fact that most women don't seem to buy computer games which feature them. In short, creating games based on Nancy Drew books has made our lives relatively easy when it comes to appealing to a female audience because if we do our job right, it's Nancy who's doing the appealing, not us.

(Collins-Ludwick)

Reaching a Broad Audience Age Range

Avoiding violence, profanity, gender stereotypes, and gore while including social interactions and courageous compassionate female characters helps to create games that attract females, but HeR Interactive still has to achieve their stated goal of appealing to the broad age range of ten to adult.

One of the major ways they achieve this is that the game has two difficulty levels—Junior and Senior detective. As you may have noticed at the end of The Critical Path example shown previously, the Senior detective puzzles are much harder. Availability of hints is another major factor as Collins-Ludwick explains:

Telephone hints (which are usually given by Bess and George, although in some games Ned Nickerson, Nancy's boyfriend, or Carson Drew provide them) are only available to Junior Detectives, as are many of the more pointed VOs. And while all Players have access to Nancy's Journal, in which we can and quite often do clarify or emphasize pieces of information that Players come upon during the game, only Junior Detectives can look at the Task List, which reminds Players of what they've done and, based on that, what they still need to do.

(Collins-Ludwick)

Different difficulty levels may be the major reason that the Nancy Drew games can be enjoyed by a wide age range, but HeR Interactive also tries other techniques to include the older audience. The *Secret of the Old Clock* game provides a good example of this in its use of the 1930s Nancy Drew books as source material and in setting the game in 1930. The game makes good use of the 1930 setting with period music, slang, photographs, and clothing styles. This is a clear attempt to appeal to older gamers who may have been introduced to the original Nancy Drew books. This is not to say that they read the books in the 1930s, but that the books they read 20 or 30 years ago were the original books set in the 1930s.

Perhaps the last major item that helps with broad audience appeal is that, even though each Nancy Drew game uses the same basic game engine, each new game includes some enhancement to the engine so there is something new for the player to experience. In the *Secret of the Old Clock* game, the major innovation was that Nancy could drive her car around town. Adding to the interest and complexity of driving the car is that gas gets used up and tires get worn out, especially if you drive over potholes. Gas and new tires both cost money, another new issue for Nancy to face.

Meeting the Challenge of Completing All of the Tasks Described Above and Still Staying on Budget and Schedule

When writing a book or a short story, a writer can create elaborate actions, scenes, and multitudes of characters without affecting the budget of the final book. Unfortunately, in film, TV, and computer games, these same elements can quickly inflate a budget so the product is no longer profitable.

In addition to building great games, HeR Interactive's key to success is building these games on schedule and on budget. Each game has a six-month schedule, and in most cases, the same budget as the previous game. This has allowed HeR Interactive to price their games correctly for their market and still turn a profit.

Keeping within budget while writing a game is an important skill for the writer. A writer will often be asked for an alternative way to accomplish a game goal that is less expensive but equally effective. In the *Secret of the Old Clock*, this was a particular challenge because this was the first game that was set in the 1930s period and the first to allow the character to drive the car and thus visit more locations.

Some of the solutions to staying on budget are built into the game specifications to begin with. The same basic engine is used for each game, but something new is added each time to keep it fresh. All of the Nancy Drew games are also limited to four speaking, on-screen characters besides Nancy Drew. This means that other interactions have to be handled in different ways. As discussed previously, the *Secret of the Old Clock* makes very effective us of voice-over to solve this problem. For example, in the scene pictured in Figure 19–6, Nancy has "parked" at the gas station but instead of seeing the attendant, we see a photo of a 1930s gas station and hear the interaction with Nancy in voice-over. This use of old

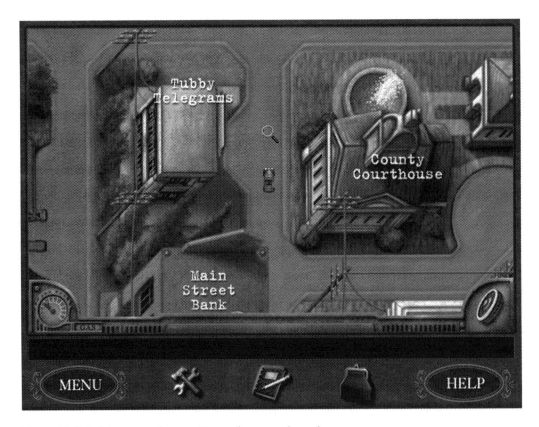

Figure 18–7 Driving map of town, Cursor drags car through streets

photos is also a very effective way to enhance the 1930s setting without great expense. When Nancy delivers her telegrams throughout the town, many locations are pictured with photos and a lively voice-over. Other locations are pictured on the animated map (Figure 19–7) of the town that allows the player/Nancy to drive to various locations. In these cases, the images on the map are all we see of the locations, but these are supplemented with amusing voice-overs, often coupled with effective sound effects. To keep things fresh, the writer wrote more than 60 interactions around telegram delivery.

The 1930s setting was further enhanced through opening narration in the style of a 1930s radio play, 1930s music, songs, radio shows, print material, and conversational slang, particularly by Emily and Marian. Here's an example from Marian's dialogue, "She probably just needs to spend some time with a bearcat like you instead of some dumb Dora like me."

Other things that help keep costs down include puzzles and games that have potential for repeated game play, such as the mini-golf game. In general, good games and puzzles were emphasized over elaborate special effects and unlimited characters. Last, sometimes non-essentials just have to be cut if they can't be done on time. For example, one idea that was discarded was to allow the player to watch 1930s movies when they clicked on the movie theater in town.

The end result of all these efforts is an effective game sold at a very reasonable price.

Conclusion: Response to the Project

The Nancy Drew games from HeR Interactive have won numerous awards including: Children's Software Revue—All Star Award; iParenting Media—Great Holiday Award; Parents Choice—Gold Award, Best Software, ages 10–19; Amazon.com—Best Children's Software; Family Life Magazine—Favorite Software; SuperKids Software Review—Best Software for Girls, and many other awards.

Commercial acceptance of these games has matched the critical acceptance as each game has sold better than the previous game as the word spreads and the audience grows for Nancy Drew games.

References

Collins-Ludwick. Anne. Telephone interviews with the author
Collins-Ludwick. Anne. Emails to the author
Nancy Drew Games, Awards and Accolades, HeR Interactive, Inc.

19 Using Interactive Narrative to Present Information

The New England Economic Adventure

Summary

Name of production: *The New England Economic Adventure*
Writer: Maria O'Meara
Developers: Jeff Kennedy Associates, Inc., Northern Light Productions
Audience: Primarily students and teachers of economics and history
Medium: Theater with live presenter, large video screen, and touch pads for audience
Presentation location: The Federal Reserve Bank of Boston
Subject: Economic History of New England
Goal: Teach
Structures: Linear with scene branching for audience input

The script samples and images used in this chapter are courtesy of the Federal Reserve Bank of Boston. © Federal Reserve Bank of Boston.

Program Description and Background

Program Description

The New England Economic Adventure (NEEA) was an immersive exhibit that was part of the education program of the Federal Reserve Bank of Boston. The exhibit was at their headquarters in Boston, Massachusetts, serving the economic education needs of students and teachers in the New England area. An immersive exhibit involves some combination of live presenters or actors, video, animations, physical objects, and audience interaction with the program through an input device, such as a PDA. The NEEA is a good example of interactive narrative used to present information, in this case the story of the growth of the New England economy.

See Figure 19–1 for the setup of *The New England Economic Adventure*.

The New England Economic Adventure (NEEA) was part of a larger program delivered by the Federal Reserve Bank of Boston educators in an adjacent gallery. In addition to visiting the NEEA and the gallery, most groups would also participate in workshops in the Fed's economic labs.

The NEEA explored three important events in New England's economic history: the founding of the textile industry, the mass production of bicycles with interchangeable parts,

Figure 19–1 The New England Economic Adventure (NEEA) with live host, screen for video and animation, related objects in front of video screen, and audience interaction with the electronic program through PDA touch pads (inset picture)

and the successful introduction of one of the first mini-computers for a mass audience. The program took users back in time and used a game show format to test their economic knowledge and skills at making investment decisions.

NEEA writer, Maria O'Meara, explained that there are three types of interactivity for each of the three economic stories in this program. The activities occur in this order.

• The lightning round—players answer multiple choice and other questions presented on the video screen and their PDAs to build up their fictional bank accounts.
• The investment round—players view video on each economic event, invest money, or make similar business decisions.
• Round of risk and reward—an audience member is invited to spin a wheel of chance, which selects a random event, such as a natural disaster, that affects players' holdings.

The narrative video material presented in the large center screen (see Figure 19–1) involves two young, energetic, time travelers who journey to the past and visit the three New England economic events: textile industry, bicycle manufacturing, and the mini-computer. The time travelers take on contemporary roles in each period, such as one of the investors in the textile industry. They also present background information, questions for the audience, and the correct answers to the questions using video, animations, graphics, and audio.

At the end of the game, each audience member's total fictional dollars earned from investments and correct answers in the lightning round are displayed on their PDA screen. The person with the highest dollar amount wins the game!

Figure 19–2 The New England Economic Adventure time travelers who appear on the video screen in various historical periods

Use of Stories to Present Information

The New England Economic Adventure (NEEA) could have presented its information as a set of well-organized facts that the user could assimilate. The NEEA, however, chose to present the bulk of its information in the narrative video of the two time travelers described above. The time travelers essentially take on our role as people of the 21st century, and take us back in time to participate in the great economic stories of New England.

User's minds are particularly open to information presented through storytelling. Before the printing press and extensive access to written works, much of human knowledge was conveyed through the oral tradition of storytelling. Where non-narratives deliver information through argument and description, narratives allow the user to become part of the information by becoming or identifying with a character in the story. Information embedded in a story is also linked by time and events and thus large bodies of information and the connection between different elements can be easier to remember through narrative. In addition, curiosity is a crucial component in learning. The user has to want to know what happens next. This is hard to accomplish in a logical presentation of information, but is a key element in any good story.

For the reasons discussed above, and others too complex to discuss here, story has always been and will continue to be an effective way to present information, particularly information related to human behavior and actions. Narrative to present information is a common technique in many types of interactive media, including: edutainment programs, such as *The Oregon Trail* where we follow a family by wagon train across the untamed American West; training programs that allow users to role play key characters in performing essential tasks, such as selling or marketing a product; and immersive exhibits, such as *The New England Economic Adventure* discussed in this chapter.

Popularity of Immersive Exhibits/Experiences

Presentations, such as *The New England Economic Adventure*, that include large screens, live presenters, theatrical lighting and sound effects, audience interaction, and other elements to bring the audience fully into the experience are called immersive exhibits or experiences. These types of exhibits are popular in museums because they provide a unique experience that you cannot get sitting in front of your TV or computer.

Even when standard computer screen kiosks are used in museums, there is often an attempt to make them more immersive by creating a set, such as a car sticking out of a wall, an ATM machine, or any kind of structure that will attract users. Immersive exhibits/experiences are also popular in theme parks, casinos, major conferences/conventions, and even the wired classroom. Some schools now have classrooms set up similarly to *The New England Economic Adventure* with audience touch pads, big screens, and accompanying software/media programs. With all these markets, developing immersive exhibits/experiences is a big business and the writing skills studied in this case study can apply to most of the situations described above.

Production Background

The Federal Reserve System is the central banking system of the United States. The Federal Reserve System is headquartered in Washington, D.C. with 12 regional Federal Reserve Banks located in major cities, including Boston. The Federal Reserve regulates banks, implements monetary policy, maintains the financial payments system, performs economic research, and presents economic education to the public.

To fulfill its mission of presenting economic education, the Federal Reserve Bank of Boston, one of the 12 regional banks, engaged Jeff Kennedy Associates to develop *The New England Economic Adventure* (NEEA). Jeff Kennedy Associates is a Boston-based museum planning and exhibit design firm. Their work for history museums, science centers, and children's museums often involves the design and development of highly interactive role-playing games and immersion environments.

To help the exhibit designer, Jeff Kennedy Associates, develop the content for this project, the Federal Reserve Bank of Boston assembled an academic advisory board of economic historians. This advisory board, led by economic historian Peter Temin, Elisha Gray II Professor of Economics, M.I.T., made significant contributions to the treatment over the many months the project was in development. Once the exhibit designer, the client, and the advisory board had identified the three case studies for the NEEA, Jeff Kennedy Associates commissioned short papers by historians on the events to be presented in the show. Based on all this research, the treatment for the NEEA was developed and written by Jeff Kennedy, principal, and Marjorie Prager, exhibit developer for Jeff Kennedy Associates.

Jeff Kennedy Associates hired Northern Light Productions to develop the video and programming for the NEEA. Northern Light Productions is a Boston-based film and video production company. They create motion picture and video installations for museums and visitor centers, plus work for broadcast and independent projects.

Northern Light Productions hired Maria O'Meara as the writer on the project because of her extensive experience with interactive museum exhibits. Working with the Federal Reserve and the production team, O'Meara developed the script treatment and the final script from the initial treatment originally created by Jeff Kennedy Associates.

The writer, Maria O'Meara, has written for interactive media for more than 20 years. She writes extensively for family audiences, developing interactive scripts for museums, publishing companies, and the web. She especially enjoys working on museum projects that blend video, interactivity, and theater to create a unique visitor experience. She has worked on a wide variety of museum projects, including the Atlanta Federal Reserve, the Newark Children's Museum, The Franklin Institute, California Science Center, North Carolina State Museum of Natural Sciences, and many more. While at D.C. Heath, a textbook publisher, Maria was the head writer for a series of immersive interactive media programs focused on natural history including the Everglades and the Sonoran Desert. Maria holds a BA in English from the University of Notre Dame and a MS in Broadcasting from Boston University.

Goals and Challenges Writing *The New England Economic Adventure*

Goals

The writer had the following goals for this project.

- Teach the audience the history of the economic engine of New England and how key technologies built upon each other.
- Make content fun and engaging for student audience.
- Bring historical figures to life.

Challenges

The challenges the writer faced were with both content and presentation technique.

- A substantial amount of historical content was needed to understand the contexts of the economic choices.
- This dense content worked against creating an exciting narrative.

- The target student audience often considers economic issues dry.
- Because this immersive experience has a live host, video, objects, and audience interaction through a PDA, the writer is required to have the skills of a writer of video, interactive media, and theater.

Writing *The New England Econonomic Adventure*: Meeting the Challenges

Defining Presentation, Basic Content, and Narrative: The Initial Treatment

After considerable research and discussions with the economic advisory board and the client, the first major written document was a treatment created by Jeff Kennedy and Marjorie Prager of Jeff Kennedy Associates, the museum design firm on the project.

A treatment is a preliminary written document used on many types of interactive media and film/video projects. The major part of the treatment is a narrative prose description of what will occur in the proposed program. Technical information is fairly limited in this type of document; the goal is a clear description of the proposed projects sequence of events and activities. There are no set rules for treatments, however, and they can include other elements important to explain (and sometime sell) the project. The initial treatment for *The New England Economic Adventure* (NEEA) included the following components.

- An introduction explaining the rationale and setting for the project.
- An overview of the game elements.
- Economic themes.
- A detailed description of all three stories in the NEEA.
- A presentation walkthrough.
- A presentation outline.

Following is only one segment of the full treatment—the presentation outline. This outline gives an overview of the complete program.

To read the complete treatment and other script samples, please refer to the book's website.

The Presentation Outline, Part of the Initial Treatment

Presenter welcomes group, takes audience photo	Presenter
1st time travel effect, spotlight lands on textiles	Lighting/fx
1. SCENARIO #1 WHO WILL JOIN ME? a) Story video #1, sets up life in 1820 (post Waltham, pre Lowell) & intros Boston Associates	Story Video/ meet Mr. Lowell
b) Advisors jump in with rules, tell you how much $ you have, argue pros and cons of investment (shipping vs. mills)	Advisors on Video
c) Presenter takes it back to audience for choice	Presenter
d) PDA input of investment (all, half, none)	PDAs
e) Presenter introduces wheel of risks/rewards, volunteer spins	Presenter, volunteers

Presenter welcomes group, takes audience photo	Presenter
f) Results come up on PDAs and screen	Data
g) Advisors debrief, recap impact of mills on standard of living	Advisors on Video
2nd time travel effect, spotlight lands on bicycles	Lighting/fx
2. SCENARIO #2, IS BIGGER BETTER? a) Story video #2a, sets up life in 1890	Intro Video
b) Advisors jump in with Standard of Living quiz; last questions re bike (how many, what cost)	Advisors on video
c. PDA quiz (possibly with on stage volunteers?)	Data
d. Story video #2b, intro bicycles, Col. Pope	Story Video/ meet Col. Pope
e. Advisors set up investment decision, argue pros and cons of banking money or making investment or borrowing/investing	Advisors on video
f. PDA decision (bank your $, invest, borrow/invest)	Data
g. Wheel determines year (1890, 1893, 1896)	Presenter, volunteer
h. Results come up on PDAs and screen	Data
i. Advisors show what would have happened for each of the years; sum up standard of living benefits of mass production	Advisors on Video
3rd time travel effect, spotlight lands on PDP8	Lighting/fx
3. SCENARIO #3 NEW PRICES, NEW USES? a. Presenter asks "what is this?" (PDP8)	Presenter
b. Advisors jump in with quiz (re computers in 1962: how many, how big, how much they cost)	Advisors on Video
c. PDA quiz, results on screen	Data
d. Story video #3, sets up life in 1960s, rise of early computers through Ken Olsen and DEC	Story Video
e. Advisors explain that our $ is now DEC stock, intro the pricing/marketing decision to be made, argue pros and cons	Advisors on Video
f. PDA decision re market to invest your R&D $ in	Data
g. Presenter asks volunteer to spin wheel for economic conditions	Presenter volunteer
h. Results come up on PDAs and screen	Data, Advisors on Video
4th time travel effect	Lighting/fx
4. FINAL RESULTS/WRAP UP/PHOTO a. Presenter leads into grand totals, asks those who made the most to stand and be applauded	Data, Presenter
b. Advisors jump in to liven up ending and summarize teaching points; segue into showing surprise audience photo, those who will reinvent the New England economy in the future	Advisors on Video

Presenter welcomes group, takes audience photo	Presenter
c. Presenter has last word, turns the Advisors off with remote control	Presenter
Lights up, walk-out music, audience exits	Lighting/fx/music

The outline gives a good overview of the project, but an important part of an historical content-based program such as this is a clear narrative of how the content will be presented. This is handled in the next sample, The Presentation Walkthrough, which is also from the treatment. Later in this chapter, the script for this story will be presented for comparison to see the changes the writer made.

Presentation Walkthrough from Initial Treatment

Welcoming the Audience

The presenter, an FRBB staff educator, welcomes the visiting group to the New England Economic Adventure, has them settle into their seats and says that we always like to take a photograph to add to the Adventure visitor book (the flash of a strobe accompanies picture-taking).

Suddenly, the room comes alive with an environmental "time travel" effect, a combination of sound and light. As it ends, a spotlight illuminates the part of the stage that presents a loom and bolts and hanging samples of textiles.

Now the large video screen at the center of the stage comes into play. The title of Scenario #1, WHO WILL JOIN ME? fades up and holds as we plunge directly into the first "story video," finding ourselves in 1816. We get a sense for what life was like at that time for average folks, then meet Francis Cabot Lowell, who addresses us directly from the screen as if we are the highly successful group of men known as the Boston Associates, investors who, having taken a flyer with him to start a prototype mill at Waltham, he believes he can now convince to invest in a much larger scale operation in a location he tells us our colleagues Nathan Appleton and Patrick Johnson are excited about – a little town with plenty of water power and a great location for attracting the right kind of mill girls (God-fearing young farm girls who will work hard for low wages).

As on-screen images illustrate his pitch, Lowell outlines the basic idea of large-scale textile manufacturing, reminding us that we trusted him before to take what he observed in the mills of England and manufacture good, cheap cloth. Waltham, while it has its drawbacks, is enough of a success to make him sure that, by pooling our money – something we can now, for the first time, do with a new innovation in financing called a joint stock company, which lets you buy shares in a venture and sell your shares when you want to get your investment out – we can build on a scale that will make us all part of the most exciting experiment in industrial history: the creation of a profitable textile industry here in New England. Summing up, he asks if we are ready to join him in an enterprise so daring and revolutionary that it just might change the American way of life.

Suddenly, footage of our two contemporary Advisors interrupts Lowell's entreaty. They jump right in with the basics of our game, telling us that we each, as wealthy mercantile shippers of spotless reputation, have a healthy bank account of X. That bank account is kept in the funny little device we find at our seats (our PDAs). With those PDAs, we will make choices and make investments.

The Advisors plunge into an entertaining argument (one which reveals their characters of conservative and liberal spenders, with wit and energy) of the pros and cons of keeping one's money in shipping or joining with Lowell and others to back the new enterprise, the mills. They summarize the key points on each side in a spirited way. Briefly, Advisor 1 might challenge the idea of investing in the mills by asking why someone would want to own just a little part of something big instead of being the top guy in control (as in shipping); why should we assume the world will want to buy cheap cloth; how we will be able to avoid the horror of the "dark Satanic mills" that fester in England; and why not stick with a sure thing, shipping, something you know how to do and how to get a quick return on investment. Advisor 2 would respond, point for point, making the case for an investment offering freedom from the stress and anxiety inherent in the shipping business; describing the huge and new markets for cheap cloth that will make the venture successful; pointing out the dangers and risks of putting all one's money in shipping; and being part of the next big thing.

The presenter interrupts the Advisors' back and forth repartee and says it is time for the audience to make its first decision. He or she reminds us we have X amount in our accounts and asks us to now choose how to invest our money, using the PDAs at our seats. Our options are presented, first for shipping and then for textiles: invest it all, invest half, or invest none.

The audience now inputs its choices using the PDAs, and the data collected goes to a central computer.

The presenter asks for a drum roll (and gets one) as a large "wheel of risks and rewards" is spot lit on stage. The presenter asks for two volunteers to come up to pull the lever that controls the on-screen spin of the wheel (the lever is mechanical and the wheel is electronic; sound effects of a ratcheting wheel of fortune augment the effect). The first wheel that appears is marked for the shipping investors and includes a range of possible natural disasters and catastrophes (shipwrecks, piracy, storms at sea); the second wheel that appears is filled with events that would have an impact on investments in textile manufacturing (protective tariffs, production problems, scarcity of supplies, customers who cannot pay their bills on time, unavailability of skilled laborers, etc.). Each sector of the wheel has a monetary impact attributed to it (i.e., lose everything, double your money, etc.). The two volunteers pull the lever in turn, first for shipping, then for textiles.

When the computer tabulates results of the wheel spins, the large screen shows the impact of chance on the audience's aggregate investments, and audience members also see changes to their own results on their individual PDAs.

The Advisors immediately reappear on screen to debrief, their
comments general enough to relate to the way this audience chose to
invest. They show us the success of Lowell through illustrations that
appear on screen as they speak, and making a direct connection between
the impact of joint stock companies, large scale textile manufacturing
and average peoples' rising standards of living: the availability of
affordable cloth has ramifications on many fronts, including health and
hygiene as well as comfort, style and practicality.
Now, for the second time, our environmental "time travel"
effect fills the room with light and sound. At its end, a spotlight
illuminates the part of the stage on which bicycles are displayed.

Refining the Content and Presentation: The Script Treatment and Script

When the writer came onto the project, she was handed the complete treatment described in
the previous section. Writer O'Meara said that compared to other projects, the presentation
and content was well developed by the museum designers in this treatment. The stage that
a writer joins a project like this varies widely. Sometimes, writers are given no more than a
single paragraph and have to write the initial treatment themselves.

On this project, the writer's primary task was transforming the initial treatment into a
script treatment, do research, and create a final production script.

Making Content More Interactive—The Script Treatment and the Lightning Round

O'Meara explains the process from initial treatment to production treatment:

> We (writer and Northern Light Production team) got the initial treatment from Kennedy
> (museum designer), read it and then had a kick off meeting with them to discuss their
> content, messages, audience, the exhibit space and set up, how audiences would use this
> space, review floor plans, and discuss results of their focus group testing.
>
> After these meetings, we then wrote a script treatment. In this treatment, we came up
> with the lightning round as a way to break down some of the background information
> you would need in order to make an informed investment decision. We were really try-
> ing to get away from having the kids sit there with all these buttons, but not get to push
> one until they had watched about twenty minutes of video. The lightning round idea was
> readily accepted by everyone because they could see its benefits to the game.
>
> (O'Meara)

The lightning round concept presented the background information in an interactive game
show format. The writer suggested presenting a series of questions that the audience members could answer individually. So instead of having a solid stretch of video, this content
was broken down like this:

1. Brief video, animation, graphics, and audio background appears on the main screen introducing the question.
2. The question appears on the main screen and the student's individual PDA.
3. The student answers the question, and a light blinks on the chairs of the students
   who choose the correct answer. The students with correct answers also get additional

game dollars added to their bank account that they can use later in the investment section of the game.

4. Brief video, animation, graphics, and audio appear on the main screen explaining the correct answer.

O'Meara said that the above issue with the background content and the lightning round is an example of one of the main problems that faces a writer on a content intensive project like this. The client is concerned that the desired content is included in the project. Because of this, the client will often want to add more content than can be easily digested by the target audience.

When this happens, it is part of the writer's job to come up with better ways to deliver the content and present these options to the client. One technique that O'Meara likes to use is to stage readings of the material with the client. She said that a simple out loud readthrough of the script with the client will often demonstrate that a particular segment is too content dense and needs to be shortened or presented in a different way. In general, readthroughs are a good tool for the author to hear how his/her work will play to an audience. O'Meara said she is not averse to gathering friends or family to be a mock audience for one of her scripts. On this project, there were also formal readthroughs with the target audience. A group of high-school students were gathered in a classroom and the script was read by the writer and members of the team. Lots of valuable feedback was gained this way to fine-tune the script.

Based on the readthrough experience and the writer's suggestions, the team adopted the lightning round game show approach and thinned the amount of linear content presented. With this major change in place, Maria created a script treatment. This is somewhat similar to the walkthrough shown above, but has more production detail and far less background material.

An excerpt of the Script Treatment follows including the introduction of the lightning round. Notice how it is different from the previous sample of the initial treatment. The script treatment:

- has more detail, such as actual examples of questions, details of scoring, and the role of the host
- is broken down into clear sections with headers all in caps
- includes approximate timing information to get a sense of project flow and run time.

Excerpt of Script Treatment

```
GROUP PHOTO
    Prior to the game, the audience lines up for a group photo.
    The photo could be taken in a designated area that would be set up
so they could stand close to one another, possibly on a grid painted
on the floor. This area would be pre-lit and could possibly have
backdrops of the mills, a bicycle scene and an early DEC office setting
that could be placed behind the students. Taking group shots in a
designated area allows for better lighting and composition.
```

HOST 1:00
The Host opens the show with a welcoming speech and general description of the game.

LOG-IN :15
In some way to be determined, the visitors log-in. This activates the station and allows the host to see on the computer screen which seats are occupied.

The players are immediately given a predetermined amount of money in their account. The host explains this is only the beginning. In this game, as in real life, they will soon have opportunities to increase - or decrease that amount through work, investment and luck (good or bad.)

SCORE A
A predetermined amount is given to each player. Depending on how difficult such calculations are, we could designate the amount in 1816 dollars. The host could explain the approximate value in today's dollars. At the end of each story, the amount would be recalculated to reflect its worth in today's dollars.

LIGHTNING ROUND 2:00-3:00
(This a different name for the pop quiz referred to in the treatment.)
The lightning round allows visitors to earn money and add to their initial amount by answering questions about the time period they are entering. Although the questions are knowledge based, with a little thought some of them can be deduced. The question appears as an attractive graphic on the main screen. The PDAs allow the visitors to select the correct answer. Once the selections have been made, video highlighting the correct answer plays. The video answers should be short - 10-30 seconds at the most in order to keep the pacing quick. Each video should focus on only one piece of information.

General or background information required to set up the investment story can effectively be communicated through these questions.

For example:
QUESTION
It's 1816. What war ended just two years ago?

- The American Revolution
- The Civil War
- The War of 1812
- World War II

A very brief video about the War of 1812 focuses on the dilemma our investors, who made their money as merchants, are facing. While great fortunes were made in shipping, embargos during the war showed how risky the business was. When the war ended, wealthy men who made their fortunes in shipping looked to invest their money in something that would be profitable, more secure, and long-lasting.

Writing the Script: Using All the Available Tools

After the treatment was approved, the writer started working on the script. A lot of research went into writing the script, and the client, the Federal Reserve Bank of Boston, was a great resource. According to O'Meara:

> The key to the success of this project or any project is the involvement of the client. In this case, the Boston Fed was extremely helpful. They themselves are very knowledgeable about the time periods that we were writing about and provided good leads on research. They gave us helpful feedback and listened to our suggestions.
>
> (O'Meara)

When the research was completed, the writer could execute the script. For an immersive script, the writer has many of the same concerns as a typical interactive media project, such as interactivity, structure, pacing, and strong dialogue. However, a script for an immersive exhibit has special challenges because, as mentioned previously, the writer is not just creating an experience that will happen on a computer or video screen, but also has to write for a live audience, host, and physical objects in the room. Some understanding of theatrical writing has to be added to interactive media writing skills.

One key issue is how to integrate the host. The writer, O'Meara, wrote that:

> The host's role would be subject of many discussions as we went through script development. We (writer and production team) were nervous because a live host is something that is out of our control. You are afraid that if they get someone awful, the whole program will stink. At a certain point though you have to say, well this is what the client wants, so these are the things you need to do in order to make it work (i.e., pick people who have stand-up experience, make sure they are trained to use the program and make sure you have enough of them in case someone gets sick or goes on vacation!). In the end, I think the program benefits from having a live host who is involved at key points in the game.

The initial concept for the host was to have him or her introduce the presentation, and then the rest of the program would be self-running. But this did not make full use of the advantages of having a live host who could fine-tune the presentation and answer questions for this specific audience. So, the decision was made to give the host some control over the pacing of the show through controls at their podium. By clicking a "Next" button, the host could move the program on to the next segment when the group was ready. This allows the host to adlib and deal with any unresolved issues or questions before continuing.

The challenge was determining just how often the live host should come into the program. Too much could feel like an interruption; too little could lose the advantages described above. The correct solution, as always, is to test and retest. The team did a number of paper tests with live audiences. A paper test uses sketches, text, and verbal description to give the audience a feel for how a program will unfold. This allows the writer and the rest of the team to get feedback on issues, such as the role of the host. The client's commitment to training live hosts also needs to be considered before including this in a program. In this case, the Boston Fed already had educators on staff that led groups and were quite capable of playing hosts for *The New England Economic Adventure*.

Another "theatrical" issue was how to use objects in the room and lighting. The decision had been made to include a large object for each of the three stories. These objects included a loom, a bicycle, and a 1965 mini-computer. The writer had to decide how these objects could be highlighted in the script. She did this by suggesting the use of a gobo lighting effect, which is a shaped light and shadow effect that can also use color. This lighting technique is used to highlight objects, the host, and even members of the audience. O'Meara said that on some immersive projects she has worked on, lighting effects are used extensively, for example an ocean-related exhibit has a blue shimmering ocean gobo to emphasize key moments in the presentation.

Even when the major elements are in place, such as the host and the lighting, seemingly small issues can have a substantial impact on the overall experience. The writer will sometimes have to fight for such elements. For example, O'Meara thought it was important that the audience member who got a correct answer in the lightning round should have the light on their chair turned on. In testing this turned out to be a hit. Students liked having their light come on and looked around to see how many other people got the correct answers.

Another "small" issue was adding more variety and interactivity in the types of responses possible in the lightning round and investment decisions. At the investment stage in the Lowell story as illustrated in the script below, the audience member has to decide what percentage of their wealth they will invest in trading or in the textile mills. It would have been easier to have a simple multiple choice for this item, but the writer argued for a slider tool that would appear on the PDA and allow the student to move it back and forth and get a wider range of investment combinations.

In general, the writer has to be an advocate for what technology and effects will be engaging for the audience and get the message across.

Segment of Script for Game 1: Will You Join Me?

After an opening section of the program where the host welcomes the audience and the program introduces the basic premise of the game and how to use the equipment, Game 1 begins. This is the section that explores the founding of the U.S. textile industry by Lowell in 1813.

Compare this script with the initial treatment that was included earlier in this chapter. It covers the same material. Notice how the treatment is executed into script form. Also notice the changes made to the script from the treatment. This is the writer's contribution. The notable addition was the Lightning Round as a way to break up the background material and make it more interactive. Also note all the elements that a writer of an immersive script is responsible for, including:

- host action and dialogue
- items that appear on audience PDA
- video images
- lighting in room on objects and people
- screen dialogue
- screen narration
- sound effects.

GAME 1

HOST	VOTE; PDA	VIDEO & LIGHTING	AUDIO, NARRATION & SFX	EFX	CUES
In our first game, we'll be visiting the year 1813 and exploring the beginnings of the textile industry here in New England. Look down at your screen to see how much you have to start with.		Graphic or animation Bank account icon from PDA.		1813 Gobo effect on queue with movie	Host – next at the word screen activates pda info
As you see, you each have $10,000 in your accounts. Remember, that's $10,000 in 1813 dollars. But in that time, just as today, you could earn money ... so let's earn a little more money right now in our Lightning Round.	PDA GRAPHIC on system shows each person how much they have.	MAIN SCREEN Graphic Bank account shows amount of money each person has.			
You'll have a chance to answer 3 questions. For each one you answer correctly, you'll earn $1,000! You'll have 10 seconds after the question to enter your answer. Anyone have any questions? ... Let's start the lightning round.		GRAPHIC Lightning Round graphic or animation flashes on main screen. Possible lighting effects flash throughout room.	SFX Lightning round theme song plays.	Host spot and blue wash fade out. Gobo Lightning effects timed to main screen.	Host – Next on the words Lightning Round. Movie starts 30 frames after lights fade out.

VISITORS	GRAPHIC & MAIN SCREEN	CHRIS (VO)		
VISITORS have a pre-set amount of time to answer the questions	TEXT BUILD, with graphics What was the relationship between Britain and the United States in 1813? a. They were at war. b. They were allies. c. The US was a British colony. d. Europeans had not yet come to North America.	First question. What was the relationship between Britain and the United States in 1813? a. They were at war. b. They were allies. c. The US was a British colony. d. Europeans had not yet come to North America.		
	ROOM EFFECTS Lights dim a bit; gaming music counts down pre-set time for voting to be done.			
	Onscreen countdown with SFX indicating that time is up.		Possible gobo effect over seats during countdown. Lighting Effect ends at 3,2,**1**....	

(Continued)

HOST	VOTE; PDA	VIDEO & LIGHTING	AUDIO, NARRATION & SFX	EFX	CUES
	PDA Correct answers add to score. Lights of people who answered correctly go on.	MAIN SCREEN Graphic The correct answer, "a." is highlighted with corresponding sound effect.	CHRIS The correct answer is, a. They were at war. If you got that right, you just added $1000 to your bank account which is displayed at the top of your screen.	Correct score pda lights go on and stay on until the show segues to the on-screen response. Possible gobo effect??	
			SFX Sounds of war, cannons, as if all around visitors.		
		MAIN SCREEN VIDEO ADVISOR 2 In simple t-shirt, possibly with life jacket or other nautical prop. Behind him, we see images a graphic: **War of 1812** images of naval battles, illustrations, cannons firing and other exciting shots. Animate a little merchant ship sinking. FLASH of cannon ends clip,	CHRIS In 1813, the United States was at war with Britain ... and the two world superpowers of the time, Britain and France, were at war with each other! The Atlantic Ocean was a dangerous place! British warships seized American merchant ships, confiscated cargo, and kidnapped crew members, forcing them to serve in the British navy. The war was literally sinking the trading business! SFX Naval battles Penny whistle as ship sinks.		

BOOK AUTHOR'S NOTE: There are several more questions similar to the one above as a way to establish context for the economic story to be told in the next section.

HOST	LOGO	SFX		
Now let's begin the Decision Round In this round, you'll have a chance to go back in time .... to the year 1813, where you'll decide how to invest your money ... and you'll see if you make a profit. Ready to make some more money? Let's begin our trip.	Decision Round	Decision Round SFX	1813 gobo effect timed to movie Lights fade out.	Host - Next at the words Decision Round activates movie Host - Next on the words our trip, starts the movie
	CHRIS and SARA on screen in modern-dress against plain background. They matrix out of the scene.	CHRIS Ready? SARA Ready.		
	TRANSITION TO PAST Lights dim as sound effects fill room. We enter a door, and then a dark, private office.	EFFECTS: 5-:10 seconds Lighting and sound effects in room take visitors back to 1813 Boston.		

(Continued)

HOST	VOTE; PDA	VIDEO & LIGHTING	AUDIO, NARRATION & SFX	EFX	CUES
		MAIN SCREEN VIDEO ADVISORS matrix into an area outside of LOWELL'S office. CHRIS and SARA materialize in costumes of the day that would make them fit in with Lowell and his friends. The sounds of "aheming" and murmuring from inside the office. They open the door and enter the office.	CHRIS (Looking at his outfit, brushing himself off, maybe little flecks of electronic time transport material fly off) (to audience) Well, it looks like we all got here in one piece! SARA (brushing herself off) Let's fill you in quickly. We are all prosperous associates of a man named Francis Cabot Lowell. CHRIS We've made our money in trading, but Lowell has called us together to hear a startling new proposal. SARA C'mon. Let's go in.		
		LOWELL is presiding over a meeting. He sits at a functional office, or desk with ledgers, papers. There are two or three other men in the room. CHRIS and SARA enter the room, the camera following as if they are leading us to our seats. They slip into a couple of seats.	LOWELL (to the advisors/ audience) Welcome, welcome. Come in. Sit down. Meet my associates. This is Patrick Jackson and Nathan Appleton. Sit down.		

Props may hint at China trade, a porcelain tea service, a silk pillow or wall hanging of a Chinese scroll.	LOWELL I've called you here with a business proposition ... After long hours of planning, I have devised a way by which we may avoid the catastrophic risks of the trading business ... a new way to invest our money.

BOOK AUTHOR'S NOTE: The scene continues as Lowell lays out his plans for setting up a textile factory. He asks Sara, Chris and the others to invest in his plan. They discuss the pros and cons and then it is time to decide.

	SARA (sipping) Thank you. I'm keeping most of my money in trading like Mr. Appleton here (aside to audience) and so should you. Trust me.	
	CHRIS Like Mr. Jackson, I intend to invest heavily in your plan, Mr. Lowell. (aside) I'm telling you, this guy has it all figured out. Go for it!	
	LOWELL (to audience) And what about the rest of you. Will you join me? It's time to decide.	

(Continued)

HOST	VOTE; PDA	VIDEO & LIGHTING	AUDIO, NARRATION & SFX	EFX	CUES
		MAIN SCREEN Illustrate slider system rolling all the way to one side for trading; All the way to other side for Lowell.	SARA (VO) So, Lowell has asked you to decide how to invest your money. Use the slider on your screen to make your decision. Right now, the slider shows that your money is equally invested in trading and Lowell's mills. To invest more of your money in trading, move the slider towards the left. CHRIS (VO) To invest more of your money in Lowell's mills, move the slider towards the right.	Host spot fades up on the word right	At the word right **screen** **fades** generic background
HOST (Host reactivates the countdown.) It's time to make your decision. You now have 10 seconds to make your choices. Enter your final choices . . . Time's up.				Gobo effect during countdown	Host – Next at the word Choices starts the (movie) countdown. After countdown movie goes to generic background.

HOST Now let's see how the money you invested with Lowell did. We'll wait until the Risk Round to see what happens to your trading investments! If you invested in Lowell's mills, the right side of your screen will show your investment and how much profit you earned.			Host – Next at the word investments – activates the DVD graphic.
HOST As you can see, money invested with Lowell tripled in value over the first 10 years. That's a good investment. Let's find out more from our time travelers.	PDA Calculates all Lowell dollars	GRAPHIC Show chart with return on investment of Lowell over a 10-year period 1813–1823 $1,000–$3,000	Host – Next at the word Travelers. Movie starts
		CHRIS matrixes back into "today." The image of a mill appears first. He brushes himself off, perhaps bits of cotton are in his hair. He looks around for Sara. She's a bit late and arrives with of all things her tea cup.	At next blue wash and host spot fade out
		CHRIS Well, we're back. (Does doubletake to see if Sara is coming.)Those of us who joined Lowell were well rewarded. Though Lowell himself lived only a few more years, the group stayed together for many years making many excellent investments....	

BOOK AUTHOR'S NOTE: Chris and Sara discuss the outcome of their investments and then it is time for the risk round. This mostly affects the students who decided to keep their money in trading. In the risk round, a member of the audience spins the wheel of chance.

(Continued)

HOST	VOTE; PDA	VIDEO & LIGHTING	AUDIO, NARRATION & SFX	EFX	CUES
HOST Can I get a volunteer from the audience to come up and help me with the Risk Round? (After someone comes up.) Just pull the lever and let's see what happens.		RISK ROUND LOGO appears on main screen.		Gobo whirling effect changes and lands on lever. The lighting effect continues until lever contact is made. On contact lights fly off and away.	Host – Next at the words <u>see what happens</u>. Movie Graphic begins.
		MAIN SCREEN Wheel/Grid/Board/Barrell comes up. Some choices may not affect everyone.			
HOST: *(during the spin ...)* *Will your ships be attacked by pirates ... or sunk in a storm? Or will you be successful trading in lumber ... or exotic spices?*	*Pirates* *Lumber* *Storm* *Spices*	*SFX* *Accompanying sfx of spinning* *Then any item chosen has its own sfx*			

One of the members of the audience spins the wheel and the results affect the investments of the traders in the audience. The final tally of each player's investments is made and displayed on the PDA. The winner is identified with a flashing light. The host introduces the next story in the program.

Development: The Prototype

Although not strictly a writing issue, another part of this project is worth mentioning. A fairly common practice used in projects is the creation of a prototype. This project required the creation of three different stories that were going to use the same technique and approach to content. In situations like this, it makes the most sense in terms of time and budget, to focus on one of the three stories first. In this case the Lowell story was the focus. This story was refined and tested until all major issues were solved before additional development was done on the other two stories. A prototype saves a lot of time in the long run because once all the issues are resolved in the prototype, then the rest of the production goes much more smoothly. Even if a project does not have multiple identical segments as this one does, sometimes a prototype is developed out of a section of the program.

Conclusion: Response to the Project

The New England Economic Adventure successfully hosted hundreds of students and educators at the immersive exhibit described in this chapter and in related exhibits and workshops at The Federal Reserve Bank of Boston. The program received enthusiastic response.

References

Jeff Kennedy Associates, Inc. website. http://www.jkainc.com
O'Meara, Maria. Emails to the author
O'Meara, Maria. Telephone interviews with the author
Prager, Marjorie, Jeff Kennedy Associates, Inc. Emails to the author

20 Adding Story to a Simulation *Amped III*

Summary

Name of production: *Amped III*
Writer: Aaron Conners
Developer: Indie Built, Inc.
Audience: Rated E-10, Main audience is 18–25 year olds
Medium: Xbox 360, and PlayStation 3
Presentation location: Home, where entertainment games are played
Subject: Snowboarding simulation, stories about snowboarding and boarders
Goal: Entertain
Structures: String of Pearls, Linear

The script samples and images used in this chapter are courtesy of Indie Built, Inc. © Indie Built, Inc.

Program Description and Background

Program Description

Amped III is the third edition of the popular snowboarding game created by Indie Built, Inc. The *Amped* games are known for their realism and the sophisticated AI behind the snowboarding action, as opposed to many other snowboarding games, which tend to introduce more fantasy elements and unrealistic courses.

The producers of *Amped III* wanted to stick with the realistic snowboarding game play that had been successful in the previous releases of the games, but they wanted to add something different. That difference eventually evolved into character customization and several off-the-wall story segments.

The player of this game takes on the role of one of the snowboarders in a rowdy crew. The player's character is customized at the beginning of the game in gender, appearance, and attitude. The attitude can be either cheeky or chill. For this reason, there are four player voice options: Male/Cheeky, Male/Chill, Female/Cheeky, and Female/Chill. In most instances, four different lines of dialogue represent each personality. This customization can change considerably the player's experience of the game.

The game features snowboarding in seven different resorts: Northstar (California), Snowbird (Utah), Valle Nevado (Chile), Laax (Switzerland), Avoriaz (France), Zugspitze

DOI: 10.4324/9781003430612-25

(Germany), and DC Mountain Lab (Utah). In order to move from one resort to another, the player must solve a series of story challenges. The story challenges in each resort are presented by one of the player's snowboarding crew. Each challenge requires snowboarding and other skills by the player to solve.

Each challenge is told from the point of view of one of the crewmembers. Because of this, each challenge/story varies widely in tone and presentation, including anime, stop motion, animated hand drawings, Jib-Jab (collage style) animation, and several other techniques. This diversity of styles and the stories themselves make the story challenges a sometimes fantastic counterpoint to the more realistic snowboarding action.

In addition to the story challenges, the game also has a back-story that runs throughout the piece. Part way through the game, the player is accused of taking money belonging to the crew for a trip to South America. The player has to clear his/her name to be reunited with his/her friends and complete the game. The player is helped in his quest by a mysterious snow goddess.

Figure 20–1 Main snowboarding interface for *Amped III* showing realistic mountain action

Production Background

Amped III was produced by Indie Built, Inc., originally named Access Software). Access created both adventure games and sports titles. Its Tex Murphy futuristic detective games won numerous awards including the Software Publishers Association (SPA) Adventure Game of the Year award. The most successful Access sports game was the *Links* golf game released through Microsoft.

Microsoft bought Access and changed the name to Indie, which participated in the launch of Xbox with the successful *Amped* snowboarding title. Indie Built, Inc. was purchased by Take Two Interactive Software (TTWO) as part of the 2KGames brand.

Indie Built, as a subsidiary of Take Two Interactive Software, focused primarily on sports titles, such as *Links*, *TopSpin*, and *Amped III*. Nate Larsen, the Art Lead at Indie Built, is an avid snowboarder and the driving force behind *Amped I* and *II*. Larsen believed that *Amped II* lacked "soul" and brought writer Aaron Conners onto the *Amped III* project to create a story to reenergize the franchise.

The *Amped III* writer Aaron Conners has been a pioneer in interactive storytelling, writing and co-designing the games *Under a Killing Moon*, *The Pandora Directive*, and *Tex Murphy: Overseer*, the first two winning the Software Publishers Association's Adventure Game of Year awards. Aaron has also published novels and non-fiction books.

Goals and Challenges Writing *Amped III*

Goals

Writer Conners' goal on *Amped III* was to add story elements to a snowboarding simulation. These story elements had to appeal to its core audience and add to the fun of the game without restricting the snowboarding sim activities.

Challenges

Conners summed up the main challenge of this project, "How to tell a story in an environment (sim) not conducive to story and to people who don't necessarily want a story" (Conners). This general statement can be broken down into the following specific challenges:

- Coming up with the right type of story and humor that will appeal to this game's 18–25-year-old audience and gain consensus from the *Amped III* production team.
- Structuring the integration of the story in a simulation in a way that does not negatively impact the snowboarding sim part of the game, while adding to the enjoyment of the overall experience.

Writing *Amped III*: Meeting the Challenges

Meeting the Challenge of Determining the Right Story for This Game

Presenting Story Options

Unlike the Nancy Drew game in the earlier chapter, in *Amped III*, there was no existing story material to draw upon. All options were open. At the beginning of the story development process, there were a wide variety of opinions on the team as to how the story should be presented, or if there should be a story at all. Before starting serious discussions on the narrative, writer Conners immersed himself in the type of material that is a hit with the intended audience of 18–25 year olds.

Based on his research, Conners came up with an initial story discussion document for the team. His document laid out six different types of stories on a scale from realistic to fantastic. Conners said that the writer should always come in with a set number of defined options for initial story meetings. This works better than having a wide-open discussion with no defined options on the table.

Conners said that having defined options considerably speeds up the discussion process and keeps it focused. Another benefit of a structured discussion is that it is easier to get consensus by the production team. On this project, according to Conners, gaining consensus was a key issue. "Maybe the biggest challenge I faced was coming up with a story that everyone could (mostly) agree on" (Conners).

As you read his Initial Story Discussion Document, notice the following sections:

* Story Golden Rules: these rules lay out the core assumptions about the story that have already been determined. It is important to include these core assumptions to set a starting point and limit for discussions.
* Story Tone: tone is the style of the story telling (e.g., realistic, fantastic, dark) and is frequently overlooked or minimized by inexperienced writers. Conners knows that tone is essential for the development of the story and makes this one of the main points of discussion early in story development. Under tone, he also included discussion of genre. Most stories fall into categories or genres, such as adventure or science fiction. The conventions of these genres are well known by the audience.
* Story Concept: this section builds on the Story Tone section, providing examples of each type. He also provides discussion points for each type both pros and cons to guide the discussion in relationship to *Amped III*.

Initial Story Discussion Document

NOTE: *Pyro* was the working title for *Amped III*.

STORY "GOLDEN RULES"

1. The story shalt incorporate players' customized characters.
2. The story shalt be tied to players' escalating experience/gear/ skills/access.
3. The story shalt work within integrated gameplay modes.
4. The story shalt be entertaining.

STORY TONE

In my opinion, the central storyline should have a **relatively consistent tone** (though story "tangents" can certainly have widely varied tones). Everyone agrees that the story should be humorous and entertaining, however there are at least *six* potential, fundamentally different approaches:

(A) High Adventure:	A rollicking tale involving a mystery and/or quest, colorful characters, good humor; player is swept into the action and, by accomplishing tasks and overcoming obstacles, goes through a variety of twists and turns and gradually reveals the existing back-story, leading to a big payoff (or several, with pathing).
(B) Faux Fantasy:	A story set in the real world, with the focus completely on the player, who may interpret reality in a fantastic way, have a double (fantasy) life, display his thoughts in a unique way, etc.; For this concept, the back-story is less important than the player's reaction to what's happening around him.

(C) Sci-Fi (Lite): This encompasses lighter sci-fi elements, such as time travel, alternate history, urban legends, aliens, etc. Levels of humor, technicality, and weirdness vary a lot from story to story.

(D) Parody: A tongue-in-cheek approach to storytelling that pokes fun at clichés, pop culture, movies, books, people, genres, etc.

(E) Pythonic: A unique style of humor that walks a fine line between wildly zany and ridiculously stupid; In Monty Python's full-length features, the story is structured on a well-known quest and utilizes elements of parody.

(F) Fantasy: The broadest category of all, this can be anything from sci-fi to anime, limited only by the creators' imaginations; humor isn't precluded, but can be more difficult to pull off without the standard perception of reality to play against.

STORY CONCEPT "A": HIGH ADVENTURE
[EXAMPLES]

- Indiana Jones movies
- XXX
- Robert Ludlum/John Grisham novels

[PROS]

- Most reality-based
- Most natural transition from gameplay in *Amped I* & *Amped II*
- Easily integrated with career and/or players' escalating experience/gear/skills/access

[THE BIG QUESTION(S)]

- Will the game be built around a substantial storyline (which, in my opinion, this story concept requires)? Do fantasy elements have a place in this type of story? How well will this story concept gibe with the Pyro Soul?

STORY CONCEPT "B": FAUX FANTASY
[EXAMPLES]

- *Big Fish* (story/flashbacks)
- *Scrubs*, Andy Richter (protagonist POV fantasy sequences)
- *The Fisher King* (protagonist-only perception of reality)
- Calvin and Hobbes (protagonist-only fantasy life)

[PROS]
- Reality-based, but with lots of creative leeway
- Good opportunity to use a wide variety of graphic styles
- Possibly best fit with the Pyro Soul

[THE BIG QUESTION (S)]

- Can the story content be customized? (This is the most player-centric story concept, so each player's experience should be at least slightly different.)

STORY CONCEPT "C": SCI-FI (LITE)
[EXAMPLES]

- *Back to the Future*
- *X-Files*
- *The Butterfly Effect*
- *Sky Captain and the World of Tomorrow*

[PROS]

- Unique story concept for a sports title
- Freedom to create our own "rules"
- Appease Brenner's Chupacabra obsession

[THE BIG QUESTION(S)]

- Can a sci-fi story be hilarious? Should it be? Should we consider sacrificing some of the humor for an extra helping of weirdness? Will the sci-fi lean toward reality or fantasy? What does our target audience think about sci-fi?

STORY CONCEPT "D": PARODY
[EXAMPLES]

- Austin Powers movies
- Beastie Boys videos (*Sabotage, Intergalactic,* etc.)
- *Kill Bill*

[PROS]

- Hip, intelligent humor style (if executed properly)
- Opportunity to poke fun at ourselves, gaming conventions, snowboarding culture
- Good counterpoint to THUG II's "in your face" jackassness

[THE BIG QUESTION (S)]

- Can this concept be hip, smart, and entertaining without crossing the line into *stinky* cheese? Can fantasy elements be added without disrupting the tone?

STORY CONCEPT "E": PYTHONIC
[EXAMPLES]

- *Holy Grail*
- *Baron Von Munchausen*
- *Roger Rabbit*

[PROS]

- No restrictions on humor or realism
- Greatest potential to achieve cult status
- Good fit for Snow God, Snow Sharks, Snow Weasels

[THE BIG QUESTION (S)]

- Is it just too much? Are we going for cult status or broader appeal?

STORY CONCEPT "F": FANTASY
[EXAMPLES]

- *Wizard of Oz*
- *Yellow Submarine*
- Heavy Metal

[PROS]

- Anything goes
- Opportunity to create unique Pyro Universe
- Most differentiation from *Amped I & II*

THE BIGGEST QUESTION OF ALL: REALITY VS. FANTASY

Amped I & Amped II provided an essentially realistic snowboarding experience with little zaniness and no fantastical (*i.e.* unrealistic) elements. Currently, *Pyro* is headed in a very different direction with proposed elements such as Snow Gods, Snow Weasels, Awesomeness Displays, etc., and this raises some fundamental questions:

1. Is a realistic snowboarding experience still a vital element of *Pyro*?
2. If so, will the game be based in reality with forays into fantasy? Or will this be a fantasy world that features realistic snowboarding?
3. If we're offering a *non*-realistic snowboarding experience (*i.e.* a unique Pyro universe), do we need to explain this to the player? Should we use the story to transport the player from the realistic world of *Amped I & Amped II* to this new universe (*a la* Wizard of Oz)?
4. Could *Pyro's* new direction alienate fans of *Amped I & Amped II*?

The previous sample is a good model of an initial story document, which might include discussion of:

- tone
- genre
- well known examples of works using a certain tone and genre to reference the discussion to something concrete
- pros and cons of each option including questions to consider for this particular project.

Focusing Story Discussion: Tone, Scope, Storytelling Devices

The well-defined options in the document above made it much easier for the production team to quickly eliminate options that won't work and begin discussing the type of story that they want. The next step is to focus in more detail on the approach to the story that was determined in the first step.

The agreements from the first meeting and continued points of discussion are outlined in the document that follows, which includes some of the elements from the previous document but eliminates others. For example, science fiction, adventure, and total fantasy genres were eliminated as options in the first discussion. The basic tone has now been defined as fun, good-hearted parody with fantasy elements. The author adds more examples of the agreed upon tone and expands the "Golden Rules" from the first document into Story Scope, which lays out the specific rules for story implementation as it pertains to *Amped III*. The new material introduced is a discussion of specific story characters (Snow God) and story elements.

Tone, Scope, and Storytelling Devices Discussion Document

NOTE: *Pyro* was the working title for *Amped III*.

STORY TONE:

"PARODY":	A tongue-in-cheek approach to storytelling that pokes fun at clichés, pop culture, movies, books, people, genres, etc.
Reality/Fantasy:	Alternate, exaggerated, or distorted pseudo-reality (aka fantasy lite – mostly realistic foundation with fantastic elements of varying degrees).
Theme/Moral:	Story elements will be fun, funky, and good-hearted, rather than dark, cynical, or bitter; the focus will be on the positive side of snowboarding (and youth) culture with an underlying message of "What's so funny bout peace, love, and understanding?".

[EXAMPLES]

* Austin Powers movies
* *Airplane*
* Beastie Boys videos (*Sabotage, Intergalactic, etc.*)
* *South Park*

[PROS]

* Hip, intelligent humor style (if executed properly)
* Opportunity to poke fun at ourselves, gaming conventions, snowboarding culture
* Good counterpoint to THUG II's "in your face" jackassness

[THE BIG QUESTION]

- Can this concept be hip, smart, and entertaining without crossing the line into *stinky* cheese? Can fantasy elements be added without disrupting the tone?

STORY SCOPE:

- ❖ Will incorporate players' customized characters;
- ❖ Will be tied to players' escalating experience/gear/skills/access;
- ❖ Will work within integrated gameplay modes;
- ❖ Will be entertaining;
- ❖ Will offer customized content (for different types of player characters), but to what degree is TBD;
- ❖ Will not conflict with "real world" boarding mechanics;
- ❖ Will motivate players to complete the game with a strong narrative thread;
- ❖ Will have levels of content so players can (partially) control story intensity;
- ❖ Will integrate real-world locations, pros, etc.;
- ❖ May have some pathing and/or multiple resolutions (TBD);

POSSIBLE STORY INSPIRATIONS & STORYTELLING DEVICES:

- *It's a Wonderful Life* (Clarence the Angel, changing the future [save snowboarding, *et. al.*])
- *Star Wars* (Obi Wan, the Force)
- *Big Fish* (story/flashbacks, act out tall tales, legends [chupacabra], etc.)
- *Scrubs*, *Alley McBeal* (protagonist POV fantasy sequences)
- *The Fisher King* (protagonist-only perception of reality, hero/quest elements)
- Monty Python (myth parody, animation blended with live action)
- Calvin and Hobbes (protagonist POV-only fantasy life, animation)

POSSIBLE STORY INSPIRATIONS & STORYTELLING DEVICES:
Snow God

- ❖ Could be a guardian angel;
- ❖ May be a loveable loser trying to earn his wings (think *It's a Wonderful Life*);
- ❖ There may be an entire pantheon of Snow Gods (of which ours is the most junior or misfit member);
- ❖ Some Snow Gods may be evil and be in conflict with good Snow Gods (think the Council of Wizards in *Lord of the Rings*);
- ❖ Snow Gods could provide story direction, help, incentives, task intros, etc.;
- ❖ Snow Gods could appear in different guises;
- ❖ Snow Gods may appear only to the player (and maybe a few other NPCs) and be invisible to most other boarders (think *Harvey*)

Bruce Lee, Che Guevara, etc. We've discussed the idea of seeing someone fall off a cliff (to his death, presumably), and then reappear later in advancing states of decomposition (think *American Werewolf in London*). If we tie the player's ability to see a dead person to his/ her association with the snow god, then maybe we could justify the appearance of other dead people, such as Bruce Lee or Che Guevara? The snow god could even introduce them as his buddies. . .?

Snowboarding Lifestyle/Xen

❖ The "Moral of the Story" will be along the lines of South Park episodes (". . .You know, I learned an important lesson today. . .");
❖ Keep the message very positive and life-affirming;
❖ Use themes of acceptance, diversity, and goodwill

Defining the Objective and Plot Discussion Document

NOTE: *Pyro* was the working title for *Amped III*.

The previous discussions determined the type of story, basic approach, and introduced some of the possible elements and storytelling devices. The next document begins getting into more specifics on the story for this game particularly the theme and the back-story. A back-story in a novel or a screenplay is usually the underlying story that provides the background for the main story we are viewing. One of the most famous back-stories is from the film *Casablanca*. The aborted romance in Paris happened years earlier and provides the context for the two lovers when they meet again in Casablanca.

The way the *Amped III* writer is using the term "back-story," he is referring to the main story of the game. But because the main focus of the game is snowboarding, in this context the main story is more of a back-story that provides context for the snowboarding and the other story challenges.

STORY OBJECTIVES

- Strong Single Player Experience
- Limited Multiplayer Experience
- Crew Interaction
- Complement (not Obstruct) Gameplay
- Male AND Female Player
- Reality/Alternate Reality Blending
- Clever Premise
- Humor (smart and/or silly); Allegory; Irony
- Snow God
- Strong Payoff
- Theme: "Freedom"
- Theme: "Selling Out Snowboarding"
- Theme: "Gaminess/Gaming Conventions"
- Theme: "The Magic of Snowboarding"
- Fight the Power
- Beat the Game
- Freedom
- Take the Long, Strange Trip

- Freedom tastes nothing like chicken. Hang with your crew. . .trick to shock and awe. . .chase the Yeti. . .maybe even save the world as you know it. Do what you want to do.

PYRO BACK-STORY IDEAS

1. **The Haunted Mountain.** Mysterious happenings, ghost sightings, etc., are scaring the boarders off the mountain. You and your posse decide to investigate. One by one, your buddies disappear and it's up to you to find out what's happened to them. Eventually, you discover that it's a nefarious ploy concocted by Old Man Withers from the Amusement Park.
2. **The Snow Job.** Someone on the mountain is on a crime spree. What starts out as petty vandalism and tagging soon escalates to putting sugar in the ski patrols' snowmobiles' gas tanks, and then cutting the lift cables. Worst of all, it seems that someone is trying to pin the crimes on you and your posse. Can you identify the villain(s), catch them in the act, and clear your name before you get busted and/or someone really gets hurt?
3. **The Treasure of Monte Bordo.** Rumors of a lost silver mine are confirmed when you and your crew discover the frozen corpse of an ancient telemark skier while carving up the back country. An oilskin pouch found in the dead skier's jacket contains a yellowed map and a number of clues. You must locate both natural and manmade markers scattered around the mountain in order to find the secret mine entrance.
4. **The Unbearable Lightness of Boarding.** After a near-death fall, you are revived by a strange, *Obi Wan*-type character who then mysteriously vanishes – or was it only a dream? His whispered words lead you to investigate and you find out about the legend of the Mountain Man. Many have attempted to find and ride the paths (or *chutes*) of enlightenment hidden around the mountain, but only the truly pure of heart will commune with the Mountain Man and reach snowboarding nirvana. But beware! There are those of the dark side who would reveal the Mountain Man's secrets.

This story discussion process continued until the final story was determined. It involves a mysterious snow goddess and a backstory dealing with the supposed theft of the crew's funds by the player. With the basic story defined, the large problem still remained of how to integrate this story into a simulation.

Meeting the Challenge of Integrating Story into a Sports Simulation

Problems with Story in a Sim

When the producers brought the writer Aaron Conners onto the project, they told him that they wanted to add something different, some new life to their snowboarding game. They had not settled on this new life necessarily being a story.

In an interview for this book, Conners explained that the producers' initial hesitancy about adding story elements was because in the past, story in games of this type has been often handled badly. "Problems with story in past games were interruption or intrusion into the main action. This is something that the gamers hate" (Conners). In a simulation, whether it is driving a car, flying a plane, or snowboarding, the main appeal is doing the activity not the story. If there was going to be story in this simulation, it had to be integrated in a way that did not interfere with snowboarding game play.

Story Structure

Given the story limitations imposed by the type of game (sim) and the audience expectations, Conners realized that in this project, story would be a subsidiary element. The game will still primarily be a snowboarding simulation with the story elements as extra bits of fun thrown in. As Conners put it, "The story in this game is like chocolate chips in ice cream."

As noted earlier, the problem with story elements in many computer games is that they interrupt the activity. The player is having a good time solving puzzles, shooting aliens, or snowboarding when suddenly the interactivity is interrupted and they are forced into a situation where they have to go through a series of story related interactions.

Instead, Conners suggests that for a game of this type, the story elements be set up at a natural break in the action. One story element can be an introductory piece setting up information needed to get the next scene going. After viewing this introductory story segment, the player then enjoys the main action of the game, such as winning a snowboard challenge. Once they achieve the challenge, then they have the back bookend story—payoff to the setup. This lets players know they have accomplished something and can move forward in the game without interrupting the main action of snowboarding.

The overall structure of this game is the string of pearls approach discussed in Chapter 17. In a string of pearls structure, a player can perform all sorts of activities in one location (the pearl), such as a snowboarding resort, but to move on to the next location (pearl) he or she has to accomplish some tasks or meet some challenge.

This approach applied to *Amped III* resulted in a bit of introductory story to set up a scene at a snowboard resort. The user can then play at the resort for as long as they want. They can board various slopes, play in terrain parks etc. The story elements are not imposed on them. But when they are finished with one resort and want to move on, they can choose to enter a story challenge. Once they solve all the story challenges in that resort, they can go to the next resort. The story elements are indicated on the mountain slope by a rainbow image and one of the characters yelling to the player. Usually, the character that is calling to the player becomes the teller of this particular story segment.

Below is an example of a story challenge from the first act of the game. This challenge is introduced by the character Hunter. This story is told from her point of view. An unusual element in *Amped III* is that the character telling the story also controls the style of the presentation. Hunter sees the interaction with the bullies as being similar to a Japanese samurai tale. Because of this, the story challenge is presented in anime style, a type of Japanese animation (see Figure 20–2). As noted earlier, story challenges presented by other characters are presented in completely different styles, such as anime, stop motion, animated hand drawings, collage animation, etc. Conners hopes this stylistic device will help create the narrative randomness important to this game's audience. This segment below also introduces the main back-story of the game, which is that the player stole the crew's money.

Figure 20–2 Anime style scene in Hunter's Story

Script Sample from Act 1

Notes on script format and terms:

- *Pyro* was the working title for *Amped III*.
- [GAMEPLAY] indicates an interactive section where players can ride their snowboards. All scene types must be clearly labeled in the script for the production team.
- [GROVER] indicates a non-interactive scene rendered within the game with player character customization.
- [PRESENTATION] is a linear, non-interactive sequence usually from a specific character's point of view.
- SANDBOX or SNOWBOX refers to boarding on the mountain.

```
1.4: ANIME
[GAMEPLAY] SCENE 1.4.a
EXT. - NORTHSTAR RESORT - AFTERNOON
PLAYER rides into the STORY ZONE, where BULLY BOARDERS are hassling
WIENER BOY.
[10 SECONDS OF HASSLING WIENER BOY IN GROVER].
                                                        CUT TO:


[GROVER]    SCENE 1.4.1

PLAYER:     (1) Hey, you dill-holes! Knock it off!
            (2) Hey, how 'bout everybody just chill . . .
            (3) I just LOVE guys that pick on helpless kids.
            (4) I just LOVE guys that pick on helpless kids.
```

BOOK AUTHOR'S NOTE: The numbered lines of dialogue above refer to choices that the player made in customization at beginning of game. Only one line of dialogue will be played.

> The Bullies toss the Player dismissive looks and ride off. After the Bullies ride away, HUNTER rides up to Player and Wiener Boy – she has seen what happened and is super pissed.

HUNTER: Hey, you [FUDGE BROWNIE]!

BOOK AUTHOR'S NOTE: "FUDGE BROWNIE" replaces a curse word. It is a more humorous alternative to bleeping text. It is also said by a different actor.

WIENER BOY:	Don't worry about it. Those guys are just jerks.
HUNTER:	Hey, Franklin, NO ONE screws with me. . .or my friends—

                                                        CUT TO:

[PRESENTATION]   SCENE 1.4.2
CLOSE ON HUNTER'S EYES IN ANIME STYLE:

HUNTER:	(anime) —We must defend our honor!
JAPANARRATOR:	And so, it was that three of the *yuki taishou* vowed vengeance upon the [FUDGE BROWNIE].
HUNTER:	(anime) —We meet tonight! At the great tower! A price will be paid!
JAPANARRATOR:	Hunter's words echoed through the hero's mind—
HUNTER:	(anime, echoed) —We meet tonight! At the great tower! A price will be paid!
JAPANARRATOR:	But first, a quest lay ahead, for only by earning the *Night Pass of Seiyuu* could one return to the mountain and fulfill one's destiny in the legendary Battle of *Kitaboshi*. . .which happens that very night. . .around eleven o'clock. . .

[IN-GAME]   SCENE 1.4.b
The Player returns to the SANDBOX, earns a NIGHT PASS, and then goes to the STORY HOT ZONE at the Lift to the NorthStar Tower.

[IN-GAME]   SCENE 1.4.3
EXT. – THE TOP OF NORTHSTAR RESORT, NEAR THE TOWER – NIGHT
FADE IN: "NIGHT" . . . "Around 11:00" (w/accompanying Japanese characters) . . .
In Anime style, the Player, Hunter, Sebastian, and Wiener Boy are shown gathered near the Tower.

JAPANARRATOR:	Snow fell like delicate plum blossoms as *Seiyuu* returns to mountain with Mighty Night Pass. At the Tower of *Kitaboshi*, *Seiyuu* learns Fate has dealt lethal blow to vacation plans of *Yuki Taishou*!

SEBASTIAN: (anime) Someone broke into Hunter's locker and
                    purloined all our vacation cash!
WIENER BOY: (anime) If it was those jerk guys, they will feel
                    the wooden wrath of my real num-chuks!
JAPANARRATOR: To search mountain for jerk guys, splitting up four
                    Yuki Taishou: *Bishoujo*! Beautiful danger girl with
                    courage of *hitokiri* assassin and fighting hotness!
                    Oukii Nikuma! Big Pork Buns, with triple strength
                    of delicious super-size! *Gaki*! Upstart punk, super-
                    fast velocity of foot and mouth! And set of real
                    num-chuks! *Seiyuu*! Man or woman – who can know?
                    Chameleon power of customization!
                    It is *Seiyuu* who comes upon, the – let's call them
                    Colonatrons – who appear from darkness, reveling in
                    their evilness:
COLONATRON: (robot voice) So then the Pleasure Droid turns to me
                    and says: "Now I see why they call it a half pipe!"
JAPANARRATOR: *Seiyuu* sets off in heavy pursuit, oblivious to almost
                    certain peril that is awaiting.

[IN-GAME]   SCENE 1.4.c1
The Player rides after the Bullies, keeping them in sight but not
getting too close.

[GROVER]   SCENE 1.4.4
EXT. – HALFWAY DOWN THE RUN – MINUTES LATER
Midway through the run, the Bullies suddenly stop in the center of an
open area and wait until a SNOWMOBILE RIDER rides up to them.
CLOSE ON: J-DAWG is the Snowmobile Rider [Cue MYSTERIOUS WIND
CHIMES]. After a brief exchange, J-DAWG rides off and the Bullies
continue their run.

[IN-GAME]   SCENE 1.4.c2
The Player resumes shadowing the Bullies.

[GROVER]   SCENE 1.4.5
EXT. – BOTTOM OF THE RUN – MINUTES LATER
At the end of the run, the Bullies ride up to a STORAGE BUILDING and
around to the other (blind) side of the building (out of the Player's
view). Moments later, they come roaring out on snowmobiles and take
off.
                                                              CUT TO:

INT. – STORAGE BUILDING
There is ONE REMAINING SNOWMOBILE. The Player climbs on and takes off
after the Bullies.

[IN-GAME]   SCENE 1.4.d
The Player follows the Bullies on snowmobile. Eventually, the Bullies
ride over a crest and disappear from view. When the Player rides over
the crest, CUT TO-

[PRESENTATION]   SCENE 1.4.6

In ANIME: PLAYER is surrounded by the Bullies; J-Dawg appears and pulls up alongside the Player; they ride beside each other and talk:

JAPANARRATOR: And so it was, *Seiyuu* surrounded by evil
                   Colonatrons. And then appears J-Dawg, who rides up
                   to *Seiyuu* and makes starting crazy talk of stealing
                   crew money:

J-DAWG: (anime) You stole our crew money!

JAPANARRATOR: Also, there is video, it seems, of *Seiyuu* breaking
                   into locker and stealing money!

J-DAWG: (anime) There's video of you breaking into the
                   locker and stealing the money!

JAPANARRATOR: And what about Colonatrons? Why was J-Dawg riding
                   with them? The answer, it seems, all are now working
                   for mysterious new sponsor!

J-DAWG: (anime) You're out of the crew, dude! [beat] Quit
                   staring at my hair!

JAPANARRATOR: And so began legendary Battle of *Kitaboshi*—falsely
                   accused, honorable *Seiyuu*, escaping evil Colonatrons
                   down treacherous Cat Tracks of Doom!

[IN-GAME]   SCENE 1.4.e

The Player races down cat tracks, pursued by the Bullies on snowmobiles. Eventually, the Player reaches a snow bridge, which disintegrates as s/he rides over it, allowing the Player to escape into the darkness.

The Player escapes from the Bullies on snowmobiles by going off a JUMP.

                                                              CUT TO:

[GROVER]   SCENE 1.4.7

FREEZE THE SNOWMOBILE IN MID-AIR! Dandelion voices-over the frozen image:

DANDELION: Looks like that player's gotten into a little bit of
                   trouble.

[PRESENTATION]   SCENE 1.5

CLOSE ON Dandelion's Scrapbook and a series of scrapbooked pages:

DANDELION: Oh, I knew my friend didn't steal the money, but it
                   sure did look bad. J-Dawg's mysterious sponsor flew
                   the rest of the crew down to Chile the next day.
                   And that's how my friend ended up all alone. Well,
                   not TOTALLY alone. I had plenty of room in my van
                   and, before you knew it, we were on the road to Salt
                   Lake City! While I was at the scrapbooking expo, my
                   friend would be looking for work at Snowbird to try
                   and earn back the money that had been stolen. What a
                   super special person. OUCH! But how d'ya earn 5,500
                   bucks in just a few days? Well, if I'd just quit
                   ramblin' on, maybe we'd find out . . . !

END OF ACT I

Adding Interactivity and Randomness to Linear Story

Narrative Interactivity and Character Customization

As discussed in the previous section, the decision was made not to have complex interactivity in the story elements. Conners decided that the player would find that intrusive in a snowboarding simulation, where the basic goal is boarding challenging trails and terrain parks. Because of this, the story elements are linear, setting up action scenes and offered as fun rewards after the player achieves a boarding challenge.

Conners did want to add some limited interactivity to the story elements. He achieved this through allowing the player to customize his/her character at the beginning of the game. The game opens with an introduction of the player with his/her crew. The player is completely dressed in a pink bunny suit so the player's character cannot be seen at all.

After the crazy first scene introducing the characters, the player is taken to a customization area, where he/she can customize the character. The player can choose gender, appearance, and attitude. The attitude is determined primarily by choosing the player character's voice. Choices include male, female, cheeky, and chill.

For example, Sebastian offers to show the player his "special place".

The chill male response is: "(1) You hittin' on me, big man?"

The cheeky male response has more attitude: "(2) Uh. . .your *special place*?"

The female lines show similar attitude changes: "(3) I don't think I wanna go there" and "(4) That sounds nasty."

The customization of the player's character, particularly the voice, affect the player experience of each scene, even though they do not affect the actual direction of the story.

Adding Randomness

When Conners researched what was successful with the game's target audience, he discovered was that one of the major appeals in humor and story is randomness. Look at films and TV, such as *South Park*, *The Simpsons*, and *Family Guy*. Much of the humor is generated by odd, random elements that are completely unexpected and sometimes seem to come out of nowhere in terms of the story. Conners decided to try to capture the same feeling of randomness in the story elements of *Amped III*.

The main way this randomness is achieved is that the story elements are each controlled by one of the characters' point of view. Their point of view not only controls the content of the story but the actual style. As noted previously, Hunter's story in the long script sample earlier in this chapter is in Japanese anime style. Each of the other characters' story is also told in a widely different style. See Figure 20–3 for an example of one of the other styles—Sebastian's animated sketches. Conners explains that the story gets even crazier towards the end. Like Monty Python, it combines animation with live action and puppets. The narrative becomes wild and off the wall.

Of course, this crazy approach to the narrative is mirrored by the story elements themselves, such as a wiener mobile that looks like a giant hot dog and a snow goddess that eventually comes to the player's aid.

In addition to making the story elements a bit wild, the writer also made minor changes to the snowboarding sections of the film. These changes don't affect the mechanics of the boarding but are window dressing that add to the fun. For example, one of challenges is to run an obstacle course. It is tracked by passing through big rings on the slope. The player has to complete all the rings to win the challenge. The writer named the challenges after old rock albums and songs, such as *Magical Mystery Tour* and *White Rabbit*, with images to

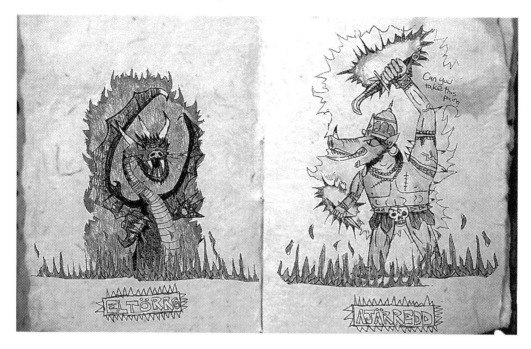

Figure 20–3 Animated sketches shown as part of Sebastian's Story

match, such as a ring composed of psychedelic images. On other challenges and resorts, a similar technique is used by parodying RPG (Role Playing Game) elements, such as alchemy challenge, wizard challenge, etc.

Figure 20–4 The psychedelic introduction for the Magic Circles Challenge in the computer game *Amped III*

Conclusion: Response to the Project

The off-the-wall story segments of *Amped III* received a positive response from most of the critics. With quotes like, "With a story mode that demands to be finished and pacing so good that it'll steal big chunks of your life, Amped 3's one of the best extreme sports titles since the original SSX." "The story and presentation for Amped 3 is the funniest, most tripped out, wacky and bizarre thing you have ever seen! "In general, critics felt the story elements were a big plus for the third generation of this snowboarding simulation. The game won awards and award nominations for Most Outrageous Game, Best Story, Best New Character, Funniest Game, and others.

References

Conners, Aaron. Emails to the author
Conners, Aaron. Telephone interviews with the author

21 Key Points from Part IV: Writing and Designing Interactive Narrative—Games, Immersive Experiences

A Story with Interactive Potential

There are no hard and fast rules about what makes a good interactive narrative, but some things that have worked in the past include the following:

- A clearly defined goal to lead the player through the story.
  Example: Solving the mystery at the inn (Chapter 18 *Nancy Drew: Secret of the Old Clock*).
- An interesting role for the player that allows some control over the narrative flow.
  Example: In Chapter 18, the character becomes Nancy Drew.
- Various plot possibilities and choice points. Scenes can be played out in a number of ways, and the player's choices in these scenes can lead to a number of possible endings.
  Example: In the classic *The Pandora Directive* (book website), the player/Tex Murphy can choose to have a fight with his girlfriend and can decide to sleep with the evil woman, but these choices lead to his death at the end.
- A story line into which puzzles and games can be easily integrated.
  Examples: *Amped III* (Chapter 20) justifies its games by making them part of the snowboarding action.
- An intriguing, unusual world to explore.
  Example: Part of the fun of immersing ourselves in the multimedia experience is a chance to explore unusual locations, such as the past at a time when great economic decisions were made (*New England Economic Adventure* Chapter 19).

Strong Linear Narrative (Chapter 16)

Most of the writers in the programs featured in the case studies first wrote a linear story, which they later developed into an interactive narrative. The main reason for this approach is to make sure that the idea can be developed into a strong story. All the interactivity in the world won't make a bad idea interesting. It is also sometimes hard to determine the full interactive potential of a story idea until it has been fully developed.

Classical Structure (Chapter 16)

Many successful interactive narrative programs are based on classical narrative structure. Classical narratives usually have a lead character who has a need or goal that he or she wants to accomplish. When the lead character tries to achieve that need, he or she meets obstacles that create conflict. Obstacles can be another person, the environment, or inner conflicts. The conflicts build until the climax, where the character achieves the goal or not.

DOI: 10.4324/9781003430612-26

Characters

The Player (Chapter 17)

At the same time as the writer lays out the basic story, he or she needs to define the role of the player(s) clearly. Who are they in the story? The lead character? A minor character? What will they get to do? How much control will the player have over the characters' behavior? What is the player's goal? What are the key obstacles to achieving that goal? Will these obstacles be personalized in the form of an opponent?

Character Interactivity (Chapter 17)

It's necessary for the writer to devise a way for the lead character/player to interact with his or her environment. If it is limited interactivity, the writer might merely need a menu or map of options. However, if there is to be complex interactivity, the writer has to come up with a more sophisticated approach, such as interactive dialogue, moving, picking up objects, and clicking on objects and characters to get information or initiate interactions.

Architecture: Structure and Navigation (Chapter 17)

Once the writer has a clear idea of the plot, characters, goals, and conflicts, he or she can decide which interactive structure might work best. The types of structure available depend to a large degree on the authoring system—the story engine that will be used to produce the program.

Linear Structure with Branching

If the story will be primarily linear with occasional branching choices for the users that eventually loop back to the main plot, consider a scene-branching structure. This approach is used in *Boy Scout Patrol Theater*, which is described in the book's website. In this narrative, a Boy Scout patrol searches for a little girl. The player assumes the role of one of the scouts and can decide which locations to search, such as the school or a farm. Once launched on the search of a location, the scene is primarily linear until the next branching point. Although interactivity is limited in this approach, it does allow the writer more control over story elements. In this case, the writer thought that limited interactivity was the best way to maintain the suspense of the search for the girl.

Puzzle-Based Narrative (Chapter 18)

A writer whose major interest is presenting puzzles and games might want to use a puzzle-based narrative. This is the basic approach used in *Nancy Drew: Secret of the Old Clock*. The lead character (player) is trying to determine who is doing evil things to drive the current owners from the inn. To solve the mystery many puzzles of all types have to be solved. Much of the interactivity is in the puzzles, not in the narrative itself.

Hierarchical Branching (Chapter 17)

If a story has a number of major choices that take it in a completely different direction, then the writer is involved in hierarchical structure. The problem with this structure is branching explosion. Five options with five choices each equals 25 scenes; five choices for each of those scenes equals 125 scenes. This quickly becomes too much to write or produce. This is why hierarchical branching is primarily limited to the endings of stories.

Parallel Structure (Chapter 17)

A way to have multiple story paths and avoid the branching explosion of hierarchical structure is to have parallel story paths. In this case, there are multiple story paths that the user can explore, but the paths are limited, usually to three or four. Choices the user makes send him or her back and forth between these paths instead of onto completely new story paths as in hierarchical structure.

Parallel structure is useful for showing multiple perspectives on a story or various ways a story could unfold based on user choices. *The Pandora Directive* uses this structure. Its "A" path is a basic Hollywood story where everything turns out all right and the hero gets the woman. The "C" path is bleak film noir, ending in death for the hero. The "B" path is a more realistic, middle ground compromise story. This approach allows a high degree of interactivity for the user but still allows the writer some control over the story.

String of Pearls (Chapter 17)

The string of pearls structure combines a worlds approach with a narrative. In this structure, the character is allowed to explore a certain world or portion of a world, but to move on in the story, he or she has to achieve certain plot points. In *Dust: A Tale of the Wired West*, the first pearl of the story allows the player/lead character to explore a desert town at night. But to advance in the story to the next pearl, the player must find a place to sleep. The next morning is the next pearl of the story. The player/Stranger can continue to explore the town, but now he (or she) must find guns, bullets, and boots. This approach allows maximum interactivity for the player and the least writer control over the narrative.

Immersive Exhibit/Experiences (Chapter 19)

Not strictly a narrative structure, but another way to present a narrative is to make it part of an immersive experience or exhibit. This type of program includes large screens, live presenters, theatrical lighting and sound effects, audience interaction, and other elements to bring the audience fully into the experience. The narrative and interactivity is created by the combination and interaction of all these elements. In addition to the techniques of interactive media, the writer for such a program also needs to understand how to write for live theater. These programs are popular in museums, theme parks, casinos, major conferences/conventions, and even the wired classroom.

Information-Based Narratives (Chapter 19)

If you are planning an educational program, consider structuring the content as a narrative for the following reasons:

- User's minds are particularly open to information presented through story telling.
- Where non-narratives deliver information through argument and description, narratives allow the user to become part of the information by becoming or identifying with a character in the story.
- In a narrative, a user can identify with characters in a story and a story can carry emotional content.

- Information embedded in a story is also linked by time and events and thus large bodies of information and the connection between different elements can be easier to remember through narrative.
- Last, curiosity is a crucial component in learning. The user has to want to know what happens next in a sequence. This is hard to accomplish in a non-narrative presentation of information, but is a key element in any good story.

Storytelling Devices (Chapter 17)

Structure gives the overall approach to the story, but to develop narrative within that structure, the writer needs to use a number of storytelling devices. It helps the players to have some sort of map of the story and/or location so that they know where they are at any given time. Often this is an actual map, such as the map of the town in *Dust* and *Nancy Drew: Secret of the Old Clock*.

Interactive devices help make the user aware of interactive possibilities These devices can be as simple as text menus or icons that indicate what action is allowed in a certain situation. The Help feature, on-screen text, the narrator, and linear movies are other useful tools for telling an interactive tale.

Mechanics of Scriptwriting (Part I)

There are a number of organizational devices that help in the plotting of narrative, such as flowcharting (Chapter 3) and character charts (Chapter 18). The writer has to keep in mind the basic techniques of the scriptwriter (Chapter 2), such as showing the audience the story with dramatic action instead of simply telling the story with words, as in a novel. Finally, the writer must come up with a proposal and script format suitable to the project (Chapter 3).

Part V

Interactive Writing Careers

22 Conclusion and Career Tips

The World of Writing for Interactive Media

Types of Writing

Writing for interactive media is a growing field with a variety of different types of writing opportunities in various formats and industries, including:

- Software and applications
- Social Media
- Websites
- E-learning
- Training
- Museum and theme park presentations
- Games

Don't be too narrow in the types of writing jobs you are willing to consider. One of the basic premises of this book is that a strong writer should be able to write for all types of interactive media (with the proper training of course). Don't just focus on the most obvious types of writing, such as computer games or websites. There are many other types of programs being created in interactive media, such as e-learning, training, and museum and theme park exhibits. Each of these categories represents multi-billion-dollar industries that do exciting work.

Interactive Writer Titles

Depending on what type of writing you do, you could have many different titles, including:

- UX Writer
- Content designer
- Web writer
- Copywriter
- Game writer/designer
- Producer
- Writer.

DOI: 10.4324/9781003430612-28

Challenges for the Interactive Writer

No matter what type of interactive writing you do or what your title is you will face some exciting challenges that are different from what you may have experienced writing for linear media like books, newspapers, or TV/film. These include:

- Interactivity
- Limits of small screen
- Writing for many media
- Specialized writing tools
- Complex script formats
- Understanding capabilities of interactive media.

Meeting the Challenges—Getting the Skills

As discussed in the previous chapters, each type of interactive writing has some unique steps on the career path, but also a number of shared ways to get the skills needed to become a professional interactive writer.

Self-Taught and On-the-Job

More than many careers, writers for interactive media can learn the basics of the craft themselves. This is particularly true of social media writers, many of whom were creating social media posts since childhood. Unlike writing books or movies, one thing making it easier to break into interactive media writing is that you can easily publish examples of your own work. For example, you can create your own social media posts, websites, and even games. This gives you professional looking samples to add to your portfolio. Even better if you can create a successful online business with your writing skills. Some of the writers I interviewed for this book had business on social media sites with hundreds of thousands of followers and income from sponsors. This gave them credibility to later get writing jobs with major corporations.

Colleges and Online Learning Sites

But just because you may have been creating social media posts or writing a blog since you were a kid, it doesn't necessarily mean that you are good at it. There are several ways to sharpen your skills more quickly than just trying to figure it out yourself. For example, getting some formal education in the field can help you advance faster and get a solid foundation in interactive media. Your teachers can help you quickly learn the tips and tricks that might take you a while to learn on your own. Another advantage of a school is the possibility to get real experience by working on college websites, social media accounts, online newspapers, or other opportunities. It also gives you a chance to network with other media students who may someday be the person hiring you or vice versa.

There are many colleges and universities that offer courses in Communications, Journalism, Digital Media, and Social Media. These schools range from your local community college to major universities. Research them and find the best fit for your needs. Examples include:

- Carnegie Mellon University
- Georgia Institute of Technology

- MIT
- Savannah College of Art and Design
- Florida State University
- Arizona State University.

There are also a number of online learning sites, that offer courses and certification programs, such as:

- Google Digital Garage
- Coursera
- General Assembly
- LinkedIn Learning.

Books and Articles

There are also books that are focused on writing for interactive media. This book offers a broad introduction to the entire field of interactive media writing. Other books are focused on writing for a particular part of the interactive media world, such as websites, social media, or applications. A book can be a good way to start your studies in the field, because an experienced author has organized the content in a logical and comprehensive manner, as opposed to finding a bunch of articles on your own. Hard to make specific book recommendations here because new titles are coming out all the time. Ask a colleague or a professor which titles they find useful, or rely on one of the online learning sites described above or writing communities listed below for recommendations.

Communities/Information Hubs

There are a number of writing communities and information hubs that collect articles, host discussions, and sometimes sponsor writing events, particularly in the field of UX writing and content design. A few examples:

- *UX Writers Collective* (Medium)
- *Writers in Tech* (Spotify)
- *Readability Guidelines* (Content Design London).

Professional Networking Sites

The largest professional networking sites, such as LinkedIn, offer thousands of job postings, learning resources, and a strong way to connect with other writers and potential employers. You can expand your network and opportunities on a networking site by joining relevant groups, e.g. Interaction Design Association or International Game Developers Association, to get relevant news, tips, conference announcements, and learning resources.

Internships

Writing theory is great but ultimately you have to put what you have learned into practice. Writing internships are a great way to get some experience. Many companies offer internships. They are usually available through the internship program at your school if you are a student. You can also go directly to the site of your target company and look for internship opportunities in the relevant department.

Media Writing Portfolio

Creating Your Portfolio

Once you have gained the skills you need and have created some examples of writing for interactive media, it's time to build your portfolio. Most hiring managers want to see evidence of your writing skills but as importantly they want to see how you use those skills to solve a problem. Your case study should include:

- The problem you needed to solve with your writing.
- Steps you took to understand the problem and define a solution.
- Process to solving the problem: workshops, outlines.
- Your solution and how it solved the problem.
- Impact of your solution in as concrete terms as possible, e.g. 20% less errors using the feature because of improved writing, 15% more sales, etc.

As a newer writer, you may not be able to define all the steps above in detail, but do the best you can. Be sure to be honest and don't make things up if you don't have the experience in a certain area.

In addition to two to three writing case studies, it is also helpful to have a more traditional gallery of samples. It is usually better to have examples of several shorter pieces of different types rather than one long piece in your portfolio. This way you have a better chance of having a type of work that will interest the potential employer. You should break your work down into clearly defined categories, such as Instagram post, web feature story, scene for game, etc.

It is also fine to include non-interactive work if it is a professional piece and/or if it relates to the position you are applying for. For example, if you want to be a writer on a medical website, and you have published in print medical journals, by all means include this material. Many top writer-designers have gotten into writing for interactive media from linear media backgrounds, including journalists, novelists, and scriptwriters.

Even though you might be selling yourself as a writer, it will catch a potential employers' eye if you can demonstrate your understanding of interactive structure and tools in some way other than just prose text. If possible, try to develop some impressive flowcharts or storyboards to accompany your text.

Even better than charts and graphics is to get at least part of your interactive writing produced as an effective website or social media post. If you have friends with a business or a local non-profit, volunteer to write and produce their website. If you don't have production skills, team up with a classmate or colleague who does. Once this volunteer work is completed, you will have a professional piece of work. If you are currently employed, use your interactive writing skills on-the-job to develop portfolio pieces.

Presenting Your Portfolio

- You are applying for an interactive media writing job, so most employers will expect you to have an online writing portfolio. You don't need major technical skills to create an online portfolio. There are many inexpensive or free applications, such as Squarespace, that allow you to easily build a sophisticated portfolio.
- If you want something simpler to start out with, some professional networking sites, such as LinkedIn, have features for linking your work and building a basic portfolio. If

you build your own portfolio, be sure to view it in a variety of browsers and operating systems to ensure it will display well on the hiring manager's device.

- If you are lucky to get an interview, it is a good idea to bring print copies of your work as backup to your online samples. You don't want to lose a job just because the employer's system decides to crash while you are interviewing.
- In addition to the portfolio of your work, make sure you research the potential employer's media. For example, if you are applying to a social media site, be sure to analyze their site as well as that of their competitors.

Marketing Original Articles and Projects

An alternative to getting a writing job and writing the copy defined by your employer is to sell your own written articles, educational projects, or game concepts. Keep in mind that the further you can develop your idea, the better chance you will have of selling it. Before you put a lot of time into a project, it is a good idea to explore the market you are interested in and learn what the opportunities are for beginners and exactly how they want you to submit your work. A few of the main markets for original writing and projects are described below.

Articles for Websites and Social Media

Although many of the content-based sites and social media platforms rely heavily on staff written articles, there are still markets for submitting original articles to online sites and social media platforms. If you bring special expertise to your articles, you will have a better chance of making the sale. Also, if you are a beginning writer, don't focus on the top sites and platforms. Almost every industry or trade group has a website. These are often good places to start. Search "Trade and Professional Associations" on the web. If you are new, you may have to do the first couple articles for free to build up your portfolio. Other types of articles are also regularly purchased by all types of online sources. Writer sites like Writer's Digest often list freelance opportunities, but sometimes, it is better to go directly to the site or platform you are interested in to determine the policies and interest in freelance writers.

Educational Projects for Publishers

Although this is a much tighter market than it used to be, many textbook publishers are also looking for the next great digital product for the classroom. So, if you have a great idea for a better way to teach primary school math or college chemistry, this is the place to try.

In most cases, the publishers will require that their authors are certified experts in the field. Most textbook/educational materials authors are professionals or teachers. If you have a great idea, and you are not a professional in the field or teacher yourself, you can always partner with one to make your submission.

The sites of the major publishers all have links for authors or new submissions that outline the process for submitting a potential project to them. It is a good idea to review the publisher's product line first to make sure that they publish the type of product that you are proposing. Don't submit an English grammar product to a company that focuses on science. The four largest textbook publishers are currently: Pearson, McGraw-Hill, Scholastic, and Houghton Mifflin Harcourt.

Computer Games

With major games now costing millions of dollars to produce, selling an original concept to a game publisher or developer has become as difficult as selling a story to a movie studio. Your chances increase considerably if you can develop at least a portion of your game. Even a simple prototype or a series of eye-catching graphics are better than coming in with just a design document or script. Another alternative is to consider developing your game yourself in a lower cost technology.

The International Game Developers Association has a whole series of articles about breaking into the industry and submitting games, including to textbook publishers. You will need to be a member to access many of the resources, but the association offers low-cost student memberships and limited free memberships that give access.

Good Luck!

This book has provided an overview of the skills needed to be a successful writer for interactive media. You are not expected to know everything on the first day of the job. The key requirements for a successful writer for interactive media are to be a solid writer and a voracious learner because the one thing constant in this field is change.

Good luck on your interactive media writing career!

Index

Printed in the United States
by Baker & Taylor Publisher Services